Running to Catch Up

Running to Catch Up

— PETER FLATMAN —

© Peter Flatman, 2018

Published by Runnercare Publishing

A CIP catalogue record for this book is available from the British Library.

ISBN 978-1-5272-2185-7

Book layout and cover design by Clare Brayshaw

Front cover image © Photography by Mark Shearman MBE.
L–R (149) Jim Brown (1) Steve Kenyon (2) Keith Penny
(303) Peter Flatman (74) Ray Crabb.

Prepared and printed by:

York Publishing Services Ltd
64 Hallfield Road
Layerthorpe
York YO31 7ZQ

Tel: 01904 431213

Website: www.yps-publishing.co.uk

Dedication

I salute the thousands of athletes I've competed with and their sense of fairness, friendship and sportsmanship. Further, I pay tribute to the vast army of unpaid recorders, marshals, course measurers and race referees without whom this book would never have been published. In the early days results would be hand written or typed by club officials, printed by a photocopier and a queue of eager runners wanting to read their times and places. Each runner would study their verdict as if their existence depended on those precious seconds won or lost. If anyone is in doubt about the importance of results sheets, then take look at Facebook and a group called, *I was or am a Runner.*

Contents

Foreword

Stephen Wade

Peter Flatman has done something here that enthusiasts for sport, of any kind, long to know about. He has written a memoir from a viewpoint so rarely experienced: that angle on life embedded in the actual tough and rough experience of the hard discipline involved in determination and survival.

The survival was, in Peter's case, his world as a runner. We know about the 'loneliness' of the long-distance runner from Alan Sillitoe's writing, but that was fiction, stretched into a wonderful imaginative dimension which somehow opened up a mindset and a character. Peter Flatman may have the same result here, but his approach rather demonstrates the poet Idris Davies' attitude to writing: 'don't ask me for style – I don't sell it.' That is, in this book, the sinews of the muscles under pressure to win in athletics magically transmutes into words, as the writer takes the reader into the milieu of competition, timing, distances, training regimes, the stresses and strains of keeping normal life only *just* normal, and so much else.

I witnessed the genesis of the book, as a tutor but also as a general reader, one who relishes a good, honest memoir; I saw the book work outwards from a draft with plenty of potential to a full-length, detailed account of an area of life that few of us know.

The resulting narrative was a triumph; we read of a noble enterprise as the athlete faces trial after trial; we increasingly back him and will him to succeed, and when he falls short of his own aims and objectives, we feel the despair.

But in the end, as a writer myself who treasures the authentic life-writing we seem to long for today, I see here a valuable addition to the genre coming into print, and I congratulate Peter on seeing the project through.

I know that the reader will find a great deal to enjoy here, and his or her mind will open up to face a chronicle of a will to win. That has to be a moral lesson for all of us.

Preface

When I started jogging I thought it was too late, I knew nothing about running and had no idea how difficult it would be to get fit, let alone to run an eight-minute mile. Nevertheless, the mere fact that distance running takes years to perfect was, for me, its greatest attraction, and even at 28 I had time to improve. My book title is apt, because *Running to Catch Up* describes my state of mind and the treadmill I had set for myself. My fixed idea was that if I didn't make the grade before my thirtieth birthday, I might as well pack it in. Therefore, in my first full year, 1972, I ran 5060 miles, and it helped I was serving on the remote island of Anglesey as the training certainly filled in my time. Soon, I was competing for the RAF, where it always seemed I was the old man! Never mind, I was soon hooked with the challenge to get better and enjoyed the great feeling that comes from setting Personal Bests.

So how did I come to write a book about my favourite subject? In 2011, I visited the local library and saw a leaflet about a 6-year part-time degree course in Creative Writing at Hull University. What an opportunity, I could have easily missed. After six years I graduated with a Batchelor of Arts Honours degree and a 2:1, which gave me the confidence to embark on this book.

I never imagined when I began jogging at 28 that I would achieve anything of note in such a competitive sport as distance running. In the last forty years, I have run over seventy thousand miles and competed on the track, road and cross-country. I have excelled at 10km, 10-miles, 20-miles and the marathon and managed my own running shops for thirty years – advising thousands of runners on training and injuries.

In the 2000s, I coached non-club runners to a high level – including winning the men's team prizes at the Leeds Abbey Dash 10km and Morpeth ½ Marathon.

The book is not all about running: it's also a window on my RAF life, running shops, my four children, my coaching and much else.

Stephen Wade, Hull University tutor and writer of more than fifty books, gave me the confidence write freely. Daphne Glazer, Hull University tutor and author, who encouraged me to use my own voice. Jim Whitfield, former mayor of Beverley, who lent me his scrapbooks on local races. Alan Fowlie, a former administrator at Hull University and City of Hull AC runner who supplied me over 2000 copies of Athletics Weekly from 1972 to 2015. Phil Lambert, a City of Hull AC runner, who gave me elusive race reports and photographs. But last and not least my lovely partner Patricia, an avid reader, who has given me total support, patience and understanding in my quest to write my first book at the ripe old age of 74.

CHAPTER I

Masochistic Runners

In the eleven years since I left home in 1960, my Royal Air Force career took me to Singapore, Aden, Malta, Cyprus, Bahrain, Gan (in the Maldives), France and Holland. While in the UK, I served at RAF Cosford, Halton, North Coates, Linton-on-Ouse, Syerston, Fairford and Valley. As a medic at Valley, I'd flown on twenty-two squadron search and rescues over Snowdonia and attended fatal air crashes around the RAF's busiest airfield. I married Tricia in 1965 and, six years on, we have two daughters aged two and four, but now I felt the urge to feed my competitive instinct. My sports included football, badminton, squash, snooker and darts, but it was clear I was searching for an identity other than the number on my RAF ID card. One day, I saw Jim Currie, a chef, jogging around a sports field. The next day, I met him at the gymnasium. I had been including a short run once or twice a week to improve my stamina for football, while Jim had been running well, before he arrived in Anglesey, in the Lincolnshire Services Cross-Country League.

'I see you running most days – how do you stick at it?' I asked.

'When I started Peter, I could barely run a mile.'

'That's amazing, I can only manage about ten minutes before stopping.'

'Buy a diary and keep details of every session,' Jim said.

'If, I had one there would be lots of blank pages.' I said, uncertain of my commitment.

'Fill them up, Peter and soon you'll be running 30-minutes a day.'

'I really like football, and doubt I'll get out more than twice a week.'

'Let's try and find a race, Peter that will get you running more.'

'Are you sure Jim?'

'I'm running an easy five miles – shall we give it a go?' Jim enthused.

'OK, I hope your easy equals my easy.'

I sprinted off like a winger, but was forced to slow down and wondered why, I had the audacity to take on a seasoned runner like Jim. After about ten minutes, I was forced to stop, take on oxygen, and admit my lack of fitness. I was humbled by the older man but resolved to run more miles.

'You will get fitter Peter, but you'll need to give up football.'

'But I'm the player-manager Jim and we have matches till May,'

'Maybe, if you get the bug you might do enough *running to catch up!*'

Jim gave me some back copies of *Athletics Weekly*, where I found information about a North Wales Cross-Country League held at Bangor, Aberystwyth, Wrexham and Shrewsbury and I applied to enter a team from Valley. I continued to play football, but it was obvious – I was succumbing to the freedom and joy of long-distance running. Indeed, I found an advert for a four-man 3.6-mile road relay at Burtonwood, though it would mean a 200-mile round trip. I entered along with Arthur Moore, our best runner, Jim, and Paddy Murphy. On the day, I picked up Arthur in my battered, but willing, eleven-year-old Ford Anglia.

'Pete, you know how to pick a race!'

'What do you mean, Arthur?'

'Athletes like Freary, Hill and Kenyon go like shit of a shovel.'

'Oh, dear it's too late to pull out now.' I said.

'You're right there, Peter – they'll slaughter us.'

'Perhaps they'll have an off day?'

'When we finish, the timekeepers will be in the pub!'

'Thanks Arthur, seems we have a lot to look forward to.'

Then we collected Jim and Paddy and headed for Burtonwood via the Menai road bridge and along the breath-taking North Wales coast road. The venue was between St Helens and Warrington, and we changed in a primary school close to the start – a row of houses on one side and a wooded village green on the other. A powerful smell of wintergreen (methyl salicylate oil) pervaded the changing area. This was a popular warm-up liniment to apply to limbs before competition, but now rarely used. Meanwhile, 200 athletes were warming up around the sleepy village. The sound of athlete's feet slapping the tarmac; honed bodies on the green were stretching hamstrings and tendons at an angle of 45-degrees against gates and trees; and unpaid recorders and time-keepers were in a huddle, near the start banner, which set a vivid scene of raw excitement on a Saturday morning in April 1971. Serious athletes will do anything to shave seconds off their time, which included wearing string vests, featherweight racing shoes, and Ron Hill Freedom Shorts slit to the waist, and could, in a gust, lead to unwitting exposure!

The first-leg athletes were called to their marks, the starter fired his pistol, and released the intensity and fury of the race, and captivated the onlookers. Bolton's Steve Kenyon completed the first 3.6-mile circuit well clear in under sixteen minutes and looked comfortable. However, it would be left to the followers to portray the true nature of this brutal and merciless sport. I watched, while waiting to run the final lap in stunned disbelief, unable to move a muscle as runner after runner forced his enfeebled body through a wall of inhumane masochism. If a Health and Safety official had been present, the event would have been cancelled and questions asked in Parliament. Even in the shadow of defeat, each man would scrap for every yard, bear any pain to hold his place, and sense of duty for his team-mates.

3

Furthermore, the undeniable nature of the human spirit was alive and kicking in this peaceful village, and these men would remain defiant, unbowed and return on another day to do battle again. Now, I stared, in total awe, as these magnificent masochists shed their last dregs of life-force on the tarmac, regardless of personal injury. In fact, I saw an athlete, flopping like a rag doll with a hundred metres to go, his face a picture of agony, summon up one last gut-wrenching and cardiac-arresting moment to hold onto twenty-fifth place. Indeed, why did these amateur athletes run with such determination, when the only stimulus was the satisfaction that showed, on good days, that they had achieved a personal best time.

Moreover, the ultimate insult was each competitor had to pay an entrance fee. Yet this mattered not to the backmarkers without any hope of a personal best or prize: their bodies in a pitiless state – retching, puking, spitting, swearing and shouting, the runners had given their all some fell from exhaustion amongst the waiting second leg athletes – drawing blood from grazed limbs. However, this hardy, selfless breed of men wore the medals of valour, because for them letting their pals down was a fate worse than making the final sacrifice. Our team was annihilated, yet I was enriched by the sheer courage of these fool-hardy men wanting to give of their best. What I learned that day fuelled me with a desire to put my own body on the line and show the same courage I'd witnessed. How could I endure the pain of pushing beyond the limits of sanity to search for my own level and propel me to the very limits of endurance like nothing else in my life. At 28, I would have to learn fast as many of these athletes would have run since school and amassed tens of thousands of miles way before my age – their hearts delivering 140 ml of blood per beat, double that of a sedentary person, to fuel their bodies with oxygen and nutrients. Their bodies would have been honed of excess weight and track training to enable them to run 3000m in 8-minutes to 10-minutes or 5000m in 14-minutes to 17-minutes. I knew none of those facts then or what an awesome task I faced just to become an average club-runner. However, I quickly found out the truth that it would take years of dedication, and even then, I had no sense whatsoever, if I had the ability to face twice a day training or whether, I possessed the right genes. Nevertheless, I took a calculated risk without even a visit to my RAF medical officer to check me out. The relay had taught me the level of Lancashire club-athletics, but now it was up to me. Everything, I needed was around me in Anglesey: the sweet fresh air; the quiet country lanes; the empty west-facing beaches and sand-dunes; the little used golf links punctuated with fairways of heaven-sent, peat-sprung soil. My running career was launched, and my life full of unimagined possibilities.

Two Months Earlier…

This was the big cross-country race of the season. In 1971, while still a footballer, I was asked to run for Valley in the RAF Championships at Halton. I did not know what to expect but playing midfield for the station team meant I felt reasonably fit. My first posting after training to be a nursing attendant at RAF Cosford in 1962 was coincidently RAF Hospital Halton. Seven years had intervened since I worked for Sister Singer on the orthopaedic ward and, significantly, where I met my later to be wife. I booked into the main camp via the guardroom and walked to the Payne NAAFI for sustenance. This was a favourite haunt, and where I spent many an evening chatting up the nurses. However, nothing had prepared me for what I was about to witness an hour before the RAF Cross-Country Championships.

The large NAAFI was full of young men, who were, to my youthful experience, alien beings. Why did it not occur to me these were the very men who would be my adversaries on the muddy fields of Buckinghamshire? Each was there, because this day and hour would be special for them and their teams from RAF stations all over the UK – it was as if I'd attended a party without an invitation and in my former NAAFI, I had thought of as my second home. When I looked around, my sense of being in the right place at the wrong time magnified. Face after face, enthusiastic gestures, a certainty of destiny and an excitable chatter you might hear in a football stadium. The more, I gazed into their young faces of conviction, their *joie de vivre*, and the sheer exultation in their body language – the more I wanted to be in their gang. They gathered in team groups, with the best athlete or captain exhorting his team to run like the wind, give no quarter and leave everything on the course. I looked for some doubt, without success, just unblemished, fresh complexions, lack of stress and eyes so bright, so clear they could have been made of glass. I was overwhelmed by the opposition and finished in 141st place in 36:17 – ten minutes behind the winner, Roger Clark.

Signs from the Past

I was in my twenty-eighth year when felt running could be for me. Yet were there clues within me as I grew up in rural Norfolk? The walking to school. Cycling five or ten miles on deserted lanes near the river Waveney. At Bressingham School, I would practise long and high jumps, even though, I was never a natural athlete. I would practise kicking a tennis ball against our front gate for hours to be able to kick with both feet. One Saturday afternoon, I made a perfect volley with my left foot – the only downside, my slip-on shoe was catapulted towards our large living-room window. While I was frozen to the earth, my shoe went spinning in slow motion to the centre of the four-by-five feet shiny glazed aperture. My mother was incandescent, my father saw the funny side, while I found another wall, and not a window in sight.

It gleamed on that bright spring day – red and cream it was my dream.

I feathered her black pedals – while beasts in the fields stared.

My determination and sense of adventure were never better demonstrated than when, in 1948 aged four, I decided to go for a ride on my tricycle. I told my two-year-old sister:

'I'm off to Diss to buy some new shoes.'

I don't recall her answer but got on my trike to set off for the three-mile ride to town. The journey would have taken me about an hour. On the outskirts of town, I was startled by a terrifying noise, which vibrated through my body. The beast in question was a BSA B33 motorbike, which scared me so much I wet my myself! Then I saw the shoe shop at the top of Market Hill left my trike and strode in with only one thing on my mind.

'I want some new shoes?'

'Where's your mum? Where do you live?'

Meanwhile, my Aunty Joy had seen me and was trying to tell my mother. The manageress intervened.

'Why don't you come over here, and I'll show you some magic.'

'Thank you,' I said, warming to this friendly lady. 'Will it hurt?'

'Not at all, put your feet under the tube and look through the porthole.'

The pedoscope, an X-ray device, could deliver harmful radiation, especially to the young.

These machines would soon be banned.

'I see the bones in my feet,' I said, in awe of this magic box that looked right through me, 'Can't wait to tell mum and dad.'

'Now then,' she said with a frown. 'Have you got a ration book?'

I shook my head and felt the blood draining from my body. I could not believe I would be thwarted by such a tiny detail. Could she not just give me a pair of shoes – the shop was full of them. Worse was to come.

'Do you have any money, little boy?'

'No,' I said as another hammer blow took my breath away. Then I turned and wiped my eyes.

'I'm sorry,' the manageress said, 'But there's no shoes for you today.'

'Where's your ration book, boy?' I gushed, blushed, my head bowed.

My dream faded, I toddled off, and my three-wheeler no longer glowed.

I set off to go home to Nordle Corner – my legs still trembling from my fruitless ride to town. The weather had turned warmer, but a west headwind made my progress slow and tiring. When I reached halfway, I was cheered to think I would soon be home to tell my mum and sister about my great adventure. Then I saw Snow Lane Bressingham, a wooded vale of common land, with no traffic save a cyclist coming towards me. Now, I recognised my mum – I thought, *she'll never believe my story.* But I became anxious as she neared – she seemed extremely angry, yelling at me and making my ears ring.

'Why did you go without saying? Where have you been? You could have been run over!'

'I wanted some new shoes,' I said, in all innocence.

Clump! Ouch, that hurt – I still had a lot to learn. Even though the day was sunny, stars twinkled in my head. My family have never allowed me to forget that incident, which revealed traits in my personality that would shape me in the years to come. Characteristics like determination and being able to take a risk.

CHAPTER 2

Cymyran Beach

A day after I'd watched the courage and tenacity shown by Lancashire's athletes in the road relay, I was back playing football for RAF Valley vs Cefni United, who we thumped 12 – 2. I scored a hat-trick and bruised my foot. Yet, I was still not convinced about running as a sport, but a kick to my right thigh, and an immobile dead leg, meant no training for weeks, and tipped the balance. At least it gave me time to think about running as a serious sport, and about the precious time I had already wasted. In two years, I'd be thirty and *over the hill* in football parlance. The more I read *Athletics Weekly*, the more I realised my progress could take years. The average time for a juvenile runner to reach his performance plateau is eight years, so what chance would I have? By then I would be thirty-six! In April 1971, I ran ten times for a total distance of fifty miles. At the time, lots of athletes were logging 500 miles a month. David Bedford was doing 200-miles per week but, despite that, he was unable to break two minutes for 800 metres, yet he went on to set the world 10,000 metres record in 1973. In May, I managed to run on twenty-four days and began to experiment: I donned a pair of military boots, weighing three pounds four ounces, and slogged out six miles on the sand dunes at the back of the airfield. My legs ached, and my hamstrings were stretched until they felt as taut as piano wire – I never repeated that session.

My parents came to see us in Anglesey on their way to catch the Holyhead ferry to Dublin to visit relatives in Kilkenny. I didn't see much of them in the eleven years I had been in the RAF, so I shouldn't have been surprised they knew nothing of my new-found enthusiasm for long-distance running. So, when I came to greet them, wearing shorts and vest, it must have been a considerable shock for my mum and dad.

'Where are you going?' said my Dad, looking puzzled.

'Going for a run,' I said, as though he should already know.

'What does he mean, a run in the car?' Dad said, scratching his head.

'You know, Dad, with my feet,' I said.

'Well, I go to hell. How far?'

'About five miles, Dad.'

'I'm thinking of starting too,' my wife said.

'Will you win any money?' my mother said.

'It's not about money.'

'Are you any good, Pete?' Dad said.

'No, not a lot of cop, and if I don't get going I never will be.' I said.

I knew of some runners who would do anything to avoid this kind of interrogation: driving to a remote spot, changing into shorts and vest, running their session before getting dressed, and returning home as though they had just been to the shops. However, it is a good exercise to be asked such questions. I did not run for monetary gain, but for the challenge that could be measured and recorded – never knowing when I would record a new personal best.

Arthur Moore became a friend, but got under my skin at times, especially as he was a much better runner than me. Arthur's story was inspiring and courageous. He joined the RAF as an airman and thrived through education and diligence. His running was an extension of his personality and confirmation that you only get out of life what you put in. Arthur rose through the ranks to sergeant when he qualified as a navigator. About a year before we met, he was commissioned as a Flying Officer and worked in Air Traffic Control at RAF Valley. I found him to be a mild-mannered man with a sense of fun enlightened by irony, but he also possessed a keen sense of humility. He would say, 'I run a few miles on the beach every day at a steady six minutes per mile.' I would see his footprints in the sand and, given his stride length, this would confirm his assertion. He was a few years older than me but a determined competitor, whom I needed to find a way to emulate.

This was a period of transition, when I ran more and played football less. I wanted a one-circuit run that was interesting, testing and a joy and it has remained my favourite course. The criteria: the route had to start and stop, at my front door in Maes Minnfford Caergeiliog. The first mile took me past the medical centre on the left and Lake Penryn on the right, where silky, black cormorants clung to time-less rocks, waiting for their oily feathers to dry before diving in for more fish. Onwards, I ran towards the main entrance to RAF Valley's airfield and followed the perimeter fence. The road would take me through undulating soft and golden sand and over a dune to reveal a glorious vista. To my right, jutting through the beach, were Precambrian rocks dating back 4.6 billion years to the beginning of Earth's formation, and provided a stunning backdrop to a glorious seashore which stretched three miles to Rhosneigr. The wind and tides always assured me of a unique experience. Wind speed was determined on the Beaufort scale, and gales so frequent the Station newsletter was called *Force 8!* Some days, the tides and wind would deposit large amounts of sand onto the airfield runways, making my progress tardy. On another dawn, the beach could widen by a hundred metres, and with a backwind my body would all but take to the air.

About halfway, the beach juts into the sea with a collection of stalagmite-shaped, black rocks teeming with sea birds and fish. Close to Rhosneigr, I turned left at a tributary adjacent to columns of steep sand dunes, which were perfect to sprint up for leg-strengthening sessions. Then without warning, the path thinned with gorse fighting for space with adders now the trail was parallel to the Holyhead to London railway line and a pedestrian crossing accessed through gnarled, wooden gates. On the other side, another joy: an under-used golf course with soft undulating turf ideal for fartlek, a session of sprinting and easy running. In the distance, I could see the rocky wall and some steps to the sports fields. The smell and comfort of my home quickened my pace and our front door beckoned – another run, full of interest, surprise and exhilaration.

In June, I took my wife Tricia and our two girls Jayne and Sarah on our first package holiday to Lloret de Mar on the Costa Brava. I ran a few times in the heat of the day and it was a relief to join my family in the hotel pool. However, my mind was never far away from thinking about my first road race at Winsford on 4th July 1971 and, at seven miles, my longest. The day was hot and sunny, and I'd failed to drink enough before the start. I was soon drenched in sweat and suffering from the heat and no surprise, I only manage 111th place in 42:21. Still at least I'd have a chance next year to win the Most Improved Cup awarded to the athlete with the best reduction on time. I increased my training to 150-miles over the next three weeks and I was aiming to run every day as soon as I could. A friend gave me a book written by Jim Peters. In 1952 aged 33 his coach, Johnny Johnston, decided Jim should increase his weekly training to a hundred miles, with an emphasis on running them at his marathon pace. This soon paid dividends as he broke the marathon world record four times, the last one 2:17:39. Jim's book, *In the Long Run* was inspirational and I would often remember his inimitable quote: *'When I line up for the marathon I ask myself if I have run every day, run further and faster than before, if I've eaten and slept well, and in a nut-shell have I lived the life of a monk!'*

A lot of club runners then, and more now, give track training and racing a wide berth, but I believe it is the only way to improve basic speed. Therefore, I was including interval training at 100/200/400

12

metres twice a week. A couple of weeks later was Station Sports Day, I came third in the 800 metres in 2:09.9 and won the 1500 metres in 4:35.1. No great shakes, but I had never run that fast in training. These performances would enable me to run quicker at longer distances on the track, road, and cross country. I made a nostalgic return to RAF Cosford to run the Training Command 10,000 metres Championship on 6th August 1971 on the feast of Jesus's Transfiguration on Mount Tabor. Would I be equally transfigured, and win the race without fatigue? Perhaps not, as the main man present was Flt Lt Roger Clark, who relentlessly pursued a personal best and lapped me four times! The track was made of loose cinders and the crunching of his size 12 track spikes grew louder each time he passed me and sapped my morale and self-belief. Even so, I placed 11th in 36:03 a personal best and I had taken another learning curve in my quest to run with the best. To cap it all, I suffered a severe stitch from two laps, which lasted till the finish.

Now was the time to say goodbye, to breathe a sigh: my dear, old, sweet 1960 Lady Anglia was showing her age and not able to take me to distant races. Dark rings were appearing around those once sparkling frog eyes; now she would moan, not in pleasure, but in pain and exhaustion. My Dad said she was thin and indeed she was, but slowly slipping away from me. How many more races could my dear old Lady take me to? I had rescued her from a cruel travelling salesman in 1964, but now I took her for granted when she needed to feel cared for and loved. Further, she had become stroppy on cold mornings and often refused to move. Once or twice, I had to take the crank to her. She never liked that but, after a few turns she'd splutter into life and tears would fill those dark eyes for the master she still loved. She could still pull the young car-less men but cared little for them. If only, I could have held onto her, cherished and loved her, she'd be with me still. Alas, I was short-sighted and should have taken her on a weekend retreat to restore her body and bring back those beautiful, bygone days. The excuse was lame, of course, the kind that leads to losing all that we hold so dear. A long-time admirer called round and offered me thirty pieces of silver which, I like Judas, accepted.

CHAPTER 3

Percy Cerutty

I found a book called *How to Become a Champion* (1955) by Percy Cerutty, which soon became my template and I was living in the perfect place to follow his thesis. Percy was the brilliant motivator and coach of Herb Elliott – the athlete who won the 1500 metres at the 1960 Rome Olympics by an unprecedented fifteen metres. His training camp was based at Portsea, near Melbourne empty beaches, steep sand dunes and tough terrains. The remoteness of his training camp allowed Percy to preach his philosophy of the inner self – he believed this was where all was possible and where ordinary runners could run beyond their wildest dreams. Then, I realised this corner of Anglesey had all the positives of Portsea and I began to believe.

In September 1971, I ran every day and an average of sixty miles per week. My favourite session was a seven-mile tempo run at lunchtime around the quiet roads of the island. Soon I was running comfortably under six minutes a mile. This session was interspersed with a spin around the Valley beach, and cross-country circuit. On the last Saturday of September, I competed in the Chris Vose Seven-mile Road Race at Warrington, on a cloudy day, with a moderate breeze and an air temperature of 55 °F. I placed 72nd in 39:19 from 168 finishers. The course was over distance by 385 yards, which meant my average per mile was 5:27. I was ecstatic and yet chastened at the same time – it was a good performance, but seventy-one athletes were ahead of me.

Every Star has a Silver Lining

What was the motivation that drove me to excel in life? I think the main stimulus for me was learning or doing something where the reward was the sense of self-satisfaction of achieving a goal that seemed impossible. In a few months, my running performances had improved dramatically with more miles and greater intensity. I put this down in a diary of training and races, which noted distance, time taken and weather. For me, the perfect method to focus my single-minded intent and get the best out of myself. On reflection, I had learned this lesson before aged thirteen. I was a pupil of St Thomas More's Secondary School, Colchester in a disruptive class taught by Sisters of Mercy nuns. Mr Rastall was drafted in to establish discipline, and to create a work ethic. The former was controlled by lines, and the latter by the liberal use of the cane. Every piece of class-work, set by our teacher, and successfully completed was awarded a merit star, for all to see, around the walls of the class-room. Very soon, large gaps appeared like a road-race alright for some but for others may not have been effective teaching, though for me it was the perfect way to learn and succeed at the same time. Within a term, I had an unassailable lead and my teacher asked to see my mother.

'Please take a seat, Mrs Flatman. Your son has become my star pupil.'

'So, he should, I passed the 11-plus for Slough High School for girls.'

'I think he should take the 13-plus exam, so he can get some GCEs.'

'Not sure we can afford the extra year at school.'

'I feel sure he'll be successful,' Mr Rastall said.

'He works in a poultry killing shed, so he can buy his own clothes.'

'I see, not easy, but please let me know.'

I was not sure of another year at school either. There would not be much time for homework and what if I failed the GCEs? My pay for working in such a dirty job, killing chickens, was a derisory one shilling and a penny an hour! Eventually, I got the green light, passed the test, and joined East Ward Secondary Modern School in September 1958.

In July, August and September 1971, I had run 626 miles. In the previous month, I ran every day and comfortably under six minutes per mile for my seven-mile road run. On 5th October, I organised a time trial around the beach and golf course which went well in anticipation of the first fixture of the North Wales Cross-Country at Bangor on Saturday. I was taken ill two days before with severe right-sided stomach pain and went to bed, but there was no way I would miss the race. The course was part road, and partly through hilly woods. Our best runner was Arthur Moore, 7th in 30:28, while I struggled with acute stomach ache and placed 50th in 36:57. On another day, I would not have run, but felt morally obliged, because I'd organised the first team from RAF Valley to compete in this event since 1958. The abdominal pain bothered me for most of October and in fact located in my liver.

Skinny Dipping

In July 1963, I was nineteen, serving as a nursing attendant at RAF Hospital Halton and I asked my wife-to-be if she would like to go out for an evening drive in my 1949 Sunbeam Talbot. The evening was warm, sultry and the air was full of insects. We saw a stretch of water and I was hot and sticky.

'Do you fancy a dip in the lake?'

'I don't have a costume,' Tricia said.

'I don't either, are you coming?'

'Not likely – there could be mosquitoes or rats in there.'

'Well, I'll be in and out so quick they won't stand a chance!'

Famous last words. I'd contracted hepatitis B and would spend two weeks in hospital. The thought of food made me feel sick and my skin and the whites of my eyes turned yellow. I was ill with glandular fever for several months, and intermittent, unattractive yellowing for about two years.

Now, it reappeared after nine years. At first, I thought it was a stitch but on reflection, I had put my body through the ringer in September 1971 and my liver was overwhelmed. I deduced that all the hard training had left me low on antibodies.

I gradually recovered from the stomach cramps and tried to cram in more miles, but instead suffered injuries to my knees and ankle. My body wanted a rest and I eased off through November. Despite this, I had a significant breakthrough on 23rd November in a ten-mile road race at RAF Henlow and came 30th in 55:41. Runners' training shoes then were very basic, with little support or cushioning and I was still wearing Onitsuka Tiger Cubs, with only a slight heel and an upper of canvas, which gave very little lateral support. This meant the Achilles, knees and ankles were susceptible to strains and ligament damage. Nonetheless, I ran the North Wales Cross Country league at Aberystwyth in football boots and improved to seventeenth.

To be fair to myself, I was probably trying to improve too quickly. For example, eight months earlier I was unable to break 7-minutes a mile, yet now I was running under 6-minutes per mile. Indeed, I averaged 5:34 per mile in the Henlow Ten. Unfortunately, niggles and injuries stopped me running further each month. My last three months' mileages of the year were October 202, November 142, and then I made a dramatic increase in December – the last week of the year of 83-miles was my highest.

CHAPTER 4

Emergency Delivery

In January 1972, I kept my weekly mileage in the eighties. I was determined to make this year the best, because I would be leaving the RAF in the autumn of 1973, so this would be the only complete year for me to train through. Running in the seventies was very simple: the athlete needed so little in comparison with today. He needed shoes, and Tiger Cubs were light, flexible with a decent grip. Best of all was the price, as they could be bought by mail order for £1.95! A pair of white silk shorts on permanent loan from Valley's gymnasium, a long-sleeved tee-shirt for winter, and a sand-coloured tee-shirt printed with a scorpion and the slogan *A Sting in the Tail*. Today, there is a paraphernalia of kit. Shoes for every running surface; running socks, lycra tights/shorts, sweat-wicking tops, rain jackets, gloves, hats, shades, nasal strips, water bottles, a belt to carry drinks bars, energy drinks, isotonic drinks and recovery drinks. Gadget must haves: GPS watches giving distance and time, heart-rate monitoring, cadence, VO_2 max, lactate threshold; but do these devices make for better runners than, say, in the eighties? Of course, products are different, and today's runners prefer to stay dry and warm. I think it's great for a small club like East Hull Harriers to have over three-fifty members and their enthusiasm as expressed in social media is a joy to read. If, I could have had GPS watch in my heyday it would have made me a better runner. For example, trying hold a pace in a twenty mile when the split times are five-miles apart is almost impossible. I found it hard enough to judge pace on a four-hundred metre track let alone five-miles and why I usually went hard from the gun in ten-mile races like Tipton, because I knew the pace would drop in the second mile allowing me to stay with the lead group and maintain my pace.

On 19th January, I competed in the Training Command Championships at Hendon for the first time. The course had to be changed to multi-laps around sports fields, so not a true cross-country event. Even on a day barely above freezing, I was soon sweating on the seven-mile event, coming 6th in 40:05. An official RAF photograph of me nearing the finish said it all – I looked and was totally numb with exhaustion. I was pleased with the race, which was four weeks prior to the RAF Cross-Country Championships.

My wife was eight months pregnant, but I was so preoccupied with running, I did not pay due care and attention to her and our two daughters – something I would later regret. My strength and stamina had improved each month, but I had yet to reach my performance plateau. I decided I would keep my training at a constant level and would even run on the morning of an event. This would add to the stress, but conversely make me physically and mentally stronger. The 1972 RAF Cross-Country Championships was an important indicator towards my dream of making the RAF team for the Inter-Services the following year. I decided to train as normal: twice a day including track and hill work, and a long run on Sundays. **Results:** 1. Roger Clark (Innsworth) 29:27 2. Mike Hurd (Abingdon) 29:48 3. Ray Donkin (Lindholme) 29:57 4. George Edgington (Lyneham) 30:13 5. Ian Forster (Halton) 30:23 6. Kevin Daykin (Cranwell 30:27 7. John Wild (Marham) 30:38 8. Tony Brien (Honington) 30:45 9. Viv Blackwell (Rheindahlen) 30:52 10. Sandy Keith (Waddington) 30:58 Arthur Moore was 19th in 31:57 even so, my run surprised many, I came 21st 32:04 – an improvement of four minutes and 120-places. Other RAF Valley placings: JT Goodall 179th, SAC Shey, 248th, LAC Ashcroft 262nd, and SAC Armitage 266th. Valley were 23rd team.

On the contrary, back to the real and important world, my Tricia was admitted to Bangor Hospital in labour on the 9th March 1972, a beautiful day with an early morning mist giving way to warm sunshine and a still atmosphere. Meanwhile, I was anxious and felt out of touch as I ran along the beach. On another day this would have been perfect conditions for running, but I couldn't wait to get back to the gym, get showered, and dressed. In my head I was somewhere else as I raced to my Vauxhall estate and promptly reversed into a bollard, however, I suppressed an expletive and shook with the fear of not knowing how my wife was coping on a Bangor maternity ward. I could not have known, that was the precise moment my wife and son were being wheeled to theatre for an emergency Caesarean nor that my son kept returning to the transverse position, or that they were both in danger with elevated blood pressures. I was in the wrong place at the worst possible time. Meanwhile, my wife thought this was her lucky day,

'It was amazing, I knew the baby was due, but there was tightening, but no pain. I thought this is good.'

However, this could so easily have been a tragedy with unimaginable consequences. If my wife dies, the girls will be marked forever; if our son dies, I will take the blame; if they both die, so will my reason to exist. That they both survived was, in my mind, a miracle. Tricia spent three weeks in hospital, and many months recovering from her severed abdominal muscles. In our marriage, there was only one hero and my wife dealt with this terrifying, life-threatening experience in a calm and matter of fact way.

Meanwhile, I barely broke stride in my quest for eminence in the running world. In 1972, I was determined to run 5000 miles, and average a 100 a week. I was constantly asked how I found time to run so many miles, especially as I now had three children under six.

'Well, I run five miles on my way to work and then seven miles in my lunch break!'

'How do you find time for lunch?'

'Finish at 12:15, rush to the gym, change and on the road in five minutes. Run seven miles in forty minutes, bolt some sandwiches, and back at the medical centre before 13:30.'

Soon, I would add a further five-mile run from my workplace. In any era, it is best to conform to normality to avoid endless ridicule. Then, the UK was awash with distance runners clocking 100+ miles a week yet on this remote island, I felt in a minority of one. The taunts and teasing I received daily, made me more single-minded to succeed. One day, I was running the final mile of my lunchtime seven in under five minutes when a random, pot-bellied man shouted, *'If you were meant to run, you'd have been given four legs!'* I suppose I remember it, because it was literate.

On 4th April, I returned to the Burtonwood road relay which had such a profound effect on me the previous year. My performance of 18:39 for the 3.6-mile lap was more than two minutes quicker than 1971, which did not put me with the superstars, but closed the gap between us. A short race like this improves leg speed and was an ideal warm-up for my next race, the North Wales Ten-mile Championship at Wrexham. I travelled to the venue with John McCarthy, a friendly Irishman who worked in the supply flight at Valley and ran 56:25 in the Henlow Ten. The race was over two laps, starting and finishing at Wrexham AFC stadium and perversely known as the *Racecourse Ground.* The most I remember was feeling fitter than my opponents and wearing them down until, I took the lead. My winning time was 53:09 and over two and a half minutes quicker than Henlow. The title and trophy convinced me, after less than a year's training my high mileage was paying off and that winning races and setting personal bests was the only drug I would ever need.

Shortly after this, I was sent on an attachment to RAF Fairford, where the magnificent Concorde was being tested. My route took me through the wonderful Vale of Evesham, it was spring, and full of birdsong, beauty and an abundance of Nature. Once again, my wife did not complain, I'm sure her need for me so soon after the birth of our son was greater than the Royal Air Force's need to send me to Fairford. Next, I located a route of seven-and-a-half miles, which was a road circuit around the huge aerodrome. Picture yourself in my shoes, I am running through the verdant Gloucestershire countryside, passing postcard cottages to the sound of Nature's honey-bees on an idyllic sunny day. Then, to my amazement, I heard distant thunder getting louder and ever more threatening. I looked above and saw what looked like a metallic version of a prehistoric reptile as it streaked across the huge sky. Such was the Concorde's impact: at odds in this ancient world of Victorian hamlets and old men sitting outside taverns smoking clay pipes. I could not be more exhilarated, or impressed, if I was sitting beside Concorde's chief test pilot Brian Trubshaw.

On a balmy evening, I went to RAF Abingdon to run 5000 metres on a Tartan track. The weather was quite warm, and I was well pleased to finish second and taking almost two minutes off my personal best in 15:41.6. The 5000 metres is over twelve-and-a-half laps and made me feel as if I was running on a tightrope and making the experience feel surreal and tense, with every lap like a race within a race.

Next, I returned home for the christening of our son, Simon George, at the Catholic Church in Holyhead and to thank God and the surgeon, for his safe deliverance. I managed to get Wednesday 16th June off, so I could drive to Cosford to compete in the Training Command 5000 metres on the same track where I had been humiliated by Roger Clark a year earlier. Warming up, I felt confident: for twelve months, my diary was filled with hill work, with interval training, long runs and a weekly average of a hundred miles. This was the station where I did my boy's service. I was ready when the starter said, '*On your marks, feet behind the line.*' Then, fifteen pairs of feet obeyed. The starter's gun fired, as did a shot of the athlete's drug adrenaline to fire the engine inside us all with more oxygen; a quickening of the heart to feed nutrients to the muscles and an opening of the airways to supply more oxygen. I steadied up and trusted my fitness, which rewarded with another title and a new personal best of 15:34.4. I enjoyed the applause from the grandstand. Even though I'd started running late in life, I knew it would take another five years to reach my potential. My RAF service would end in fifteen months and how would I fare in civilian life, where I had to get a job, a mortgage and a house? There was no magic formula. The activity of distance running is rudimentary yet uplifting and a sport which repays those who train hard. My dedicated winter training had been withdrawn from the runner's mileage ban, and now I could enjoy the praise and glory with compound interest.

During the summer of 1972, I ran a lot of track races. This was deliberate, because it makes all runners faster and stronger. The distance around a track is precise and there is no hiding place. I would never make an 800-metre runner and never broke two-minutes, yet I knew it would make me better prepared for the 1500 metres and when I ran faster at that distance, I would be faster at 3000 metres. I ran seventeen times on the track in 1972 and achieved ten personal bests. Club runners often say the track is too boring, but if they are serious about improving their speed, the track holds all the answers.

The previous summer, I had competed in the Winsford seven-mile road race, coming 111th in 42:21. I had made a mental note about a cup awarded to the athlete who reduces his time by the biggest margin. So, I made sure to enter and compete in this race being held on Saturday 5th July 1972. My full support team was on board: my wife Tricia, Jayne, Sarah and four-month-old Simon. We had such a lovely time going through Bangor and I was reminded of this song by Fiddler's Dram: *'Didn't we have a lovely time the day we went to Bangor, A beautiful day, we had lunch on the way and all for under a pound you know.'* Everyone was in good spirits and I hoped I could win that cup.

The nearer we got to Winsford, the worse the traffic, not a surprise, with it being the first weekend of July. We were dawdling along, while I kept looking at my watch, calculating, fretting and still not sure we would make it. There was only one thing to do, *Throw me my kit please love, I'll have to change while I'm driving!* I ripped off my Clark Kent gear and transformed into a runner without a hope of winning the Best Improved Cup. Meanwhile, the car judders and stalls and the kids were stunned by their dad's manic behaviour. I had done everything but tie my laces on my red, white and blue Onitsuka Tiger Cub shoes, which had tangled around the clutch pedal and caused the stall. We crawled until a break occurred near the town centre. Then, we saw the start and I still hoped the race might be delayed. Finally, I stopped the car near the start, but there was no sign of runners instead the Winsford mayor in full regalia and a race official. I'd waited a year for this race to arrive, so I could challenge for the Best Improved Trophy and could not even get to the start on time. We were minutes from the venue, and I hoped the race might be delayed.

'Which way have they gone?' I said, tying my laces and unable to see any of the backmarkers.

'They went that way,' a race marshal quipped.

My poor wife, still not recovered from childbirth, now had to find somewhere to park in a strange town, tend to three kids, and meanwhile her husband just ran away! I turned several corners before I saw the tail of the stragglers, but I could forget any chance of winning that cup. Then I thought: *All that training, never missed a day, yet now I've missed the sodding start. Reckon I'd be late for my own funeral.* At last, I began to pass some slow runners, but I was flat out and knew the race would be finished soon and I would not be anywhere near the front. When I reached the finish line, I was physically and mentally exhausted and placed 38th in 38:24. At the prize-giving, I was staggered when they announced me as the winner of the Best Improved Runner Cup. Somehow, I managed to run almost four minutes faster than the previous year. Plus, a bonus, because the time I lost at the start could enable me to challenge for it again the following year. I showed the girls the cup. Jayne said, 'That's great, dad.' Simon was sleeping, and Sarah gave me one of her grins. *On the way home, I was never alone, and we opened a bottle of cider, singing a few of our favourite songs as the wheels went around.*

CHAPTER 5

Bad News

Apart from all the recent happenings with my family, my running, and my final year in the RAF: my demob would lead me to a very different life. I was determined to become as near as possible the best runner in the RAF, but I had a far bigger responsibility to care for my wife and three children. In that respect, I owed it to my family to sign on for another ten years I would be able to continue improving my running, leaving at the age of forty with a pension and still be able to pursue a civilian career. I sought an interview with the station commander, Group Captain Brian Huxley, who told me,

'Corporal Flatman, you are an airman that the Royal Air Force can least afford to lose, but we are a contracting organisation and opportunities will become fewer and fewer, and if you leave now, you will have the best chance to seek a new career to provide for your family.'

I could not fault his advice, as he probably knew more than I about the future direction of one of the world's premier air forces. RAF personnel at that time numbered 133,000 – by 2015 it had dropped to 37,000. This rate of reduction would certainly hamper opportunities and promotion, yet from a running point of view, it would also be detrimental to my athletic career. I applied to be a probation officer, but my Senior Medical Officer politely informed me, after a psychological test, that I was not suitable.

There was a further possibility, but this also came with a dilemma: I could join my younger brother Paul and our Dad in a chicken processing business. I worked in this trade before joining the RAF thirteen years earlier, so was aware of the hard graft involved. My father was fifty-four and EU rules meant a large investment in modern machinery would be necessary. Paul was an extremely ambitious young man of twenty-four and already planning to take over the business. The parable of the prodigal son came to mind. I had left home as the older son to seek a life elsewhere while the younger son would eventually inherent my parents share of the business, which he used along with his own endeavour to make himself a multi-millionaire within twenty years. So, when I returned in 1972, I suffered the fate of the younger son, and would need to seek my own fortune. I sought solace on the Colchester Garrison track in an open 5000 metres race. My father came and watched me for the first time. When we came home, he told everyone, *'It was a one-horse race. Pete led from start to finish.'* I was pleased too, with another personal best of 15:28.6.

I decided to increase my training mileage to 125 miles per week. I wanted to be ready for the winter season and ready to challenge for the RAF Championships in February. This was an outrageous ambition, as the current champion Roger Clark was in his prime and finished 6th in the International Cross Country held at Cambridge in 1972. I occasionally ran with, new arrival, Flying Officer Ian Wilton-Jones, and I lived his line: *If you aim for the stars, you've got a good chance of landing on the moon.* He became a good friend, who was training to be a fighter pilot and drove his Mini Cooper as if it was a fighter aircraft. Ian would forever be telling me about his 1500 metres personal best in 3:58.2; not once, but twice! I returned to Warrington to run the Chris Vose 7.2-mile Road Race and placed 26th in 37:08 – a two-minute improvement, and an average mile pace of 5:09. This earned me a phone call from Roger Clark, who was impressed with my run and said I had beaten some good club runners. He offered me a run for the RAF First Eight vs Oxford University.

The first race of the 72/73 North Wales Cross-Country League at Bangor was on Saturday 7th October 1972, and I needed to beat 50th place from the previous year. The course was rough and hilly, but there is no substitute for fitness, and I won in 28:29 with Arthur Moore second in 28:41. I made another breakthrough, and this would keep me enthused through the winter. In some ways, the win made me a little nervous that I might get carried away with my form and race too hard before the crunch race at Halton in February.

I got my light-blue RAF vest when I ran on 21st October 1972 against Oxford University. Now, I started to beat runners I'd only read about in *Athletics Weekly*. The course was through undulating, ancient forests, with the *Dreaming Spires* serving as a stunning backdrop. I was delighted to finish 5th in the five-mile event in 26:00 minutes, and we easily beat the boys in dark blue. A week later, and the Second North Wales League at Aberystwyth, which I won with Duncan Gaskell second from the home club. Just four days later, I was due to run for the RAF vs Borough Road College, and British Universities. My training was good, and I was firing on all cylinders. Running was fluent and a complete joy. But had I hit peak form too early? I was twenty-nine, and still a novice of sixteen months. Against much better opposition, I placed 4th in 27:55 for the 5.75-mile race against some serious athletes. I finished ahead of the National Youth Champion Neil Saunders, and it all seemed easy. Sometimes, an early breakthrough can make an athlete over-confident and I hoped I could find this form again at Halton in February. Despite my overarching ambition, I had proved myself at the highest level yet.

We took a strong team from Valley to compete in the RAF Henlow Ten-mile Championship. The course was point-to-point, starting at RAF Cardington, famous for housing the gigantic R101 airship built in 1929. On 4th October 1930, the R101 was brought down by gale-force winds and heavy rain, and crashed on a hill in Beauvais, France. There were only six survivors from fifty-four on board, and it spelt the end of airship development in the UK. The race was held on Wednesday 24th November 1972, on a sunny but cool afternoon with a slight northerly breeze. The 200-plus runners gathered near the massive green airship hangar, listening to the starter's instructions to keep left on the public roads we were using. I had kept my recent good form, felt eager to set a personal best at ten-miles. Roger Clark also wanted to set a personal best, and he was closely followed by Mike Hurd. I was astonished to be in third place, consoling myself that these athletes had trained for at least ten years to reach their standard. Nevertheless, I was amazed I could hold onto third spot, and a bonus of my first sub-50-minute clocking. **Results:** 1. Roger Clark 47:53, 2. Mike Hurd 48:43, 3. Pete Flatman 49:53, 4. Ray Crabb 50:18. Roger had set a course record, but Valley won the team race with Ian Wilton-Jones 9th 51:30 and Arthur Moore 11th 51:55. Our B team came 23rd.

The third North Wales Cross-Country fixture was at Wrexham on Saturday 2nd December 1972; the course was wet, the going heavy, and I was feeling unwell. As I pushed harder, the deeper I sank into the mud – it was my worst nightmare. My lead was less than ten metres and Duncan Gaskell and Ewan Williams were snapping at my heels. On the second lap, the mud was churned up by the hundreds of feet dipping into the sticky quagmire. For me, the last fifty metres were replayed in my head as if in slow motion, and time stood still. The strain on our faces told of our toil – and that at any moment I thought I'd be overwhelmed. I threw myself at the line and collapsed into the clinging mud and won by two seconds. My last race for a while and now I could concentrate on my plan to win the RAF Championships in February. Firstly, I needed to know what it was like to run at Roger Clark's race pace for six miles, but it was quicker than anything I had so far achieved, and I needed a plan. I measured and marked a course of four miles with a surveyor's wheel and a pot of paint. The four miles was 66% of the six-mile RAF race, and if I could run the distance in training in 19:20, I should be able to keep that pace for the extra two miles. I knew that a time trial was usually up to fifteen seconds slower per mile than a race because of the lack of the race-day adrenaline. If I could do this, I truly believed it would give me a chance to achieve a medal.

The first attempt was just outside twenty minutes, but I forgave myself because, I had eight weeks to whittle the time down to nineteen minutes. My mission, though did not allow enough time to have another season on the track, another year of 5000 miles to consolidate my stamina, or another year to run with some of Britain's finest athletes, such as Roger Clark, Julien Goater, Jon Wild and Ray Crabb. This chance would end soon, but I would do everything possible to achieve my aim, which had engrossed and motivated me since 1971. I kept my training at a hundred plus miles per week through Christmas and New Year of 1973 – a year which would be momentous in one way or another.

CHAPTER 6

RAF First Eight

My next stepping stone would be the Training Command Cross-Country Championships at RAF Henlow on Wednesday 20th January 1973. After another long journey from Anglesey to the outskirts of London, we found the course had been changed because of a local outbreak of foot and mouth disease. It was three laps of the airfield perimeter, grassed, and quite flat. Someone shouted, *'Eric Delaney is running, and can run forty-eight seconds for 400 metres!'* I was already over-hyped and did not need any more incentive to run faster. But, the thought of Eric beating me to the first turn wound me up like a coiled spring. The gun fired, and I took off as though I was *the* sprinter and never looked back or heard anyone. As I crossed the line, I leapt up, as if I had just netted the winner at the FA Cup Final and made a vain attempt to knock the stars out of the sky. I won the race by nearly two minutes. Now, I proved my radical training was paying off, but should I have held back, once I knew the race was in the bag? Perhaps this was a time when I would have benefited from having a coach. Ian Wilton-Jones and Arthur Moore were second and third, which secured another team win for RAF Valley.

The penultimate North Wales League race was at Shrewsbury on a very traditional course of hills, gates, and streams on the outskirts of the town. The league had fully served its purpose and helped to put us on a par with other RAF stations that competed in service leagues around the country. Shrewsbury were a good team, and headed by a stalwart of many years, Ewan Williams. I remained unbeaten with my biggest margin of thirty-eight seconds, while Arthur and Ian took second and third. The team title for the series was out of sight, but we had given a good account of ourselves, and Valley.

Now I could concentrate on the final build-up to my make-or-break attempt to win the big race at Halton on Wednesday 24th February 1973. I got within a whisker of my target on my four-mile circuit of torture at Valley now I needed to trust to Nature and good luck. This was the place I learned to fear those bright-eyed, fit-as-a-butcher's-dog fiends, now I had become one of them. Walking the course was a popular activity before a cross-country event and could be justified to check the state of the running surface. But I considered it a distraction, when I should be getting in the zone for the terrific battle ahead. Lots of idle chit-chat and questions about one's form does little to concentrate the mental side for a big event, and this, for me, was the biggest of all.

Ahead of me was thirty minutes of physical and mental stress. I felt as ready as I could be for this race – I had kept to my plan, but now needed to produce a miracle. Heavy rain for two hours meant the grassy, undulating course had become heavy and waterlogged. The weather was around 7 °C, when 406 competitors faced the starter. My plan would be as simple as it was foolhardy: to chase Roger Clark, the overwhelming favourite, and try to stay with him. The first 400 metres were uphill, but I thought if I don't try, it would be a lasting regret. The starter's pistol startled, the leading contenders scarpered, like an ill-fated cavalry charge. Within two minutes, I was on that narrow ledge between aerobic and anaerobic calamity. The latter happens when the body lacks the oxygen to metabolise the body's glycogen and when it's breached, the breathing becomes laboured and the muscles fill with lactic acid, causing an inevitable slow-down. I had kept within two metres of Roger, but my body was screaming to be released.

I understand this delicate balance but tried through force of mind over body to ignore it. However, this is basic physiology, which decrees you cannot take more out than you put in. I had placed my body on the athlete's rack, I had tried to defy Nature and now endured the torture. Meanwhile, my body was protecting itself – while I was hell-bent on destroying myself. Somehow, I caught my quarry, one of the best cross-country runners in Europe, but now I was paying as my guts were wrenched with cramp, and legs seared and stretched to breaking point, while a battle of mind over body, or vice-versa, made me feel wretched. At this point, I even felt I might have to drop out, but that was brief, even as runners started to catch me.

I was like a car firing on three cylinders, a ship without a sail, or a man lost in the desert. My bed had been made, and now I would have to accept the consequences. All hope of winning had vanished into the thin, cold air. I would have to husband my depleted resources if I was to qualify for the RAF First Eight in the upcoming Inter-Services match. My mental ability had been my greatest strength, but now proved to be my Achilles heel. I could not match the runners who passed me but recovered to lose no more places and finished fifth. Over forty-four years have passed since that epic day – it was my big chance, and if I ran the race over again, I would never have beaten Roger Clark but firmly believe that with a different approach I could have competed for a medal. The RAF Cross-Country Team Manager Flight Lieutenant Alan Warner said, '*Pete, I never saw you making the First Eight for the Inter-Services.*' I thought, little did he know, how devastated I was to have missed the podium. **Results:** 1. Roger Clark 27:33 2. Ray Crabb 29:01 3. John Wild 29:17 4. Ray Donkin 29:36 5. Pete Flatman 30:00 6. Kevin Daykin 30:03 7. Kevin Best 30:07 8. John Clarke 30:10 9. Sandy Keith 30:12 10. Bill Tonner 30:18. On another level, I had helped RAF Valley win the bronze team medals for the first time. Team counters for RAF Valley: Me 5th, Ian Wilton-Jones 14th, Arthur Moore 20th, Dusty Miller 61st, John McCarthy 69th, Phil Goodall 91st... Gordon Sutherland 162nd, John Holmes 194th, Stan Owen 168th, and Steve Murphy 237th; 380 finished. **Teams:** 1.

RAF Brize Norton (11, 12, 21, 22, 43, 48) 157 pts; 2. RAF Wyton (2, 3, 24, 27, 35, 102) 193 pts; 3. RAF Valley (5, 14, 20, 61, 69, 91) 261 pts.

I put on my long-sleeved top and ran a lap of the RAF Cross-Country course, which had encapsulated my heart and soul for two years. My journey from the obscurity of a mere number in Her Majesty's Royal Air Force towards the top of the tree as a distance runner was all-consuming. When I joined the Service as a boy entrant, aged sixteen, I could never have imagined a sport that would match my temperament so perfectly. My early life was affected by whooping cough, scarlet fever and diphtheria, which meant I lost my first year at school. My father's bankruptcy would mean a move to another county, and with it a different 11 plus syllabus which I failed to pass. Soon I was working in a chicken processing plant, from the age of eleven to sixteen. As I continued my warm-down, I thought of my progress: 141st in 1971; 21st in 1972; and 5th in 1973, in what would be my last chance to run in this event. But now all my faculties would be needed to find work and provide a home for my wife and three children.

I made an appointment to see an RAF Resettlement Officer. I was not sure if he could help me, as I had settled on becoming a medical sales representative, but I wanted to be certain I had researched all possibilities. Squadron Leader Phelps greeted me,

'Good afternoon, Corporal Flatman. How can I help you?'

'I've found a job, sir, but need a month's leave to train as a medical representative.'

'Congratulations, I'll speak to CO Admin. It's the least we can do.'

'Thanks sir, I would have preferred to have signed on…'

'I know, the RAF has to reduce personnel.'

'I joined as a boy, sir, but I'm ready for Civvy Street.'

'That's the spirit. Now tell me what's your greatest achievement in life?'

'Easy, sir – making the RAF Cross-Country team for the Inter-Services.'

'Wrong answer, Corporal. What about your wedding day – it was mine.'

'If you knew how hard it is to make the First Eight, sir then you'd realise, it's much easier to find a wife than get into that team,' I said with a smile.

'I'm still not sure, Corporal,' he said.

'So, sir what sporting success have you enjoyed?'

'None, I'm afraid.'

'Game, set and match, sir?'

CHAPTER 7

Inter-Services

I contacted BBC Wales sport about the success, after many a barren year, of RAF Valley's cross-country team and received a favourable response. Peter Walker, the former Glamorgan cricketer came to Anglesey with a film crew and interviewed me after we had run a short distance on Cymyran beach. The camera crew would return on Saturday to film the fifth and final North Wales cross country race. The publicity was excellent for RAF Valley set in such a remote location and was aired on *Sport Wales* on 15th March.

The Inter-Service cross-country championship was held at the Guard's Depot Pirbright on Friday 9th March 1973, and my son's first birthday, which would mean a five-hour drive, and the same back. I had never competed on a Friday before or since – so it was sad not to share his first birthday with my family. The British Army are a proud bunch and many of them considered they were the superior service. Indeed, they came up with the dastardly idea of using the ferocious assault course, more suited to yomping than cross country running. Furthermore, the one in three gradient hills would surely halt those slick 'Brylcreem' boys. Next, an Army barrack room lawyer noticed Ray Crabb, who had qualified in second place in the RAF Championship was under eighteen and ineligible to compete. The khaki serge had put the boot in and sought to undermine the RAF, but would they be prepared for the sky-blue vengeance. Our hosts must have wondered what hit them when the RAF first-eight wreaked havoc amongst the squaddies, the like of which had not been seen in years, moreover, it would take the British Army twenty years to get their hands on the Inter-Services Cup again. **Results:** 1. R Clark (RAF) 35:44 2. J Wild (RAF) 37:13 3. R Ward (Navy) 37:21 4. J Goater (RAF) 37:59 5. W Venus (Army) 38:07 6. R Donkin (RAF) 38:13 7. M Hurd (RAF) 38:15 8. J Clare (Navy) 38:18 9. K Daykin (RAF) 38:25 10. P Flatman (RAF) 38:41 11. P Brazil (Army) 38:47 12. P Horwood (Navy) 39:19 13. Molloy (Army) 39:23 14. M Gue (Army) 39:35 15. K Spacie (Army) 39:41 16 R Dicker (Navy) 40:05 17. K Best (RAF) 40:15 18. T Davies (Army) 40:30 19. P Dring (Army) 40:38 20. P Chapman (Navy) 40:51 21. V McClenaghan (Navy) 40:55 22. R Meadows (Navy) 41:51 23. A Ratcliffe (Navy) 42:27 24. E Ranicar (Army) 44:05. **Teams:** 1. RAF 29 2. Army 76 3. Royal Navy 80. My run was good enough to earn selection for Combined Services two weeks later.

I joined some of my team-mates for couple of miles warm-down, and I met Julien Goater for the first time. He was a member of Shaftesbury Harriers along with David Bedford and soon he would be challenging his world-record 10,000 metres. He would also win the National cross-country race at Parliament Hill by an unprecedented two minutes in 1981. Julien was 20 at the time, and I asked him this question,

'I'm trying to run 5000 metres under 14:30 – have you any advice?'

'Run the first lap in 71 seconds and then keep to 70 seconds per circuit,' Julien said.

I thought, *if you ask a daft question you must expect such an answer.*

Then I started the five-hour journey back to Anglesey, and my family after an exhausting day. Twelve hours later, I would be competing in the final North Wales fixture on my favourite course at RAF Valley. My legs were still aching from yesterday's assault course, but I managed to win by a few seconds from team-mate Arthur to complete my fifth win. Wrexham won the title and I produced a programme in which I paid tribute to all my friends who'd made the season so memorable.

One lad was Stan Owen from Bolton, who finished in 168th place in the RAF Championships and not dissimilar to my 141st in 1971. I met Stan at a special reunion to commemorate the twenty years of unbroken success of the RAF in the Inter-Services Cross-Country at the RAF Club in Piccadilly on 14th June 2012 and was delighted to know he'd placed in the top twenty on several occasions.

I returned to the Winsford 7-mile road race in July 1973 to try and win the Best Improved Cup again. My late arrival the previous year meant I had a 2 or 3-minute cushion, plus, I thought my form made me 2-minutes faster. This time, I made no mistake and was there with time to spare. Ron Hill made a stir when he turned up in bright canary yellow vest and shorts. I tried to stay ahead of Ron to avoid being rendered blind staring at his kit! In the event, Ron kicked after 4-miles and went on to win the race, but I was more than happy to record 33-minutes 6-seconds and reduced my previous best by 5-minutes 18-seconds and retained the Best Improved Cup. The next year the organiser rang me in Hull and asked for the trophy back and I explained I was not in the form to repeat that again and sent the trophy back by post.

The Burton-wood relays had made a big impression on me in 1971, and I was determined to bring something like that to RAF Valley. With all the running I did, there was not a nook or cranny of the local roads I did not know, and one had always fascinated me. The circuit was practically traffic-free, the lane only six feet wide with undulating terrain traversed by a small bridge over a narrow tributary, which added to its aesthetic appeal. The complete circuit measured 1.7-miles and though quite short meant more people would take part. I also reckoned teams of three would also encourage a better turn-out. The first event, in September 1972, attracted a modest 27-runners in 9-teams, which doubled in March 1973. The third relay on 14thAugust

1973 encouraged over a hundred entrants, and 35-teams of 3 faced the starter Group Captain Huxley. Running-wise I was at a peak and reduced my record from 8 mins 5 secs to 7 mins 38 secs and on an accurate distance my average mile pace was 4 mins 30 secs. Apart from organising the Valley's first road relay, I also managed a Valley track and field team that reached the final of the RAF Inter Station final for the first time. During the winter, our cross-country team won the Training Command Championships and placed third in the RAF Championships. On the road, Valley won the Henlow 10 for the first time. I was very happy to persuade so many to create pride in themselves and our station. On a lighter note one of my friends had this to say, when I was presented with a trophy for my services to RAF athletics, *'To end on a humorous note, Peter would like to thank the firm of Gestetner, and the Bowmaker paper Mills for their unstinting support which helped him flood the station with circulars, posters, results sheets and the like to rally his troops in the cause of athletics at RAF Valley.'*

CHAPTER 8

Relocation

I came to the decision that raising and killing chickens was not for me. Nor did I want to cause any conflict with my younger brother. Pharmaceutical companies were on the look-out for ex-RAF medics to recruit as medical representatives. Consequently, I visited a recruitment agency in London and obtained interviews with BDH Chemicals and Roche. While this was encouraging it would still be a major challenge with only five O Levels to my name. My wife was quick on the uptake and realised with all my running training, most of my civilian clothes were old and out-of-date. In the space of an afternoon I would be transformed like a later TV make-over programme. The fifty-shilling wedding suit, worn out shirts, and terrible shoes were confined to history. A mirror told the story: I looked and saw an up to the minute Italian navy pin-stripe suit with lapels almost lapping my arms and flared trousers that would flap in the wind. Even though I was not strictly within the bounds of RAF regulation, I was already cultivating bushy side-burns.

All I knew about Preston was its football club, and Sir Tom Finney. He died in 2014. Sir Stanley Matthews said of him, *'A truly great player and on a par with Pele, Maradona, Best and Di Stefano.'* My interview took place in the Station Hotel Preston in July 1973. The room was spacious, and I sat at a chair opposite Sid Richardson area manager for Scarborough, York, Hull and Doncaster. On his right was the Northern Regional Manager for BDH chemicals. Sid checked my name, address, and asked if I wanted a tea or coffee. I refused as suggested by the agency who put me forward. Polite conversation ensued for a few minutes, as Sid waxed lyrical about Liverpool, and I said I supported Colchester United! Then out of the blue the Regional manager said,

'Would you tell us about your life so far?'

'I was born in Diss, Norfolk in 1943 – lived on a farm where my dad bred ducks for Smithfield Market … we moved around a lot and settled near Colchester in 1955…' and so on.

'That's enough Peter now let me tell you about our great company…'

A week later I received a letter offering me the position with a starting salary of £1850 plus generous expenses and an Austin Maxi motor car. I travelled to London on Sunday 2nd of September and stayed at a hotel in Elephant and Castle and each morning took the tube to Allen & Hanburys Victorian factory at Bethnal Green. Besides, this the factory had become a training site for Glaxo and its subsidiaries, which included BDH chemicals and later Duncan Flockhart pharmaceuticals. The course would last a month and for part of which I would shadow an experienced representative around his patch in central London, then in the middle of a heatwave, sticky and very uncomfortable. I did my best to keep up some training and getting to know London at the same time – I even ran a 10,000-metres at Crystal Palace in 31:22. An Austin Maxi was allocated to me, which meant I was able to drive to and from Anglesey. My running was taking a backward step, but the needs of my family must take centre stage.

The following weekend I drove home on Friday in the company car. Next day, I took my wife and three kids to East Yorkshire to find somewhere to live. My area was extensive, and it was difficult to know where to live to minimise my travel time to call on GPs, consultants and chemists. Even though we had lived at Cleethorpes and York in the 1960s, it never occurred to me to venture to Kingston upon Hull.

We stayed over at, *'The Ship'* in Shiptonthorpe, but our room was directly above a noisy bar. There, we found a jug of water in a large bowl and under the bed a piddle pot in lieu of a loo! The next day we found a seaside let in Bridlington, available till March and snapped it up. The flat was on the second floor, so not especially suitable for three children aged 7, 5, and 7-months. However, the flat served its purpose and we moved in on 2nd October 1973, after a long journey from Anglesey.

The following weekend I journeyed to Hull via Market Weighton and Beverley the latter dominated by the Minster which is larger than a third of English cathedrals, but conversely it is only one of two parish churches in the town. Beverley Minster was rebuilt in the thirteenth century and widely considered to be a gothic masterpiece. I reached the outskirts of Hull in the half light and was astonished to see several high-rise flats that made a dramatic backdrop against the fields of East Yorkshire. So, this was the great city of Kingston upon Hull, that had endured destructive bombing in WW2 and always referred to as a, *North East coastal town,* in the war-time media. Although it was apparent the city had seen better days, I was impressed by the dual carriageways towards the centre and the sense of space. Unfortunately, I lost my way in Queen's Gardens and must have circuited them at least four times before crossing North Bridge to Holderness Road and now in a desperate search for a B&B. A right turn to Southcoates Lane seemed to change my luck in the shape of a pub called, *Highland Laddie* and a painted sign offering accommodation. On a Saturday night, the pub was heaving, I fought my way to the bar,

'Do you have a room for the night?' I said without response.

'Have you a room for tonight?' I repeated in her ear.

'Sorry, we stopped doing rooms in 1969.'

I thought, *what a welcome from this famous port – probably got a lot going for it, but a bed for the night was not one of its attractions.*

Underwhelmed, I trudged out from whence I came and drove back towards North Bridge and turned left to a quiet industrial street and made myself as comfortable as possible on the back seat of my Austin Maxi. At dawn, I roused myself, and found a transport café on Cleveland Street for a bacon roll and tea. Next, I drove on to Hedon road passed the Prison towards the Docks and BP at Saltend. At last I had something that seemed familiar close to the estuary and a sign to Withernsea. In fact, on that sunny morning, I was reminded of family trips to Great Yarmouth, when all was right with the world. This city of Hull was different to any other in my experience and I resolved to make the best of it. I headed back to the centre and strolled through Whitefriargate and was amazed to see an airman from RAF Valley talking to friends on Monument Bridge. Then I drove home to Anglesey.

We had lived in 12, Maes Minfford, Caergeiliog for four years, which was, by far, our longest stay in one place in our eight years of marriage. As this property belonged to the MOD it wasn't just a case of handing the keys back. For a start, we had to check an inventory of every item provided which was substantial, furniture, beds, tables, chairs, pots & pans, cutlery, plates, saucers, kitchen utensils and even gardening equipment. The process was dehumanising and the term, *Marching Out*, akin to confessing one's sins at St Peter's Gate. The only way to sleep at night was to leave the house better than when we *Marched In* four years earlier. But worse still for my wife Tricia, because I had been training to be a Med Rep in London for the previous month so all the cleaning and caring for our three children fell on her shoulders. The march-out day arrived, Monday 2nd October at 10am. As I waited for the housing officer, I looked around our spotless married quarter of four years and the contrast with a second-floor holiday flat in Bridlington was more than I could bear. When I turned towards the kitchen, I was petrified because my wife had her head buried in the gas oven. How could I tell the kids? Thankfully, she was just cleaning a greasy shelf. Presently, the march-out team arrived wearing white gloves to find ledges undusted, which they did, but allowed us ten minutes to dust. We passed the *Marching Out* ordeal, and for the moment we were homeless. Nevertheless, I could not leave without musing about this fabulous corner of Anglesey, the traumatic birth of our beautiful son, where I found the joy of running and how the course of my life would be changed forever.

Finally, a journey of a lifetime as we packed our possessions into the Vauxhall estate, and the Austin Maxi. I led our mini convoy at a gentle speed along the A5 with Jayne for company – it would be many years before I would see Anglesey again. Meanwhile, my wife was driving the other car with Sarah, and 7-month old Simon. We had sandwiches and drinks and agreed to stop at Hartshead service station on the M62 and the scene of an IRA atrocity, four months later, with the loss of twelve lives. As a serviceman, I had grown accustomed to the nomadic life, of living in different places, where nowhere felt like home. However, in these two cars were all I held so dear and now I was cut adrift from the world in a way only a refugee would understand. The M62 ended at Ferry-bridge and we followed the signs to Selby. At last after five hours we saw the sign to Bridlington and 65, Trinity Road, top flat of a holiday let, and our thirteenth abode since our marriage in 1965. We unloaded the chattels, put the kids to bed and I ventured out for run along the prom – just to feel terra firmer again. But the zip had gone from my legs and worse still I had lost my appetite for slapping my feet on cold pavements.

The next day, I was at work visiting GPs in Hull with a target to see five a day. Every surgery was playing the same, homely wireless known as Radio Humberside and permeated a warm and friendly ambiance. The presenters had captured the essence, particularly in Hull, of a large village with integrated family ties many of which were forged through the highs and lows of deep-sea fishing. At lunch-time I walked down Jameson Street, and wandered into the Hull Daily Offices where I learnt the daily circulation was an extraordinary 131,000 and more than all the national dailies combined. The Mail was the glue that moulded the great city into a super-sized village.

At the end of the day, I was glad to get back to the flat we now called home and listen to my two daughters having fun with the local accent. Then I went to the car and brought back a black and white kitten, which soon captivated the girls. Sarah named the kitten Alison, as it was her favourite girl's name. However, their mum was not best pleased to have an untrained cat in a top floor flat, but Alison would be with us for another three moves in the up-coming years.

'How did it go?' my wife said.

'It was OK, but I met a very miserable Doctor on Holderness Road.'

'How do you mean?'

'Well he made me feel useless, and a drain on the NHS.'

'Did you see your area manager?'

'Yes, he told me to stay in the second lane on Willerby Road dual-carriageway.'

'Why is that?'

'So, I was not swerving to avoid parked cars.' I said

'I bought Jayne and Sarah a school blouse and cardigan.'

CHAPTER 9

East Hull Harriers

I went into the bedroom and filled in my call sheets, and orders taken from chemists. After a busy day, I needed to run, and found a road known as Wold-gate which led to the village of Kilham. The light was fading fast, and I became rather nervous as a thicket of overhanging trees transformed the gloaming to the black of night. Even though I ran this route many times I always felt a chill when I passed under that tree cover. Imagine my surprise, when recently, I went to see a David Hockney exhibition of his life-time works of art at the Pompidou Centre in Paris. His paintings are full of colour, vitality, but what I saw in the last hall blew me away, a series of large pictures of, *Wold-Gate the 4 Seasons*. I had run there many times, and often felt uneasy especially in the dark, but to see such wonderful depictions brought a feeling of peace, I never felt, at the time, on that evocative road. At least I was running daily, but still feeling unfit. One day, I met an old couple from the bottom flat as I came home from a run.

'I know someone called Dick Dobson, who used to work with me on the Hull to Hornsea railway. He's being laying trails for East Hull Harriers for years – I'll tell him about you.'

'OK thanks,' I said and thought no more of it, then a few days later I saw him again.

'I've had a letter from Dick Dobson inviting you to East Hull's club house.'

The letter was quaint, gentle and written with careful thought. As he knew I was a Southerner he'd drawn a map showing Salts-house Road, the club-house adjacent to Sutton Hospital, and a block of council flats opposite.

The afternoon of 21ˢᵗ October 1973 was cool, the air damp from recent rain, as I stood opposite a ramshackle, turn of century, wooden hut, amongst a thicket of trees. Moreover, the sign above the door announced to all the importance of *East Hull Harriers & Athletic Club*, originally formed in 1893, but then known as, *The Holderness Road Presbyterian Harriers.*

I lifted the time-worn latch and stepped into another world of service and duty. The old hut was first used, when the club moved, in 1908, from the Presbyterian church to the Crown Inn on the opposite side of Holderness Road, but quite what the church elders made of the Harriers' transfer to a public house is unknown. As my eyes adjusted to the dull interior of the hut, I noticed race posters attached to a notice board, and wooden benches along white-washed walls. The club-hut was damp, which made the air humid, and acrid. But for me, the memories made here on raw Saturday afternoons – the battle over the clinging clay on Castle Hill; negotiating water filled drains, and the chasing down of the slower packs of harriers. Memories seeped from every nook and cranny of this revered shelter. On Saturday afternoons, the slow-pack of older members would recall when they were the fast boys, the medium-pack would work together to keep the fast-pack at bay. On the good days, all three packs would finish within seconds of each other. There was a great cheer as Dickie arrived to lay the paper trail, on the drain banks, and sticky clay-based farm-lands. Despite constant enquiry Dickie, as ever, never divulged the route of the day's pack run.

'Are you Peter, the RAF lad I invited to the club?'

'Yes, thank you for your kind letter, Mr Dobson.'

'Let's have none of that, call me Dickie. I'll let Peter Dearing know you're here.'

Veteran runners complained of sore knees, tendons, shins, and would till they could run no more. For me, being in this time-served hut was akin to the time-doctor's Tardis with its ability to connect me with harriers of past generations. The smell of winter green oil applied to worn-out limbs was like an incense burner being wafted at Holy Communion. At the back of the hut was a doorway, only partially hidden by multi-coloured plastic streamers. Inside were two galvanised tin baths, fed by a Belling boiler, which would often overflow with clogging mud.

Peter Dearing was the club secretary, dedicated and determined to raise the profile of a once respected sporting team.

'Peter this is the RAF lad I spoke about,' Dickie said as if he'd had a win on the pools.

'Can we have a chat after the pack run,' the secretary said as he made eye-contact with me.

Dickie looked on and wondered why he'd not signed me up right-away. But his duty called: he removed his bicycle clips, adjusted his bag of ticker-tape and started to lay the trail as he had done for thirty years.

'Not over the castle mound please, it's knee high in mud,' Ken Keats pleaded.

'And that bloody drain-bank near the hospital needs a canoe,' Johnny Crawford chided.

The slow pack did just that as they jogged into a winter's afternoon, some recalling their relatives who'd obeyed the subaltern's whistle, only to be cut down by enemy machine guns at Oppy Wood. The medium pack followed ten minutes later, some with vivid recollections of their city being devastated by the Luftwaffe. There were just five in the past pack, including me, which were now twenty minutes behind the slow pack. I was thankful my thirteen-year RAF career was relatively peaceful. Without a thought, I set off at my normal pace, and was soon fifty metres ahead, when the wags started,

'Who does he think he is, Derek Ibbotson?'

'Dickie will have him on heavy plough today.'

For me, it was an adventure to follow a paper trail, and gave me a sense of adventure missing on the athletics track. I should have run slower as I was amongst the first back to the club house and a relatively clean bath of hot water. When I changed, Guy Buckley, a Frenchman, who came to Hull in WW2 greeted me,

'Well done, you're a good runner, but you must win the club championship to have their respect.'

'Thank you. I noticed you won three times after the war.'

'Yes, and then I was respected as one of them.'

So, there it is, I'm an outsider like Guy, and need to prove myself. The club secretary beckoned me,

'Did you enjoy the trail?' Peter said.

'Yes, but the plough was deep and sticky.'

'I noticed you ran ten miles in 49:53 last year, and wondered if we are the right club for you?' Peter said

'I didn't belong to a running club in the RAF, maybe it's not so important,' I said.

'None of our runners will be able to give you enough competition.'

'Thanks for being so honest, I'm happy to sign up for East Hull,' I enthused.

I was shocked Peter Dearing, an avid and ambitious club secretary thought, I might not want me to join his club. But his was an act of integrity above personal ambition.

In 1957 the club changed from an all-white kit to red vest and white shorts – perhaps, so the club would not be confused with Real

Madrid? East Hull Harrier's president, Graham Brummitt was old school, a prodigious organiser, and an official measurer of road races. His house on Rosmead Street was used for committee meetings, and if we were lucky a pint in the local before time was called. He also wrote the club newsletter, with a brief note called *With the Racing Members*, it was short on content, because not many harriers ventured into races. These were the active members at the end of 1973: John Crawford, Eric Chambers, Peter Dearing, Guy Buckley, Gary Foulson, Alan Hugman, Brian Jones, Brian Jennison, Graeme Jenison, Ronnie Kemp, Brian Kitchen, Dave Leveson, Richard McKowen, Ron Mason, Alan McColl, Derrick Pickering, Dave Stutt, Alan Wiles, Les Wiles and myself. Hull was quite isolated, at the time, and it was difficult to get a team of three to run any out-of-town road race.

On 1st January 1974 I travelled north to run in the famed Morpeth to Newcastle road race. A record field of 170 got off to a slow start into the teeth of a bitterly cold headwind. Jim Alder won, but five minutes slower than his best run. Furthermore, a measure of the severity of the wind was that only 24 runners beat the first time standard as compared to the usual 60-70. **Results:** 1. J Alder (Morpeth) 69:50 2. D Pratt (Sheffield) 69:56 3. A Spence (Bingley) ... 34. P Flatman (E Hull) 75:36. **Teams:** 1. Morpeth 26 2. Sale 27 3. Kendal 43.

Although I was running most days it lacked the purpose of the previous year when I was hell-bent on winning the RAF Championships. We were house-hunting in earnest, and we finally chose a three-bedroomed house on Belvedere Drive, Bilton for £7,900 to the East of Hull. Our girls could walk to Thanet Primary, I was well placed for my busiest part of my territory and we lived only a mile from East Hull's venerable club-house.

I had saved with Guardian Building Society for six years, and enough for the ten per cent deposit. But when I applied for a mortgage, it was refused, saying, *I'm afraid you have insufficient status!* I withdrew my savings and closed the account. In Beverley, I received another rebuff when I went into *Dee & Atkinsons* and asked about properties in the £8000 range. She peered at me quizzically, in the practised manner of one who had to deal with the impoverished class, *Oh, we never have anything available at that price.* A visit to Beverley Building Society restored my faith in the town. I put down a lump sum into a new account, and we moved into our new home in February 1974. The house was built in 1952 by a well-regarded local builder with a good front and a small back garden where, I installed a children's swing. I have a treasured photo of Jayne, Sarah and Simon dutifully washing their bikes against the house wall.

Absent Without Leave

My girlfriend Carol wearing a pink patent leather mac, and silk headscarf came to see me off at North Station Colchester to join the Royal Air Force in September 1960. She still couldn't understand why I'd signed up for thirteen years. I brushed her cheek to wipe a tear and we promised to write every day, but it would be three long months before we'd meet again. Three trains and four hours later I was at RAF Cosford, wearing civilian clothes, we were marched, with our baggage, to pre-war billets – our new home. We each had a steel bed, horse-hair mattress and a neatly arranged bed pack but looking like a giant triple decker sandwich. The next three days passed in a blur of activity: sarcastic, screaming, swearing NCOs informing us we had lost our mums; lights out, lights on, and a screeched reveille at 06:30. Later that morning, we were herded into an unheated hall, where we stripped off to be examined, and coughed on command. Then we had a series of war lectures, and kitted out with every conceivable piece of clothing, even down to bag called a housewife, with a sewing kit inside! On the 22nd September 1960 almost four hundred of us gave the oath of allegiance to her majesty.

After the shock of the initial week there was a structure of daily trade training, and a semblance of order ensued. I wrote to Carol every day, and sometimes received two or three in return. Corporal Gunga Din, aptly named for his swarthy face and tough attitude, announced a thirty-six-hour weekend off, but we'd still be confined to barracks, and I wondered if I could outwit the system. The boy-entrants could wear civilian clothes from midday on Saturday, which might enable me to avoid the scrutiny of the guard room. I was determined to make the five-hundred-mile round trip from Wolverhampton to Colchester and return undetected within the time limit. We had been warned of a bed check at 10pm on Saturday, but my pals said they would cover for me. By late afternoon I was on the last leg from Liverpool Street to Colchester singing this song '*Got no bags and baggage to slow me down, Travelling, so fast my feet aren't touching the ground!*' In those days, there was no easy way to let her know I was coming. Imagine, Carol's shock when I arrived at her front door – now all those paper kisses could spring to life, like so many rose petals on a scented garden. The affirmation of true love till we die, and her lovely perfume would linger on my clothes for the weekend. I saw my sisters and brother and returned to Cosford by early evening the next day. Once again, I slipped into camp undetected, but was nervous I might have been missed. The lads were full of it, how they had used pillows under bedclothes to depict my body and the end of a broom to portray my head as I slept. Indeed, it was just as well, because there was a late-night check, yet thanks to my pals, I'd evaded detection and a stretch in a military prison.

After the upheaval of moving from Anglesey starting a new job and buying our first house, it was not a surprise my enthusiasm for running through a dark, cold winter, had waned somewhat. I found a route of about ten miles to and from my front door, which took me through Bilton toward Sproatley, and passed Burton Constable Hall on to

Coniston/Thirtleby Lane, and on to Swine Loop and Ganstead Lane and home. For the most part, the roads were not busy, and reasonably well-paved. While not, as inspirational as my favourite RAF Valley course, I managed to paint half-mile, mile marks on the road surface as measured by a surveyor's wheel. This was ideal for speed endurance sessions: 8 x ½ mile, 5 x 1-mile, 4 x 1.5-mile or 3 x 2-mile – particularly suitable for longer road races such as ½ marathon, 20-mile, and marathon races. I had hoped to have at least another season on the track, but East Hull did not have a track team, so the season was reduced to occasional Hull & District meetings, which never ran to time, and lacked competitive athletes. Consequently, I never broke any of my track personal-bests from my RAF days, which I am convinced meant slower personal-bests in long road races too.

I saw the gleaming *East Hull Harriers Members Cup* and wondered if my name would be engraved on the venerable 1920 trophy. There was quite a lot of interest, and a bit of needle, because as I was a newcomer, it would have suited some the older runners if I was thrashed, and sent home with my tail between my legs, and Johnny Crawford was the man for the job. All he had to do was reach the first style in Sutton, about a mile from the start, and injure me, in such a way, so it would seem an accident. I got to hear of the dastardly plan and had my own idea. Just to be sure, I would run close to 4:30-mile pace to the gate, if he's still with me then he's too good. I was on edge at the start and when the gun smoked, I sprinted and soon breathing like an old steam train, but I could not hear any followers. The rest of the run was more comfortable, and it was an honour to win the Member's Cup at the first time of asking. Later Dickie Dobson, who'd introduced me to the club, presented me with a varnished, hand-crafted wooden gate with my name, date and distance on the top bar of the trophy.

At the end of March was the next club event was Captain's team vs Vice Captain's team over a 6.2-mile course from the clubhouse around Bilton and back. I have never been able to understand why handicapping is condoned in a sport that is so basic and honest. Perhaps politicians might wish to incorporate a handicap scheme for parliamentary elections, because they would only need to pay off the handicapper, to be in government. The system works like this: the handicapper decides the slowest runner who receives a start time of say, 15-minutes before the best runner sets off, and is called, *off-scratch*, the intermediate runners are allocated start times to suit their perceived pace. So, for the runners, who want a little glory, only need to run slowly in a few events to have their handicap increased and then run their normal pace, win the handicap, but cheat their fellow members, and themselves. I was off scratch, starting my race fifteen minutes after the slowest runner and did not beat the handicapper, but ran 31:57 for the fastest time of the day.

Despite all the training and racing, I was doing very well in my new job, a medical sales representative for a company now renamed Duncan Flockhart Ltd, but still a subsidiary of Glaxo. The company's beta-blocker was doing well on my area and I had advanced to third best sales from the countries' sixty areas. My chemist sales were also increasing with multi-vitamins, locan cream, and aero-mycil – an anti-fungal agent for athlete's feet. All the sales force attended a three-day conference at Helier in Jersey, which included a lot of banter and sing songs. Then a surprise as the company had hired the island's only go-cart track for the afternoon. Amongst the boy-racer reps there seemed quite a few who competed seriously. But it was the first time for me. In the first-heat I was dead last and about to be eliminated, then I got the hang of racing go-carts and it was simple, flat-foot the accelerator, don't touch the brake and hope for the best. Somehow, I qualified for the semi-final and went from the gun and I won through to the final. Once again, I took the lead and built up an unassailable gap until, I saw the chequered flag, but the engine stopped, and I had to push the cart over the line to finish third.

On Saturday 1ˢᵗ June 1974, I ran East Hull's 20-miles road race incorporating the Yorkshire Championships for the first time. I often found June races to be warm and muggy, but this was even more so. Indeed, I wasn't the only one as other athletes were coming back to me and by 14-miles I was fourth and could see the village of Wawne. Middlesbrough's Tom Flory and I were vying for third place and I prevailed to come third in 1:55:37. Imagine my surprise, when I was presented with the Yorkshire winners' medal, because the two runners in first and second, Don Ritchie and David Wright (1:50:28 and 1:54:17) were from the Midlands. What happened next was surreal enough to make the national papers and the Yorkshire Post. I was asked to give my medal back, because I had not lived in Yorkshire for nine months and yet I'd lived in York for more than a year in the mid-sixties but didn't mention it. I was interviewed for the Yorkshire Post by Granville Beckett, *Had I won the race itself, I would be even more disappointed, but it was the first time I'd ever taken part in a 20-mile race and I did not do too bad.' The same article continues, Flatman (30) was stationed at Anglesey when he left the RAF after thirteen years, he is now living in Bilton. He says, 'I took up athletics three years ago, to keep fit for football, but became more and more interested. Anglesey with its beaches and sand-dunes is a great place for training and I started running 100 miles a week. I represented the Combined Services at cross country and won the North Wales ten-miles championship two years in succession. Recently, I have not been doing a lot of training, but when the autumn comes, I hope to have built up to 100-miles again and would like to represent Yorkshire in cross country events and win the Hull and District championship.' These* quotes are from a time when everything seemed possible. **Results:** 1. D Ritchie (Birchfield) 1:50:28 2. P Wright (P Beeston) 1:54:17 3. P Flatman (E Hull) 1:55:27 4. T Flory (M&C) 1:56:34 5. C Jackson (B'field) 1:56:57 6. T Hunter (E Hull Ind) 1:58:43 7. W Padgett (Bing) 2:00:21 8. D Bennett (Roth) 2:01:21 9. C Bricher (M&C) 2:02:10 10. 10. D Skidmore (P Beeston) 2:03:11. **Teams:** 1. Bingley 16 2. East Hull 19 3. Middlesbrough) 23.

I was so busy with work and training that, I neglected the front garden. Our once pristine privet hedge was spilling over the driveway and would need surgical intervention. I cut the hedge back so much that a heavy goods vehicle could park on the drive! However, my nearest and dearest was underwhelmed with my rough pruning. *'I see Peter the hedge hacker has done his worst.'* Then she shot me a look of disdain, such as given by Roman Emperors despatching underperforming gladiators.

Peter Dearing put his heart and soul into East Hull Harriers, but the apathy and lack of success must have dismayed him. I think he saw me as some latter-day, *Pied Piper of Hamlyn*, who might inspire others to train harder and to want to win. Peter ran up to 100-miles per week and hoped his new club record for the marathon of two hours forty-four minutes and nineteen seconds might trigger some enthusiasm. Peter was also the club's press officer and a very good one too. Then a nice surprise as East Hull's better athletes Johnny Crawford and Tom Hunter decided to increase their training to compete in out of town road races. We agreed to run as a team in the Ripon ten-miles race. I placed 4th in 52:24, Johnny 11th 54:03, Tom 12th in 54:11, and Brian Jones 18th in 56:02. Peter Dearing had his Hull Daily Mail headline, *'East Hull produced the finest performance in their eighty-year history.'* The result sheet said it all: 1st Team (3 to count) Bingley Harriers 14pts 2nd Team East Hull Harriers 27 pts 3rd Team Holmfirth 31 pts.

I continued to get fitter and ran in the East Hull Harriers summer league 6.2-mile and 8.2-mile event which I won and reduced the course record by 12-seconds (30:55), and by 56-seconds (41:08) respectively. My form must have been good, because I sneaked into second place in the handicap! As if to prove a point, my next event would test my distance running training, the Major Stone half marathon held on 14th September 1974, and would be my first attempt at this distance. I was unable to stay with seasoned athletes like Bingley's Alan Spence, who had won the inaugural race in 1970, Harrogate's Tim Godolphin, or Rowntrees' Jim Craven. My 4th place time 69:26 proved, to me, I had yet to find my old RAF form. **Results:** 1. A Spence (Bing) 66:02 2. T Godolphin (Harrogate) 66:05 3. J Craven (Rowntrees) 68:04 4. P Flatman (EH) 69:26 5. W Padgett (Bing) 70:34 6. A White (Long) 71:04. **Teams:** 1. Longwood Harriers 19 2. Harrogate AC 30 3. Bingley 31.

My area manager asked me to make an appointment to see the GP, who looks after Ampleforth College for their supply of influenza vaccine. Little did I know the far-reaching consequences of this simple request from Sid Richardson. The next week I drove to see the GP in his surgery in Ampleforth village. He was very hospitable and spoke with great feeling of his time as a student and how the Catholic school had shaped his life. Then he suggested I go to the college infirmary and see Matron for an order for influenza vaccine. I was heartened by his welcome and by the glorious sunny day as I parked my car at the rear of the college. The school was founded in 1802 by the Benedictine monks, and their guiding principle is to provide pupils with, *A Spiritual Compass for Life*. As I opened the rear portal I heard the monks practising Gregorian Chant in the Abbey church. My emotions were uplifted, and I felt privileged to be in such an awesome place when I walked along a corridor of memories. To my left were two large plaques for the Captains of Association Football and the Captains of Rugby Football Union. I turned right to a wider passageway illuminated by streams of bright sunshine. The sun was beckoning me to a large door, as if to tell me something special, and something I would never forget.

I opened the door and all I could do was simply stand and stare at the magnificent panorama before me. Two thousand acres stretched two miles across a beautiful valley, and for as far as I could see the vale was dotted with rugby pitches. Furthermore, a theatre, a running track, a cricket pavilion, a sports centre, a swimming pool, three fish-stocked lakes and mature woodlands. I was overwhelmed by all I'd seen and remembered living through family hardships, but an idea began to form in my mind. This feeling was not for myself, nor a mere trinket collected on life's journey, but another memory I'd experienced at my grandma's knee. She pointed out a large poster on her sitting-room wall with a single, staring eye, and two ways to live a life: the depiction on one side was of gambling, stealing, drinking, debauchery and violence; on the other caring for others, good deeds, visiting the sick, charitable works, reading the scriptures and everyone you meet be deemed more important than yourself. The message was plain and simple: Earthly happiness is only possible with a pure soul. And then the revelation, in those unforgettable moments looking across this beautiful North Yorkshire valley, and I thought, *how marvellous, if my son could come here.*

A year had passed since, I'd left the Forces and I was still struggling to find the right races and competition to be as fit as I was at RAF Valley. The local clubs were short of members and would rather run pack-runs or handicap races than seek out stronger competition in the West Riding and beyond. I figured the Hull & District one-hour, track race, being held on the last Sunday in October would be a new experience.

'Peter are you running?' asked Peter Moon.

'Yes, I must be mad to run around in this storm,' I said.

'I wish I'd stayed in bed and read the sleaze in the News of the World.' Peter said.

'Guess it will be between the two of you,' Alan Hugman pronounced.

'I'm sure it will be an uncomfortable race for all of us.' I said.

The weather got worse: gale-force winds gusting to storm-ten; slamming doors and rattling windows in the track-side changing rooms and a sky full of litter. Even the three high-rise flats, named after the triple-trawler-tragedy, with loss of fifty-eight men in 1968, seemed to be swaying in the colossal wind. Who could run the furthest and who wished they hadn't turned up? The track was aptly named, Alderman Kneeshaw, but it had the nick-name of *knees sore*, owing to the uneven and bumpy running surface. The officials out-numbered the five brave souls who lined up at the start line:

'You couldn't have picked a worse day,' the starter said.

'Do your best, you never know we could be the *Famous Five*!' Peter Moon joked.

'More like the battered and winded five!' I said.

'Guess, it'll be between Peter Moon and Flatty,' Alan Hugman said.

'Hi Brian – well done for showing up on such a day,' Peter Dearing said.

'I feel sorry for the recorders and time-keepers in this weather,' Brian Smith said.

'OK lads let's get this show on the road – feet behind the start line,' the starter shouted.

The starter's gun fired, and the runners faced a wall of wind and ducked their heads with limbs akimbo – the whole scene disjointed as the competitors forced themselves to overcome the storm. Finally, the runners reached the bend and the blast was side-on and then a powerful back-wind pushed them down the back straight. Their fifteen-millimetre steel spikes screwed into glove-like moccasins pierced the cinder track and released gritty particles into the mad atmosphere causing shin abrasions on the following runners. The sky grew darker and a thunderstorm ensued: arching lightening arrowed across the black clouds and the thunderclaps clattered ears now brittle and cold. The officials shouted times, circuits and distances to ears deafened by Nature's cacophonous din. As expected Peter Moon, Hull Spartan and I had forged ahead.

My adversary continued to fight the storm in a fearless fashion putting more distance between us for the dubious honour of being the Hull & District one-hour track champion immortalised with a soft alloy medal without inscription. Peter Moon, the local man, clutched his right side and began to falter, I seized my chance, went past him. With just ten minutes remaining it looked as if the title was mine, but I was caught short and rushed to the loo. When I returned Peter had a lead of almost 400-metres – Nature's turbulence had played havoc with our heads and our innards. Once again Moon faltered, but could I catch him again in the dying seconds then alas the whistle blew, the athletes stopped on a sixpence and the distances were calculated. Peter won by eighty metres and he threw his arms aloft to acknowledge his victory.

That day, I learned more about the indomitable spirit of competition: that does need the stimulus of material wealth; all the victor had was a non-descript medal that would soon be lost at the bottom of a drawer, but the memory of that day will stay with us for the rest of our lives. In fact, Peter Moon would be immortalised, because the Hull & District One-Hour championship was the final one to be held so Peter Moon remains unbeaten to this day. The remaining competitors would continue to improve, and seek to exceed their capabilities, because as quoted by Johann Wolfgang von Goethe, *'To be pleased with one's limits is a wretched state.'*

Hull & district one-hour track race 27th October 1974 – **Results:** 1. Peter Moon (Hull Spartan) 11-miles 500-yards 2. Peter Flatman (East Hull Harriers) 11-miles 419-yards 3. Peter Dearing (EH) 9-miles 1709-yards 4. Alan Hugman (EH) 9-miles 942-yards 5. Brian Smith (EH) 8-miles 1132-yards.

My running-fitness was still well short of my peak form while in the RAF and I still hadn't found the answer to reach that standard and continue to improve. I am certain, given another three-years-service, my path would have replicated others. In three attempts at the RAF Championships I had gone from 141st, to 21st, to 5th – I'm convinced a top three-place would have happened. My form on the track also had a long way to go – in fact none of my track personal bests improved. There was not a thriving track club within a fifty-mile radius, and Trafford track at Stretford was over a 100-miles away. I felt isolated and cut off from the talent and buzz of my RAF buddies. East Hull Harriers would never be a track-club – far from it, and within a few months I was training on East Hull's 20-mile course on Saturday afternoons. My track personal bests particularly at 800, 1500 and 3000-meters were impossible to replicate, it was as though I had changed a sporty coupe car to a land-rover, which might be good over country but never stay with a racing car on a grand-prix circuit. I was receiving great notices for road races at long distances, but my leg-speed had become slower. At the time, the marathon was thought to be the preserve of athletes becoming too slow for track-racing. Indeed, running too far, too soon has destroyed many promising athletes and the potential personal-best performances of many others. I had been sucked into this athletic world of long and ultra-distance running, where how far you ran was becoming more important than the time taken. My environment for improving my basic speed had reached an abrupt halt.

East Hull Harriers were the hosts for the, 1975 Hull & District Cross Country championships – the start and finish was on wooded land near the Sutton Royal Infirmary on Salts-house road. The host club had never won the team or individual title since the first annual championships in 1890 and many thought this would be the perfect opportunity to redress the balance. I hoped the omens were good, despite the significance of the date Saturday 15th March, which was known as the, *Ides of March,* when Brutus assassinated Julius Caesar in AD44. Should I beware of this sense of foreboding or was it just a myth – what I did know was the course was the muddiest in many years, and

I preferred firmer conditions. My role was to win the individual race and lead East Hull to the team title too. No pressure then. The rules of the race decreed that clubs had to be within a 35-mile radius of Hull, so it was a surprise that York Rowntrees were competing even though beyond that radius. Oh well, I did not know their runners, and would have to beat whoever stands on the start-line. Quite soon, I would get to know Rowntrees lead athlete, John Davies, as we swapped strides over the heavy dark earth. I opened a 50-yard gap on the deepest plough only for Davies to peg me back. Along the drain bank I pushed on and yet again he drew level – was this Brutus reincarnated? I raced to the finish and yet again he drew level then finished ahead of me by the thickness of the assassinator's blade. The finish judge gave the nod to Davies, while I had given my all. When the results were in it was even more dramatic. East Hull and Rowntrees (York) had equal points though Rowntrees' last scorer was in front of East Hull's which meant by the merest margin York Rowntrees had won both titles. **Results:** 1. J Davies (Roundtrees) 45:38 2. P Flatman 45:38 (East Hull) 3. P Moon (Hull Spartan) 46:43 4. T Hunter (EH) 47:06 5, J Clark (Grimsby H) 48:14 6. C Vodden (CoH) 48:25. **Team:** 1. York Rowntrees 55pts 2. East Hull 55pts 3. City of Hull 60pts.

Our kids were growing up fast Jayne would soon be nine Sarah seven and Simon three. We had bought a second-hand super 8mm cine camera from a farmer in Lund and captured lots of magic moments we still enjoy. My job was becoming easier as I became more proficient with paper work and made more contacts. Our family life was serene, and we arranged a holiday and booked a caravan at Perranporth near Newquay. We may not have been rich in money terms, but as a family unit we were rich beyond measure.

One week after the Hull & District I stood at the start of the very same course determined to keep the historic Member's Cup for another year. The only opponent I feared was Tom Hunter, who was as fast over mud as he was on the road. With the memory of a virtual dead heat the previous week, I was taking no chances, and took off from the gun. But even Tom was suffering from his terrific exertion in last week's race and was not really a threat to me. If anything, the course was even tougher than a week earlier owing to deep soggy ruts of hundreds of feet from the Hull & District race. However, I had a winning margin of 5-minutes 18-seconds which tempered my disappointment and possible escape from the dreaded *Ides of March* omen. **Results:** 1. P Flatman 46:16 2. T Hunter 51:34 3. B Jones 51:50 4. A Hugman 51:58 5. P Collinson 54:38 6. D Pickering 55:23 7. P Dearing 55:25 8. T Waudby 57:30

I looked at the Member's Cup, and wondered if the first recipient in 1920, Eric Wilson was still alive. He certainly was and living on Gillshill Road not far from East Hull's Peter Elletson. Eric was thirty-two when the Member's Cup was presented to him. I felt it was a great honour to meet this fine gentleman and his daughter. Eric showed me old photographs, one of which depicted the start of a three thousand field of military men running in the 1916 Northern Command cross-country event. When Eric won the cup, he was working at Wilmington Flour Mills in Wincolmlee, Hull. He also persuaded a fellow worker Joe Bullamore to join East Hull Harriers.

I found out where Joe lived on Maybury Road which was a prefab built in the late-forties as a stop-gap, after the devastating bombing of Hull in WW2. The prefabs were only supposed to last ten years, yet Joe and his wife were still living there twenty-five years later. Joe remembered Eric and his invitation to join the harriers in 1921 and he went on to win three consecutive senior titles in the mid-twenties, but became disillusioned, when he competed and won a mile race at Brough sports in 1928. In those days, all sports people were supposed to be amateur and this ethos was promoted rigorously by the wealthy, ruling classes, who had the money to play sports for fun. This hypocrisy lasted for many more years. Joe worked six days a week and dedicated precious time to become a good athlete. The promoter of the mile race offered a canteen of cutlery worth eight guineas which Joe duly won, and he was still angry that accepting the prize meant he was disqualified from athletics, and he never competed again.

On Easter Monday 1975, we woke up to a late spring snowfall and Jayne, Sarah and Simon set about building a snowman. Within an hour, the sun emerged, and I drove our family to the north east to watch me run the Billingham to Hartlepool ten-mile road race. I was aware of Dave Cannon, the reigning fell-running champion, and Ray Donkin, who was one place ahead of me in the 1973 RAF XC Championships. Cannon took the lead from the gun and won easily from North Shield's Mike Goddard who beat me to the finish by four-seconds. Further, I got the better of Ray by 1 ½ minutes for a change. **Results:** 1. D Cannon (Kendal) 51:22 2. M Goddard (North Shields Poly) 52:14 3. P Flatman (East Hull) 52:18 4. R Dunn (Morpeth) 53:06 5. R Donkin (E&S) 53:50 6. S Jonsson (Durham Uni) 53:56 7. C Vaux (M&D) 54:12 8. D Kelly (Salt) 54:15 **Teams:** 1. Morpeth 2. Saltwell 3. Middlesbrough & Cleveland 4. South Shields.

About this time, I ventured into Hull City centre in search of white running shorts and tried ARCO sports and leisure on Jameson Street. I was shown thick rugby shorts, nylon football shorts, which had tight elastic bands guaranteed to hasten any call of nature. A visit to branch of Suggs on Paragon Square fared no better. I was exasperated, and then tried Allsports on Ferensway where the staff went through drawer after drawer of sportswear without success. Surely a city the size of Kingston upon Hull should have been able to provide me with a pair of running shorts, without me having to resort to mail-order. At the time, I was making a pair of Adidas 72 running shoes last over 3000-miles. The only runner's shops I knew of were Ron Hill in Hyde, and Sweatshop in London.

The East Hull 20-mile now had AFOS Ltd as their sponsor, and the date was brought back from June to Sunday 13th April 1975. In the interim, Hull, East Yorkshire, and North Lincolnshire were collectively and controversially known as Humberside. Former East Hull member, Peter Moon was entered, but was forced to drop out at ten miles. This was my second 20-mile race, and I was determined to give it my best shot. Race favourite was Wakefield schoolteacher, John Newsome and I shared the lead with him till five miles in 25:30. A risky strategy in only my second 20-mile, but I wanted to be involved with the leaders even if it meant I might be forced to slow down later. Newsome forged ahead to reach 10-miles in 52:32, Jim Craven was second in 52:36 and I was third in 52:58. I have always been prepared to run hard from the gun and mostly with a positive result. Newsome and Rowntrees Jim Craven were first and second, while I placed third nearly seven-minutes faster than my previous 20-mile race. **Results:** 1. J Newsome (Wake)1:47:10 2. J Craven (Rowntrees) 1:48:15 3. P Flatman (East Hull) 1:49:24 4. D Quinlan (Bingley)1:50:30 5. F Day (East Cheshire) 1:50:47 6. D Gaskell (Wakefield) 1:51:04 7. T Godolphin (Harro) 1:51:58 8. J Turner (Wake)) 1:53:54 9. J Berry (Wake) 1:54:15 10. P Wright (Pless) 1:54:56 11. J Harmon (CoH) 1:55:36 12. T Flory (M&C) 1:56:40 13. G Duff (Liv) 1:57:44 14. C Jackson (M&C) 1:58:06 15. F Drozda (Pless) 1:58:51 16. K Moughan (M&C) 1:59:19 17. D Longman (CoH) 1:59:32 18. R Train (EH) 2:00:19 19. B Jones (EH) 2:00:26 20. D Hart (EH) 2:01:21. **Teams:** 1. Wakefield 2. Rowntrees 3. City of Hull 4. Plessey.

I had competed in several gruelling races and needed to ease up, but I had already entered the Lincoln 10k on Whit Monday, and was surprised to record 30:51. The next race, East Hull's 6.2- mile road race would be my last for three months, I was off scratch and reduced my own record of 30:55 to 30:23. Now I could take a much-needed rest from racing, and it also gave me a chance to take stock of my life.

I enjoyed my job as a medical sales representative and the status that went with it even though it could be mind-numbing at times, waiting to see GPs or consultants. Whenever possible, I would run at lunchtimes if I could find a swimming pool or sports centre to change and shower. Quite a few physicians were interested enough in my high weekly mileage to conduct a stress test ECG. I was quite alarmed, because my P wave was inverted, and I wondered if this was significant or dangerous. My salary had increased by almost a third in two years, so I could, or should have stayed with Glaxo, and had more time for my family. Unfortunately, the easy option never particularly appealed to me.

How the Past Predicted my Future

My early life continued to shape my future in ways I could not have foreseen. Indeed, a chance chat from my best school friend would widen my world. I was 16 and in my last term at East Ward Secondary Modern Colchester when Rodney Seaden my best pal wanted a word,

'Peter, I've got a great idea: why don't we both join the RAF.'

'My Carol would be upset, and what about Elaine?' I said

'Listen the RAF is a great life, plenty of sport and time off,' Rod said excitedly.

'I'm not sure,' I said struggling to understand his plan.

'At the weekends, we'll pull the girls in our sports cars,' Rod said, ever the salesman.

'Still I don't mind going to the recruiting office,' I said warming to Rod's persuasion.

I made an appointment for the next afternoon – straight after playing football on the school playground for an hour. Rod's idea was embedded in my mind, and the life he promised light years away from evenings and weekends working in a poultry abattoir. His picture of fast cars and girls was irresistible. I was hooked. The RAF Officer asked me to name the photographs around the walls of his office and I could only name one. Then an embarrassing moment when I stripped off for a medical examination, my feet were black from playground football. After my medical he declared, *'You're a fine physical specimen.'* I was then given a book called Ishihara and asked to say the colour I saw but couldn't. Then I was wheeled into another room to be told by a warrant officer of my red/green colour blindness and told that all aircraft trades were closed to me. I'm still puzzled about this arbitrary test because I can see red and green in all shades, nor has it any effect on my driving skills. The officer continued, *'I'm sorry about this Peter, but I do have a vacancy as a nursing attendant, but you'll have to go to our medical school at RAF Cosford for eighteen months.'* That sounded impressive to me – exactly as the officer intended! True to my character I signed up there and then. Meanwhile, I heard Rod was not accepted as aircrew, and withdrew his application. Similarly, when I signed up for East Hull in 1973, it was despite a lack of track athletes, but instead I was sucked into long distance road races and marathons when shorter track events would have been more effective for running faster times at long distances.

CHAPTER 10

Marathon Training

At the end of August 1975, I entered the Tendring 6.5-mile road race, won by Liverpool legend Mike Turner in 31:49 second was my RAF pal Mike Hurd in 32:28 and stationed at nearby RAF Wattisham. I was happy to be third in such company in 32:59. I decided, before I had run my first marathon in October 1975 to plan for the Olympic Trials marathon to be held in May 1976. The plan would last for thirty weeks: 1-10 weeks no more than 109 miles or less than 100 miles; 11-20 weeks no more than 119 miles or less than 110 miles; 21-30 weeks no more than 130 miles or less than 120 miles. Then in March cutting down to 100 miles a week which would seem like a holiday.

I used a surveyor's wheel to measure ½ -mile segments and paint the road on my ten-mile course through Sproatley, Coniston and Ganstead. Then I could use marks to run ½ mile, 1-mile, 1 ½ -mile or 2-mile repetitions on twice-weekly sessions to boost my speed endurance for long-distance road-races. Bob Coleman, an American from Eugene occasionally came with me, and was impressed enough to write to the USA Runners World about my efforts. Bob was a good marathon runner with a best of 2:35, and a very likeable man. He loved England and Yorkshire and vowed to return. He wanted to get a runners' mail order company going in the UK, and I tried to get him a work-visa without success. In the mid-80s, Bob tragically took his own life with a leap from the Golden Gate in San Francisco.

Back to 1975, and I planned a nostalgic trip to the town where I was born. The Diss 15-mile race (held on 28th September) had long been on the road-racing calendar, and wouldn't it be marvellous if I could run and win in front of my relatives. On the day, the weather was stormy with many tree branches on the race route, and not for the faint-hearted. The race started at Diss Grammar school where my father won a place in the thirties, but my grandparents with seven children to feed could not afford his school uniform. The race around Diss was over two laps. Four of us, Colin Moxson, Mike Exton, Ron Brewitt and me, did our best to shelter from the howling gale. Then, I made up my mind to go at half-way and stole a lead and enjoyed a strong back-wind. So far, with seven miles left I felt good, but at ten-miles the course turned into the headwind and Colin Moxson caught me at thirteen-miles. Colin Moxson was not a top-ten finisher in the English national cross country for nothing and proved to be the danger man. In fact, I was running on empty and my dream of winning on home turf fading fast. Indeed, I had not calculated the energy needed to run into a force-eight wind. After the prize-giving, Peter Dearing and I went around to my Aunt Ivy's house for tea and sympathy. Then a lovely surprise, when Ivy showed me a Diss Express story about the time I biked aged 4 to town for some new shoes! **Results:** 1. Colin Moxson (Woodford) 80:31 2. Peter Flatman (E Hull) 80:56 3. Ron Brewitt (H/beach) 81:02 25. Peter Dearing (E Hull) 95:35.

The Rowntrees (York) 10-mile had gained quite a reputation for fast times on the ultra-flat course which I always considered to be a bit short, but runners needed to believe in miracles. The race was held on Saturday 11th October 1975 in sunny weather and still air. Besides, the anticyclone also had the effect of concentrating more oxygen in the atmosphere. I went through five miles in 24:25, and my final time 49:00 – forty seconds faster than 1974. **Results:** 1. Graham Ellis (Holmfirth) 48:20 2. Gareth Davies (Sale) 48:36 3. Peter Rawnsley

(Sheff) 48:44 4. Derek Pratt (Sheff) 48:48 5. Pete Flatman (East Hull) 49:00 15. Chris Vodden (CoH) 50:41 16. Brian Jones (EH) 50:45.

On Friday 24th October, I took three other runners with me to run the Harlow Unigate marathon taking place the next day. But for me it would be my first ever marathon, and I wondered if this might be the end of my career, because many say there is no way back to short distances after the stress and toil of the marathon. Well that is what I believed then. We found a bed and breakfast in the village of Sawston near Peterborough, and settled in a room that slept four, Peter Dearing, Rod Train, Derrick Pickering and me. They wanted to go for a drink, while I stayed behind, but soon after I had a visitor, who scarpered sharpish when he saw me. Moreover, what if I had gone for a drink too we could have lost our kit. I did not go because I'd been told time and again that the marathon all twenty-six miles three hundred and eighty-five yards deserves the ultimate respect.

We arrived at the venue in good time and got changed. I had a pair of seven-ounce Reebok fab-road shoes with pig-skin uppers and dusted my feet with ultra-fine mycil talcum powder and did not wear socks. The previous weekend I ran a glycogen depletion run of twenty miles, and then restricted my intake to non-carbohydrate food for the next three days. This was very unpleasant and the craving for food made me light-headed and I found it difficult to concentrate or drive. In three days, I lost six pounds. For the rest of the week, I gorged on carbohydrates which my liver and muscles would store as glycogen and I hoped this would take me through the dreaded marathon wall.

When I warmed up I felt very sluggish, owing to all that extra glycogen in my leg muscles. Then, I spotted my dear old Dad watching from a vantage point and talking to someone about the marathon his Peter was about to run. I did not speak to my pals, because I did not want to break my concentration for the marathon ahead. The gun fired, but the woolly lethargy was still there, and my legs hefty with glycogen. I usually start races quickly, but not today, I reached 10k in 33-minutes, while I had reached that point, recently, in the York ten over two-minutes quicker. This was the draw-back to the bleed-out diet and I never did it so strictly again. I ran most of the marathon on my own and was pleased to reach twenty miles 1:47:20 – two minutes inside my best. The last six miles were numbing and when I reached the finish my legs seized up. The sponsor was UNIGATE dairy and every finisher was given a pinta!

I sat motionless with my back against the wall of the sports hall and had to be helped to my feet to collect my prize from Arthur Gold the president of the AAA. Dad saw the state I was in and asked to see my prize, a leather wallet which Dad opened and exclaimed, '*I thought it would be full of green-backs!*' He just could not understand why his son would punish himself for no other reward, but a time of two hours twenty-three minutes and twenty-five seconds. However, I found out later in the 1975 Marathon rankings, I placed 40th. Also, on that day I won a priceless legacy as East Hull's marathon record-holder which I have held, continuously, for over forty years. **Results:** 1. Sandy Keith (Edinburgh AC) 2:16:18 2. R Holt (Hercules Wimbledon) 2:16:50 3. T Wright (Wolver & B) 2:17:14 4. D Pratt (Sheff) 2:17:27 5. D Faircloth (Croy) 2:17:34 6. E Austin (Tip) 2:17:41 7. C Moxsom (W Gn) 2:18:12 8. A Byrne (Bolt) 2:19:35 9. Grah Tuck (C&C) 2:19:55 10. D Cannon (Gateshead) 2:21:26 11. N Fisher (Harl) 2:23:02 12. P Flatman (E Hull) 2:23:25 13. J Keeting (E&S) 2:23:49 14. R Brewitt (Holb) 2:23:57 15. R Green (Harl) 2:24 :15 ... 43. Rod Train (CoH) 2:37:59 60. Peter Dearing (E Hull) 2:44:13 66. Derrick Pickering (E Hull) 2:47:02 122. Charley Davison (CoH) 3:08:31

I noticed a classified advertised in Athletics Weekly, '*Looking for agents to sell our road and country shoes. Contact Joe Foster Reebok International 422, Bury Road, Bolton.*' Joe was the grandson of Joseph W Foster, who founded the business in 1895 in Bolton. Joseph was soon making football, rugby boots, spiked and fell shoes. In 1958, Joe renamed, rather grandly, his company Reebok International Ltd. I had learned about them in the early seventies and bought my first pair of Tendotectors from the boot of Ron Hill's Austin 1100 car after the Chris Vose 7 at Warrington. These rugged shoes were for off road training, and a bit on the heavy side. I also purchased a of pair green World 10 racing shoes designed by Ron with black, gristle three-millimetre soles, and it's important to note that Ron was running barefoot at the time!

Two days later, I drove to Bolton and visited his shop on Bury Road it was rudimentary with no fittings, but a counter and the sound of his cobblers working in the backroom. I met Joe, who said,

'You're lucky to catch me, I'm off to the Far East tomorrow.'

'For a holiday?' I quipped.

'Our Taiwan shoes are selling like hot cakes in the States – we need more.' Joe said.

'Anything I need to know about being your agent in Hull?' I asked.

'You pay the selling price less 20% when you order and collect,' Joe said methodically.

'Seems fair enough. What about faulty pairs?'

'We don't get many, send them back and we'll repair or replace,' Joe said.

I wasn't sure why I was getting into this business that would only provide pin-money at best. Meanwhile, Dr Ron Hill, a textile chemist and the UK's best marathon runner, was experimenting, and selling his freedom shorts, which were so free you needed to wear underpants or risk being charged with gross indecency! He also invented the trackster a light nylon trouser that did not cling like the later lycra tights and perfect for the English climate. So why did I want this extra agency work, I had enough to keep me occupied: my wife and three kids, running over a hundred miles a week, a full-time job, and the gardening. Why did I feel the need to increase my burden, and what was it, I was searching for?

I decided to test my improved fitness in the Morpeth to Newcastle 13-miles 660-yards road-race on 1st January 1976. My previous attempt, in 1974, in a howling headwind proved I had not matched my RAF form. As usual, the conditions were close to freezing, the wind light and variable and I was ready for a good race. By half-way, I was catching John Newsome, who had beaten me by two minutes in the East Hull 20 and I was just two seconds adrift of John at the finish. Mike McLeod, won from Keith Angus while I was well pleased to place 11th only three minutes behind the winner. Best of all, my time was nearly seven minutes better than 1974. **Results:** 1. M McLeod (Elswick) 66:55 2.K Angus (Sheff) 66:56 3. P Gallagher (Crawley) 67:20 4. R Lunnon (Gosforth) 67:34 5. J Alder (Morp) 67:41 6. D Kelly (Salt) 67:45 7. G Carey (Liv H) 67:51 8. M Craven (Ken) 67:59 9. P Rawnsley (Sheff) 68:19 10. J Newsome (Wake) 68:59 11. P Flatman (E Hull) 69:01 12. D Evans (Card) 69:19 13. D Pratt (Sheff) 69:20 14. M Bateman (Morp) 69:23 15. R Belk (Ken) 70:40 16. R Milne (Notts) 70:52. **Teams:** 1. Sheffield 24 2. Morpeth 52 3. Gosforth 58 4. Saltwell 69 5. Sunderland 87.

My wife bought me some Adidas SL72 running shoes, and a red, thick, hooded top for Christmas. She must have had a premonition, because January 1976 came in with a vengeance when an exceptional cyclone struck the country and known as the Capella storm. Gusts were reaching over one hundred miles an hour and sucking in bitterly, cold Arctic air. But I would let nothing interrupt my one hundred and twenty-miles a week schedule. I had a circuit of fifteen-miles through the flat, desolate Holderness plain which had been drained by the Cistercian monks of Meaux in the middle-ages. The Monks also built a drain of 6-miles to the port of Wyke to transport wool to the continent and I would cross the old drain twice every night. Conversely, on a sunny day, the route would be a joy through arable lands, along little used roads with the occasional cattle grid to negotiate. I would arrive home at about 5pm, have some tea and head out of the door at 7pm to face a pitch-black night, gale force winds sub-zero temperatures, and a wind-chill effect more like minus-5C. My kit was shoes, shorts and my new red hooded top, I was shaking with the cold for the first few miles, trying to run as fast as possible to increase my core-temperature. The roads were virtually empty, the birds silent except for an occasional hungry owl. The unseen storm was battering the leafless trees, bashing my frozen ears, and blowing dead wood everywhere. On such nights, the mind becomes disorientated, shadows suggest unimagined danger. Then, the dreaded cattle grids have gaps of 9-inches and are difficult to see and one wrong move could mean an injured ankle or worse. Anyway, the last few miles were on well-lit-roads one of which passed the Lambwath pub on Sutton Road and the site of the Cistercians lamb wash in the 15th century. Contrarily, the hit record by *Pilot* summed up what I felt about that first month of the year, and I could not get the words out of my head, *January, sick and tired, You're, been hanging on me, You, make me sad with my eyes, You're, telling me lies, Just, go, just go.* But I soldiered on, hoping this would give me extra, inner resolve for my next marathon. My total mileage for January was five-hundred and forty-five miles and in February I passed one-thousand miles before the month was out. I wondered if any of my competitors for the Olympic Marathon Trial in May would be braving such an onslaught and convinced myself they'd have more sheltered conditions away from the coast.

St Botolph's Stump Cast an Eerie Eye Over Me.

In April 1964, I went home to my family, and was soon roped in to help at my Dad's new chicken processing shed in Nayland. On Sunday, my father dropped me on the road to Cambridge, so I could try and hitch a lift back to RAF North Coates near Grimsby. I was wearing uniform, which usually helped, but I soon became despondent. After about an hour I got a lift, which took me passed Cambridge, then another an hour later when a lorry stopped. This was good, because he dropped me off within six miles of Boston. However, as my watch showed 3am, my chances of another lift were almost nil and with just three shillings left, I needed luck and a good plan. In fact, I had a bit of good fortune as a car full of RAF boys stopped, *'We can drop you off in Boston if it's any good to you!'* Imagine the scene: Boston's street lights were switched off at midnight and I felt fearful in this cold and dark place. Overlooking the town was St Botolph's parish church and a steeple of almost three hundred feet. Local folklore likens strong winds, dancing around the church tower to the Devil's breath and the five lanterns at the peak resemble Lucifer's flames. Accordingly, when the Pilgrim Fathers set sail in the Mayflower for America in 1620 their last vision in the gathering dusk, was of their homeland and the twinkling lamps astride the Stump.

I felt a mixture of adventure tinged with fear as I walked to the station and found a way to the wrong side of the tracks still dressed in my RAF uniform. Previously, I'd travelled back on this train from visiting my girlfriend at RAF Hospital Halton knew the time of arrival, but I did not have enough money for a ticket. Presently, I felt the vibration of the rail carrying the early morning mail train, and then the clamour and smell of the diesel engine – my heart pounded in nervous trepidation as the mail-train came to a stop. As soon as I was sure the coast was clear, I stepped out of the shadows and scampered across the track, grabbed a carriage handle, pulled myself up and opened the window to release the door catch. What a relief, I was in, and soon found an empty carriage pulled the blinds down and feigned sleep. Now, I had to hope the train would stop at a station nearer to my destination and I was in luck when the train arrived at Willoughby in the heart of Lincolnshire. I hoped the three shillings in my pocket would be enough for the journey? Finally, at 6am, the train stopped at North Thoresby and I was confronted by an elderly ticket collector, who gave me a suspicious gaze.

'Where's your ticket?' he said with the air of a railwayman, who'd seen it all before.

'Oh, sorry I got on at Willoughby,' I said nervously.

'Airman, you must think, I was born yesterday,' he said, staring at me.

'Well, it was like this, I only have three shillings to my name,' I said, pleadingly.

'Let me see, Willoughby to Thoresby – two shillings and six pence.'

'Thank you, sir, I hope I can make the six-mile hike to RAF North Coates before 8am.'

On 7th February 1976, I was entered for running-clubs, vs cycling-clubs in the Hull area. I did not know what to expect, but imagined we'd be thrashed out of sight. Seventeen cyclists and twenty-eight runners took part. The race was over cross-country trails and part of the old Hull to Hornsea railway line. At one point, I was leading the race by a minute, but on a muddy section Tom Hunter, a former cyclist pulled me back, but to my surprise, I went on to win the event. Stuart Shallcross came third as a cyclist even though he was one the district's best athletes. **Results:** 1. P Flatman (EH) 44:21 2. T Hunter (EH) 44:41 3. S Shallcross (Hull Thursday CC) 45:53 4. M Farrell (CoH) 46:12 5. D Bettison (HT) 46:12 6. P Chapman (CoH) 47:31.

I was enjoying racing twice a week and found time to run a RAF XC league event at Lindholme on 11th February and it was a pleasure to see Arthur Moore, who had inspired me so much to become a runner at RAF Valley. **Results:** 1. P Flatman (E Hull) 35:47 2. J Fretwell (Scampton) 36:03 3. A Moore (Cranwell) 36:07

I won the East Hull Harriers senior cross-country for the third year, but nevertheless, I always felt more at home on the road. The following Wednesday I ran in the RAF Lincolnshire cross-country league at RAF Lindholme where John Hurt stopped me getting lost on the course and in consequence helped me to win the race. The base became a prison in 1985. I also won another league race at RAF Finningley, which became the Sheffield-Doncaster airport in 2005, and further evidence of the on-going contraction of the Royal Air Force over recent decades. Meanwhile, my RAF win encouraged me to enter the Hull University 4½-road race on 25th February. Although, I won the event comfortably, I never imagined, I would be going back to the University 35-years later to gain a degree in creative writing. **Results:** 1. P Flatman (E Hull) 22:11 2. A Lightfoot (Sheff Un) 22:32 3. M White (Sheff Un) 22:36 4. S Knowles (Leeds Un) 22:47 5. P McCullagh (Leeds) 23:07 6. M Parkinson (Brad Un) 23:24. **Teams:** 1. Sheffield Un 24 2. Leeds Un 50 3. Bradford Un 53 4. East Hull 59.

The following Saturday 28th February 1976, I drove south to run the Woking 10 road race, and unlike East Yorkshire, daffodils were in full bloom on every hedgerow and roundabout. Despite running a hundred miles the previous week, the warm spring sunshine put a spring in my step, and another sub fifty minute ten-mile to my tally. Yet, I would not return to run this event until I became a first-year Vet. **Results:** 1. J King (Small Heath) 47:48 2. R Newble (Invicta) 48:15 3. M Hurd (Croydon) 48:25 4. T Johnston (Port) 48:34 5. R Richardson (B'heath) 49:02 6. S McHale (Glos) 49:10 7. J Watts (AF&D) 49:17 8. P Eales (Mit) 49:42 9. P Flatman (E Hull) 49:43 10. J Hazleden (TH&H) 49:45 11. D Faircloth (Croy) 49:47 12. J Bryant (TH&H) 49:50 13. N King (Lon I) 49:53 14. H Chadwick (TH&H) 50:03 15. M Russell (Croy) 50:13. **Teams:** 1. Croydon 18 2. Thames H&H 23 3. Portsmouth 31.

The next Saturday, the Hull & District Senior men's eight-mile cross-country championship was held at Saltshouse on Saturday 7th February 1976 – the same venue as 1975, and where I failed by inches to win the title. I did not taper my training, as my big target was the Olympic Trial marathon at Rotherham two months later. John

Davies, winner in 1975 was running, but well off the pace, but this time, I had the company of Tony Bland, Grimsby and a youthful Stephen Scargill, aged 20, running the senior race for the first time. In retrospect, I should have read the preview in the local paper, which made Steve the favourite, because of his great performance in the recent Northern Championships. For me, it was like a rerun of 1975 Hull & District, but this time between Steve and me and I tried to shake him off, but each time he closed the gap. In the last mile, Steve applied the pressure, and my legs felt weary from my heavy mileage, nevertheless, Steve was a clear winner by 15-seconds. I later learned, Steve had cut his training for the week leading up to the race to just fifteen-miles, as advised by his brilliant coach, Pete Jarvis. **Results:** 1. S Scargill (City of Hull) 39:23 2. P Flatman (EH) 39:38 3. T Bland (Grimsby) 39:52 4. J Clark (Grimsby) 40:02 5. C Vodden (CoH) 40:31. Teams 1. Grimsby 2. City of Hull 3. Rowntrees (York) 4. East Hull. Post-script: Three days later I faced Steve Scargill over a 3.6-road race organised by his club City of Hull, and once again we were neck and neck, but this time I took the initiative and won by ten seconds. The club gallery was dumbfounded as Steve was quicker than me over shorter distances, however, my high mileage meant I had a faster recovery time.

The 1976 East Hull 20-mile, was on the 11th April, and on a course, I knew well: it attracted Olympic hopeful Bernie Plain (Cardiff), my RAF pal Mike Hurd, and Gateshead's Max Coleby. Although I was extremely fit, I was not sharp enough for this kind of company. Ideally, I needed quality 5k races to improve my leg-speed, and that would entail a journey to Trafford Park or West London Stadium. Bernie had spent the previous week running over the Olympic Trials Marathon course at Rotherham. The early miles were brisk, and I was with Mike and Bernie at five-miles in 24:47 with Max Coleby a further eight seconds back. At Skirlaugh, I lost touch with the leaders at seven-miles on a slight incline. Plain and Hurd reached ten-miles in 49:56 while I was timed at 50:27 and Max was twelve seconds slower in fourth place. He went on to pass me in the last five-miles to claim the Northern Counties title with seventeen seconds to spare, but I had the consolation of winning the Humberside title, and improving my personal best by four minutes and it placed me 8th on the 1976 UK 20-mile rankings.

Results: 1. B Plain (Cardiff) 1:41:58 2. M Hurd (Croydon) 1:43:27 3. M Coleby (Gateshead) 1:45:09 4. P Flatman (EH) 1:45:26 5. T Hopkins (Charnwood) 1:45:40 6. J Craven (Rowntrees) 1:50:38.7, R Harbisher (Long) 1:51:12 8. W Yates (Mary) 1:51:34 9. W Padgett (Bing) 1:51:50 10. C Vaux (M&C) 1:52:34 11. T Rooke (M&C) 1:53:22 12. T White (Long) 1:54:04 13. R Hall (CoH) 1:54:17 14. L Stowell (Charn) 1:54:44 15. J Hampson (Stret) 1:55:50 16. B Jones (EH) 1:56:02 17. M Hague (Roth) 1:56:36 19 R Coleman (EH) 1:59:07 20. G Kay (Barns) 1:59:29 **Teams:** 1. East Hull – the first open road race win in the club's history! 2. Charnwood 3. Middlesboro. Eighty started, and twenty-one ran the event in under two hours.

On Easter Monday 19th April 1976, I returned to run the ten-mile Billingham to Hartlepool road race, but I cannot imagine why just eight days after a gruelling East Hull 20-mile. I took the lead from the gun, which was not the smartest idea, because I faced a northerly headwind for the whole race. But much of my training had been in far worse conditions and I was able to make light of the adverse weather and won. Later, I learnt I was the first ever East Hull Harrier to win an open road race. **Results**: 1. P Flatman 51:26 2. J Trainor (Gateshead) 51:54 3. J Hillen (Saltwell) 52:19 … 8. C Vodden (CoH) 54:19 22. R Coleman (EH) 57:08. With only three weeks to the Olympic Marathon trial, this should have filled me with confidence, but I still had nagging doubts about the twenty-six-mile race at Rotherham. For the next two weeks, I put aside my worries, and decided to paint the outside of our house, and to show my allegiance to East Hull Harriers it had to be red and white. The weather was perishing, and a cold north wind close to freezing. My hands were blue and several times I almost fell off the ladder.

I had to do something about that lingering doubt and decided to run a thirty-mile training run, I had already measured, and painted the road with 4 x 7.5-mile segments. The weather was still cold when, my wife drove me up to my starting point on the A165 near Filey at 7 am on a Sunday morning. This would be my longest run, I'd ever attempted and just thirteen days before the marathon trial a bit risky. Would this effort on a bleak, lonesome road to help me to truly believe, could I upset the odds and claim a place for Great Britain in the 1976 Olympic Marathon at Montreal? I did not expect, nor did I see another runner for the next three hours unlike today when I might see dozens. Within the first half-mile, I settled on a pace of 5 minutes 50 per mile and maintained that throughout. I reached 5-miles at Bridlington in 29-minutes. The weather was cloudy and at 5C made for comfortable running. When I reached Beeford straight, I was thankful the boy racers were still in bed, then an East Hull Harrier drove slowly passed me and wound down his window,

'What are you doing right out here Pete?'

'I am running thirty miles from Filey to Bilton, I said

'You are going at a good pace.'

'It's my last long run before Rotherham,' I said, wishing I'd kept my own council.

In fact, I completed the run in two-hours, fifty-five minutes or about two-hour thirty-two pace for the marathon. I'd proved to myself that I could make the marathon distance in reasonable comfort. In that moment, I had forgotten the importance of keeping my powder dry; of not giving away my plans and intentions for others to discuss or condemn. My words would go around the athletic fraternity and twisted with nuance and negativity. Sure, enough it was soon coming back to me from running clubs in the locality. This racked me with self-doubt, I had followed my schedule, despite bad weather and logged 3,300-miles in 30-weeks, but still missed the vital ingredient – more races (between 3 to 10-miles) against quality opposition.

I completed the house painting and gradually reduced my training for the biggest race of my life. On Wednesday, the north wind abated and by Thursday the temperature was rising. By Saturday the sun shone from a bright blue sky and the famous 1976 heat-wave had begun. Back then little attention was given to the dangers of holding marathon races in the hottest pert of the day. Jim Peters had a lead of 18-minutes in the 1954 Empire Games marathon in Vancouver, but the event was held in stifling heat and humidity and within sight of the stadium Peters made a grotesque sight, stumbling in a state of semi-consciousness, as if his movements were controlled by an inebriated puppeteer. So, guess what? On 8th of May 1976 the race would start at 2pm, when the sun would be at its strongest with an air temperature of 26C.

Four hundred and twenty-three of us gathered at the race start on Morthern road Wickersley, all trying to win a place in the Olympic Trials Marathon. I looked across and saw European and Commonwealth champion Ian Thompson and noted he was wearing a pair of fluorescent Japanese Tiger Jayhawk racing shoes, which he had pierced in numerous places with a paper punch. Now, the temperature was close to twenty-seven degrees centigrade, when in the last few months the average had been six or seven degrees. Meanwhile, the general chatter was subdued, but significantly there were others who stood stoically as if in a trance of concentration, concealed in their bubbles like astronauts. They just stood and stared at nothing, I had seen this before, but never at this intensity. Then the starter's gun released the collective pressure of the marathon men like a surgeon lancing a boil. I was up with the leaders and most of them were already sweating profusely. The sun scorched our heads, and there was no shade, I noticed the road tarmac was melting and warm enough to fry eggs, and blister feet.

Anyway, there would be no records in this heat, it was chaotic at the inadequate drinks stations, even though a certain black camaraderie prevailed amongst the runners as sponges and drinks were passed around. At eight-miles I was already off the pace and felt like quitting. There was quite a crowd of well-wishers near Dinnington coal mine, and I spotted Tricia with Mum and Dad. I stopped and said:

'It's too hot I can't go on!' I gasped.

'What does Peter mean is he hurt?' Dad said.

'He's soft as clarts,' my wife quipped.

'The road is red hot, and the melting tar sticky,' I moaned.

'Just get back in the race – it's the same for everybody,' my wife chided.

'Well I go to hell, I hope he'll be alright,' Dad said perplexed.

My wife must have thought he has done all this training and now he wants to drop out. I trundled on when all hope had gone and as my dream faded my nightmare began. My pace was not great, yet I was amazed when, I passed Jim Alder, the former Commonwealth Games marathon gold medallist. I am dehydrating, and my legs are suffering from stinging cramps. This was the day, I would suffer the true torment and pain of the marathon. Nothing could have prepared me for it, the physical and mental strain and of being unable to deal with the sudden heat-wave, moreover, it would be long time before I'd attempt another marathon.

But at least, I would finish today come what may. When, I reached the Herringthorpe track, I faced the ultimate humiliation as a teenager passed me, but later I found out he was Alvin Dewhurst – who looked five-years younger than his real age. Then, I tried to sprint, but my body was struck by a series of cramp-stabbing pains, which had me gyrating on the track like a marionette. At last it was over and such a disappointment for me and many others who were forced to pull out. In the melee of music and battered bodies a voice, above the hubbub, came from the loudspeaker, *'The greatest challenge known to man!'* and I, for one believed him. **Result:** 1. Barry Watson (Bournemouth) 2:15:08 2. Jeff Norman (Altrincham) 2:15:17 3. Keith Angus (Sheffield) 2:15.55 4. R Hill (Clay) 2:16:59 5. B Plain (Card) 2:18:52 6. A Keith (EAC) 2:19:02 7. I Thompson (Lut) 2:19:07 8. T Johnston (Port) 2:19:50 9. A Joslyn (Cwm) 2:20:13 10. N Deakin (Stoke) 2:20:29 … 13. Alan Domleo (Derby) 2:21:41 … 30. Jim Dingwall 2:26:29 56. P Flatman (East Hull) 2:31:51…132. Rod Train (EH) 2:48:20 133. P Dearing (EH) 2:48:21 **147 runners failed to finish**.

I had been aware of Derby's Alan Domleo for many years, and who won the Morpeth to Newcastle race in 1966 in 66:16 – so imagine my surprise in August 1999 when my son Simon married Sally, and where I finally met Alan (a 2:17:24 marathon runner), and Sally's uncle at the top table for their wedding breakfast. Besides, I researched the 1976 Olympic Marathon Trial for results and spoke to Peter Humphries, secretary of Rotherham Harriers who sent me a remarkable photograph of me and Alan Domleo on my left on the start line of the epic Rotherham marathon.

CHAPTER II

Hip Injury

My next race was the Lincoln 10k on 31st May 1976 and proved to me that all my hard training would be rewarded. The weather was hot and sunny, but unlike Rotherham I had acclimatised. From the start the pace was relentless and the speed more like a 5-k track race. I was in the leading group and at three miles in 13:52 was the fastest I'd ever run that distance. The reader, as I did, might think the race could be short, however, when I checked my diary, I found I had run 31:21 in 1974 and 30:51 in 1975. Furthermore, I'd trained over 3000-miles since October 1975, and in the previous month I was doing one-minute sprints while keeping to 55-minute ten-mile runs. I believe I ran out of my skin that day, however, it was also the cause of crippling bursitis on my right hip that side-lined me for three years. Also, I'd managed to keep pace with some talented road runners like Richard Milne, Harry Leeming and Colin Kirkham. Towards the finish the front three started to race, while I shared fifth place with Phil Romaine. Roger Milne, a track specialist won in 28:57 followed by Harry Leeming who won the Finchley 20 in 1974 in 1:39:18. **Results:**1. R Milne (Notts) 28:57 2. H Leeming (Dby) 28:58 3. C Kirkham (Cov) 29:04 4. B Berry (E Ches) 29:10 5. P Romaine (Holb) 29:18 6. P Flatman (E Hull) 29:19 7. M Exton (Holb) 29:45 8. D Allen (Man) 30:00 9. W Eldridge (Notts) 30:02 10. M Palmer (Notts) 30:04 11. T Bland (Grim) 30:22 12. M White (Sheff Un) 30:25 13. C Barford (Leic) 30:29. **Teams:** 1. Notts 20 2. Grimsby 46 3. Sheff Uni 49.

The next evening was East Hull's 8.2-mile race, but the weather was very different with a westerly gale. I held the course record but wanted to put it out of reach. As expected, I was the last runner to start, and over twenty minutes behind the slowest. The more I forced my pace against the unseen power of nature the more my right hip tightened up. Nonetheless, I ran harder and searched for shelter, in vain, on the pan-flat roads around Holderness. The dye was cast and despite all, I broke my own course record by 22-seconds. The next day, I awoke with a painful right hip and it would take three years to get back to my fitness of 1976.

Over the next few weeks I started to try and think of a name for my fledgling enterprise even though the sales per annum were measured in hundreds rather than thousands of pounds. One morning, I needed to see some GPs in Doncaster. I knew I had to have runner in the title of my micro-business and the only enterprises of a similar nature were Ron Hill sports and Sweatshop, run by Chris Brasher. The eureka moment arrived, while I waited for the old Goole swing bridge to reopen, a ten-letter word and a unique name for my sport's business – Runnercare. After I had seen my doctors, I parked in the centre of Doncaster and noticed a sports outfitters shop brandishing the top brand names of the era; Dunlop, Slazenger, Lonsdale, Umbro, Speedo and Converse. I went into the shop:

'In Hull, there is not a single shop that sells proper running shoes or kit,' I said.

'There's no call for it that's why,' the owner said brashly.

'I couldn't even buy a pair of running shorts in Hull,' I said.

'Anyhow if you don't have a Slazenger or Dunlop account – you're doomed to fail.'

'I don't need them, and they sell nothing for athletes,' I said.

I was shocked at the sports shop owner's negativity, as my business was situated sixty miles away and I would specialise in athletics. Now I would have to live with my hip injury which I now believe was a swollen and painful bursa, affecting full leg extension of my right leg and I was forced to cut back on my training. Despite this on a sunny afternoon promoting my wares at King George V stadium in Grimsby, I decided to run the 5000-metres, which I completed in 14:52.4. Even so, my fitness was getting worse, and by now, my training was less than thirty miles a week.

On Saturday 16th June 1976, I drove almost to Blackpool to run the Freckleton half marathon starting at 7 pm. The race attracted good athletes, and this evening was no exception. In the early stages, I was easily staying with the three leaders, B Bowler (Staff Morlands), A McGee (Bolton) and D Wilson (Blackburn) and we reached ten-miles in 50:23. However, in the last three miles, I slowed up as my hip-tightened. **Results:** 1. B Bowler (Staff Moorlands) 66:05 2. A McGee (Bolton) 66:19 3. D Wilson (Blackburn) 66:31 4. P Flatman (East Hull) 66:57 5. R Byrne (Salford) 67:52 6. S Kelly (Border AC) 69:03 7. J Ashworth (Bingley) 69:29 8. M Flynn (Liverpool Pembroke) 69:37 9. A Roams (Staff M) 69:51 10. P Bowler (Staff M) 69:51.

In the gorgeous summer of 1976 we all went to Devon on our family holiday, blissfully unaware of how our lives were about to change forever. We were facing a dilemma: my job was getting easier, our kids were well settled, and we had a peaceful existence, yet I was contemplating starting a business which would put a strain on family relationships and holidays. We stayed at Torrington in a park of chalets with a swimming pool and soaked up the sun ten or twelve hours a day and wallowed in temperatures in the 80s or 90s during the holiday. The surrounding countryside was totally parched and barren. Our lovely kids were now ten, eight and four would have been oblivious to the changes that would reshape their parent's lives.

When we returned from Torrington, I contacted a new supplier called Carita House based in Cheshire. This was important, because they were importing EB shoes endorsed by the legendary New Zealand coach Arthur Lydiard who was rated as the best running coach of all time by Runners World. His athletes, Peter Snell, Murray Halberg and Barry Magee won six medals in the 1960 and 1964 Olympics including two golds. Lydiard designed a road shoe named EB Lydiard Road for the athlete exceeding 80-miles per week, the EB Marathon for the athlete to wear for interval training and road races over 10-miles, and the ultra-light 160-gram EB Sao Paulo for 10ks and track training. At the time, they were not being distributed in the UK and gave me some much-needed exclusivity. I went down to Alderman Kneeshaw once a week to gauge interest and to ask the younger athletes what they wanted, and the universal answer was Adidas Jet running spikes. So, I gave Adidas (UK) a ring at their Poynton office and the local representative rang me back. He said, '*Sorry Mr Flatman, we only sell to bone fide retailers, who have shop premises.*' I began to question again why I had bothered with this little bit of car boot selling. My biggest motivation, strangely, was not to have shops or a business, or loads of money – it was the awful feeling of having to say no to a potential customer.

I went to the Middlesbrough Parkland, on Saturday 11th September, and was surprised to come away with another win in the senior six-mile cross country event. But I knew this could not continue much longer with my hip showing no improvement, and very sore after races. That evening, my wife and I took a trip down Holderness Road on the look-out for shop premises when we reached Jesmond Gardens we saw a double fronted shop, with its windows white washed around a sign that read, *Shop for Rent £30 a Week*. My wife remained very quiet as she contemplated what this might mean to us and our family

'We might as well have a look,' I said.

'I don't know, it's next to a smelly take-away,' my wife said unconvinced with my idea.

'It won't cost us to see inside,' I said fearing she would not agree.

'I'm not sure – I mean you've got a good job,' my wife said with a hint of resignation.

'The shop is in a good position, easy parking,' I said.

'OK, we'll have a look, but there's a lot at stake.' She said.

I rang Mr Westmoreland and we went to see him in the middle of September 1976. When we arrived he'd already opened the premises the front shop was quite small with an area of 250 square feet. Then a short corridor, thirty inches wide to second room of 180 square feet. Although this space could be used it would be difficult for security and mean a staff of two. There was a further space that could be utilised as a changing room, then a kitchen area and a large backroom for sports clothing printing or stock. Our proposed shop was a veritable Tardis with more compartments than a bee's honeycomb.

'What are you going to sell, and will you take enough?' Mr Westmoreland said.

'It's not just shop sales, but mail-order too,' I said.

'Maybe, I could come and help you parcel the goods.'

'It's alright, Mr Westmoreland, we'll do everything to make it work,' I said.

'I'll be working in the shop,' my attractive wife said, and Westmoreland's eyes lit up.

The old boy agreed, we could have 334, Holderness Road from 1st October 1976 and he drew up the lease for us to sign. He also agreed to let us have access for any stock and fittings.

'Do you hope to open for the Christmas trade?' Mr Westmoreland enquired.

'We will be trading on Friday 1st October 1976,' I declared.

'You really do mean business don't you,' he said.

Now I had set the deadline things happened quickly. I made an appointment to see The Barclays bank manager at Holderness road and outlined my business plan. My dad lent me £2000 with no repayment date and I sought an overdraft from the bank of £2000. I could see I had won Mr Parkin over, but he wanted to come and see the premises. My bank manager came the next day and seemed satisfied with the size of the shop and how I intended to use it. We signed up for a business account and everything slotted into place:

'How are you going to use this large back room?' Mr Parkin asked.

'I think by next year it will be used for sports printing,' I assured him.

I received a call from Joe Foster the proprietor of Reebok International, who wanted to meet me at my new shop at Holderness Road, Hull, to propose a joint venture for opening specialist runners' shops across the UK.

'Nice to see you Joe. How's business?'

'Very good Peter, and in the States brilliant.'

'How would our joint venture work?'

'Obviously, I hope you would help me grow the Reebok brand.'

'Of course, but I will be stocking Adidas, New Balance, Nike and Brooks.'

'I've already, taken that as read, but I must have a good slice of the business.'

'I can't think about that right now, Joe.'

'That's understandable. Perhaps things will change. Keep in touch.'

It was too soon, it would be months before the shop would be in profit, and even then, any spare cash would be needed to reinvest. However, the more I thought about the idea of Joe pressing me for more Reebok stock, the more I disliked the venture. The brand was acquired by Pentland in 1983, and in 2004 Reebok was bought out by Adidas for $3.8-billion!

The next couple of weeks was a blur of activity: I visited Adidas UK at Poynton, Cheshire, and learnt the *three stripes* sports brand supplied two thousand independent sports shops in the UK. Nearly all used the owners name, and just one had more than two outlets and Adidas did not supply any runner's shop in the UK. But I needed Adidas because they supplied all the Olympic champions and World Cup footballers. The local Adidas rep Les Harding came to see me at my shop, which was still empty, and I explained my business. He took it on himself to open an account with Runnercare provided I ordered at least £2000 worth of stock but told me, I would not receive much more much than half of my order. In fact, the invoice for the delivered stock was £1100. For my part, it was a bit of a risk, but I knew, I'd have up to six weeks to pay. Though, the rep's decision created an outrage with other shops in Hull: Arco Sports, Allsports, Suggs Sports and Crawford Sports – although there was little they could do about it. In any case, none of these were interested in the needs of athletes, and a fair proportion of my business would be for runners via mail order. East Hull was as big as a small city, and I needed a local sporting celebrity to open the shop. Colin Hutton, was a legend in Rugby League: as a player with Hull FC, he scored the winning points in the 1956 cup final; as manager of Hull Kingston Rovers and as the coach of the Great Britain side that beat Australia in 1962. I went to see him in the *Zetland Arms* his public house on Portobello Street, and he readily agreed. Everything had been done on a shoe string. Ray Hall was a local chemist who I knew from visiting him as a pharmaceutical rep, and he gave me some brilliant advice:

'Spend peanuts on fittings, you'll need all your capital for stock and remember you can sell stock, but only give away fittings'.

Ray, a member of Wyke Round Table invited me to give a talk on my business plan the following week. The Round Table was a group of young business people and I was introduced to Bill an accountant friend of Ray's,

'I hear you're planning to open a sports shop on Holderness Road?' Bill asked

'Well, Bill it is more a runner's shop and only the second in the North,' I enthused.

'I don't think that anyone will be interested in a sports shop there,' Bill said in a pompous manner, 'It's also set too far back off the road, Peter.'

'I'm planning to sell through by mail-order and I will advertise in *Athletics Weekly*', I said annoyed by Bill's negativity.

'Peter, you've got no chance on that part of Holderness Road. You need to take two hundred notes a day to break even, and there's absolutely no chance of that!'

'I'll take pleasure in proving you wrong, Bill.'

We received doubts from locals, who said the shop had always failed. Some doubters wished us good luck, but without conviction. I'd acquired a counter and some metal shelves to stack footwear, and a new hand-painted sign was erected above the door. The front windows were left white washed until Friday 1st October 1976, when Colin Hutton cut the ribbon, and my shop was open for business. As, I looked around at the wooden counter, the sparseness of merchandise and the make-do shop window, I became a bag of nerves. This was the moment of reality: facing questions I could not answer; orders I could not fulfil and my confidence melted away. Curiosity drew customers through the door, their questions surprising, especially as Runnercare had set out to be a shop for athletes. Anyway, customers asked for everything from sweat-bands to snooker tips, from tennis briefs to judo suits, and from tee-shirts to Leeds United kits. All requests were written down, although I could not stock everything the lists were essential research for future orders proving the truth of the quote *retail is detail* coined by James Gulliver – a 1970s supermarket innovator. A delivery truck arrived from Adidas, and the boxes took up most of the front shop floor space and the consignment included running shoes, football trainers and boots, running vests, shorts, and long sleeve tee shirts for autumn training. The three stripe Adidas brand logo gave our business instant kudos. But I still had my job and dashed off for appointments and left my wife to cope. From a standing start, we took fifty-eight pounds on the first day and learnt much more about the sports trade.

I was in all day Saturday with my wife trying to get things looking attractive to buy with endless pricing of stock and lacing display footwear. A young dark-haired girl came in around midday looking very nervous and she spoke to Tricia. I did not speak to her, but my wife took her name and phone number, and said she would let her know. We both liked the look of Patricia, and Tricia rang her mother to tell her to come the next Saturday. The next week was very slow and Wednesday sales dipped to £10.80. Perhaps, the doom-merchant's prophecy was coming true and all rather worrying. However, the country was suffering from double digit inflation, and a large rise in unemployment, and I thought if we could make it now then the future should be more assured. Straight away our Saturday girl was a conscientious and willing worker, with a good memory. I was placing adverts in Athletics Weekly and from the start the advertised price included delivery to the customer's door and with the pledge that orders received by 4pm went the same day.

I bought some black and white leather trainers from Joe Foster, which were close to counterfeit in everything, but name to Adidas Kick, but at a bargain price of £4.95 a pair. The trainers were displayed in a wire basket in all sizes in left shoes only and placed outside the shop. *British Summer Time* had ended, and it was quite dark when I went to collect the basket, but it had been stolen along with the shoes. The thief was thwarted and did not notice none of the stock made a pair. When I got over my initial anger at losing the stock, I realised that this would make a humorous news story for the Hull Daily Mail. The story read, '*Police Looking For, a Thief With, Two Left Feet! Peter Flatman owner of Runnercare, a newly opened sports shop 334, Holderness Road, got a shock when he discovered that a thief had made off with ten trainers from a display basket outside. The only problem for the pilferer was they were all LEFT shoes. The police are making enquiries and are appealing for information regarding anyone possessing two left feet!* I never recovered the odd shoes, but a front-page story in the 130,000-circulation of the local paper would have cost me four times as much as the lost stock.

Later in October I went to the Rowntrees ten-mile race in York and put some EB marathon shoes in my boot with some leaflets for my mail-order service. In the event, I sold ten pairs of EB Marathon for two hundred pounds, which bolstered the slow sales in the shop. I managed to book a series of right-hand display adverts in *Athletics Weekly*, showing accurate sizes, and ½ sizes available, and often delivered the next day, which runners appreciated to keep them pounding out the miles. In fact, the mail order, and out of shop sales, helped the business survive those first few months. I was determined to make the accountant, I met at the Round Table, eat his words, but I would need a trading year to prove it.

My training had dropped to about twenty miles a week and even then, I would still have a dull, nagging ache in my hip. Meanwhile, I was juggling my time between working for Duncan Flockhart and seeing reps and serving in the shop. Of course, I realised that I could not keep this going for very long without being found out and losing my job. We were pulling out all the stops to keep our small loyal, band of customers happy, but coming up to our first Christmas we were losing out, because we were unable to stock the most popular kid's football kit, Leeds United. Admiral Sportswear was the official supplier, but it was impossible to get an account, owing to pressure from the city centre shops and that was same for Liverpool and Manchester United. We kept lists of all the potential sales lost, but then realised that even if we had dealt with Admiral Sportswear, they would not have been able to deliver till after the football season was finished. We managed to find a West Yorkshire supplier, who could supply a much cheaper, near replica Leeds shirt. Of course, this would not satisfy the savvy kids, but at least we had tried. And we had scarves, hats and sweatbands all emblazoned with the names of football and rugby league teams. Meanwhile, my wife, was constantly changing the window and her sales pitch was so over-powering that the customers just gave in. If the, 'Apprentice', had existed then, she would have been on champagne and ermine, but alas this was a dreary Holderness Road shop in the middle of the seventies recession. Christmas Eve the shop was buzzing until the pubs opened but gave us our best day's sales of £399.57!

I contacted a newly qualified accountant, who I knew, and he said I needed to take a stock check. When he came to visit me his rather haughty attitude made me feel uncomfortable. Then, he asked me for my stock list and then demanded to check my figures, but in a manner, I thought more becoming of a VAT inspector than a book-keeper. I acceded to his wish but informed him a few days later that his services were no longer required. When my father, started his new business in 1962 he told me:

'I've found a good old boy to do my books, they call him Peter Moseley.'

'What does he charge you?' I said.

'About forty quid, but he's saved me a lot more,' Dad said.

'I can't see me ever needing his services...'

'One never knows what life will throw up,' Dad said with a smile.

And now fourteen years later I needed Dad's chartered accountant. At the time, Peter was based at Brentwood and I went to see him.

He was a big man with a shock of black hair and the manner of a gentleman. I felt at ease, and confident my accounts were in good hands. In 1941, Peter Moseley, aged 19, joined the RAF and flew the Catalina, a flying boat, used to detect and destroy German U boats in the North Atlantic. I would keep him in touch with sales, but my first accounts were not due till 31st March 1978, which by then, I hoped, the business would be showing positive signs of growth and sustainability.

By January, my training had become increasingly difficult to maintain, and I made an appointment to see a famous physiotherapist in Glasgow. After a long trip to Scotland, I was met by the family of someone I knew, and they put me up. They were very hospitable, but it was difficult to understand their dialect. They used one phrase, *a carry out*, which still amuses me and simply means a take away meal. The next day I caught a train to East Kilbride in the coldest weather I'd ever experienced, it was designated a new town in 1947 on a raised plateau 600-feet above sea level. However, the town was peppered with high rise flats and on that bleak day in January 1977, with four feet of snow looked, to me, like parts of Moscow. Mr McIndo's practice was on the 14th floor. He examined me and thought my injury had been caused by an imbalance due to posture. I could understand that, but the real reason had a lot more to do with running over three thousand miles in thirty gruelling weeks. He gave me exercises to ease the joint, but this was not the magic cure I had craved for.

The shop sales were slightly up, but that may have more to do with inflation than goods sold. I was urged to take part in East Hull's senior cross-country championship in February 1977, because if I won it would be for a record fourth time. In the event, I won again even though I was not very fit. With the benefit of hindsight, and if I had joined another club, I am sure Tom Hunter and possibly Johnny Crawford's name would have been on the member's cup. In my capacity as Vice-Captain, I needed to pick a team for the annual Captain vs Vice Captain race on the 6.2-mile Bilton circuit. This was eagerly anticipated by the East Hull gallery as Peter Elletson, aged 18, was making his first serious appearance in this race. In the event Peter was stronger than me and I saw at close quarters his constant and sustained loping stride as he gathered in the miles. At the finish, I had been beaten by a hundred yards, and Peter Collinson was eager to speak to me,

'Every dog has its day, Pete!' he said.

'Anyway, Peter it's great we have a young lad like Elletson doing so well,' I said.

'He's too good for you, and you'll never beat him again,' Collinson said.

'One never knows, Peter.'

As for the business, something magical happened: the sales nearly doubled, it was as miraculous as it was unexpected. We had the spring deliveries for Adidas tee shirts in over ten colourways. The quality was first class and the demand constant, which made our cash register sing a jolly song. Mothers would come in asking what the new colours were and told us how brilliantly they washed, and it was not unusual to have a single sale for up to six tee shirts at £3.99 a time. Our average daily sales were now nearly three hundred and way ahead of what I had been told was impossible by Bill, the know-all accountant. One of my staff had been at 'Romeos & Julliet's' nightclub in the city centre and told me, '*The DJ was putting the spotlight on one of dancers and said he must have got his new Adidas tee from Runnercare*'. I had taken a big risk in ordering so many, but I trusted the representative, and it paid off spectacularly. Adidas was the only big street brand at the time, and held a cult following among the young. The big shops with budgets would not have gone overboard as I had done, and in any case, they saw it as a fad, and must have thought they might get their fingers burnt.

Adidas footwear was also prominent and has remained a North of England fashion statement ever since. Top sellers were Adidas Kick a black leather three stripe-trainer sold in all sizes infant 12 to adult 12; Adidas Bamba also had a following, but the urban favourite was Adidas Samba in soft black leather, the same design as the white/blue Adidas Rom circa 1960. I was now selling Adidas road running trainers Adidas SL 72 and SL 76 in the shop and by mail order. With the business taking off so well I gave in my notice at Duncan Flockhart to concentrate more time on promoting Runnercare. It irked me that I still could not stock other brands such as Dunlop, Wilson or Slazenger, but if I had them would I have been able to fund the extra stock? I wanted progress, and I needed a new store to make the sports trade to sit up and take notice.

David Bedford, had been a hero of mine when at the age of twenty-one in 1971 he broke the European 10,000 metres record with 27:46.6 at Portsmouth on a track that resembled a cabbage patch. I met him at a sports exhibition and asked him if he could come to East Hull Harriers and present the prizes. There were no airs and graces with Dave and he readily agreed and just asked if I would confirm that in writing. This was an amazing coup, as he was the highest profile sports star in Britain at the time. Bedford's 10,000 metres world record was still intact when he came to Hull. A listener contacted Radio Humberside to report Bedford had been seen running in Willerby that morning. He came up to see me in the shop and was looking at the shoes in the rear show room, I heard the door go, and it was one of our regulars looking for a new set of dart flights. I said, 'Dave Bedford is in the back'. 'No,' he says, you're having me on!' It was amazing what a huge personality Bedford was then. He joined East Hull on a ten-mile training run, before presenting prizes at the Hull cricket club that evening.

I was still competing, but with less and less success. My hip ache was with me all the time and worse after running. I was beginning to fear my running career was grinding to a halt. The most important publication for any runner then was, Athletics Weekly, A5 and monochrome, and it was pored over like a stockbroker does rising share prices. To see one's name on its exalted pages was the goal of every club runner. There have been many running publications since, but none have matched the in-depth coverage of athletics weekly. I had been advertising once a month, now it would be weekly with a two-day deadline to be accurate with size availability. My competitors did not do this, which gave me an edge on credibility, because I only advertised what I had in stock. I also asked for page 39 every week for consistency and a play on the title of John Buchan's book, *The Thirty-Nine Steps*, even though it would take a lot more to win any distance race.

About this time, I we started to realise the shortcomings of having a shop we now had the means for a holiday, but no way to share as a family. We opened six days a week and did not have a half day and in the first year of a new business, I never even thought of taking a holiday. Something of our free and easy life style had been lost, that sense of the unity of our family, and with no family relatives within a hundred miles, we relied on each other. Unfortunately, the non-stop needs of the business came before our family. My wife had a huge battle to get Jayne into the school of her choice but when she got her teeth in to a problem that concerned the well-being of our kids, she was as stubborn as a mule, and even took on Councillor Max Bird in his posh Beverley office. She won, of course, and Jayne became a model pupil at Newland High School for girls. Sarah was now at Saltshouse junior High and becoming a good gymnast, while Simon had already followed his sister's footsteps to Thanet Primary.

We were not a year into our start-up business and I saw an opportunity to double up with a second shop in Bransholme shopping centre in the middle of Europe's largest housing estate of fifty thousand people. The shop was three times the size of Holderness Road with a weekly rent of £120. To keep within the landlord's contract, we would have to spend around £5000 on shop fittings. Next door was an audio shop, and the other side a Frank Dee supermarket. The negotiations were protracted and complicated. Eventually, I saw a young city executive called Justin from London and terms were resolved, but with a hike in legal costs. Of course, this was a lot different from the old-world friendliness, of Mr Westmoreland for our first shop on Holderness Road.

I was still running a little, and entered the Scarborough six-mile race, a hilly race taking in two circuits of the Castle Hill, but I found the race difficult with lack of training and I had to accept my fading form. Indeed, in the last mile, I was in about sixth place and feeling cramped around my injured, right hip. Then someone said, *'Pete, you're limping.'* In that moment, I knew immediately this was the end of the road and that my injury had become chronic and unmanageable. I stopped running totally: it had been sixteen months since I had first become injured, but my growing enterprise meant, I could devote more time to my business.

Now it was all hands-on deck to get the new shop open as soon as possible, because of the ticking time bomb of costs, was gnawing through my bank balance. We duly opened our second shop on Friday 21st October 1977, just fifty-five weeks after our first shop. Brand new fittings wide aisles full of stock with the footwear department at the rear of the store Looking back, it barely seemed conceivable that the venture materialised, because I wanted it to, and possibly a result of not getting my own way in a Diss shoe-shop when I was four years of age. The shop caused quite a stir on Bransholme but must have been a thief's paradise with our open displays. On the first Saturday, there were so many browsers that I put one of my staff on the door to count how many walked around the shop between 3pm to 4pm – it amounted to over three hundred. I gave a lad of about twenty a job, who seemed affable and confident, then I noticed some strange behaviour. When he thought, I wasn't looking he would open the till draw and rearrange the notes and even count the change, so he could calculate how much he could remove from under-rung sales – it was so blatantly dishonest, I sacked him on the spot. Next, I took on a female manageress, who I trusted, but she was caught red handed selling Adidas trainers for a fraction of the price to staff in Frank Dee's supermarket. To make sure, I asked a police constable to accompany me to the shop and we entered by the rear door. When challenged, she was brazen telling me she was not a thief. She was taken back to Tower Grange on Holderness Road, put in a cell, and only then owned up to the thefts.

The shop was not as profitable as Holderness Road owing to higher costs but achieved its aim in raising the status of Runnercare as a formidable player in the Hull area. So much so that rumours were circulating that I had a financial backer, which was not true, but I took it as a compliment. At the end of our first year the takings in our original shop was over fifty thousand pounds, unfortunately I lost contact with the clever-clogs accountant who'd doomed me to fail.

This new venture, and a serious injury which curtailed my training, should have brought us closer together. Our marriage was in its thirteenth year, my wife doted on our three children, and making our house into a home. Meanwhile, I was working, or thinking about the business every day with the sole aim to make Runnercare successful for the benefit of us all. Within a couple of years, I would be looking to open a third shop in the centre of Hull. We'd bonded with a lovely RAF life especially living in France and Holland. If anything, our marriage was even better, when we left Anglesey for a good job and settled in East Yorkshire. My wife was unsettled, when I suggested we strike-up on our own, and she was probably right. We would never be as content again.

CHAPTER 12

Pain Free Running

Throughout the summer of 1977 and most of 1978, I was side-lined by my on-going hip problem: a painful inflammation of the bursa located on the greater trochanter of the femur, but a blessing in disguise, because all my motivation could be focussed toward the success of Runnercare. However, my weight increased, which meant, I could walk into the new East Hull Harrier's club-house and not be recognised. The life of the club had moved on, although there was the little matter of the Senior Club Championship in the spring of 1978. Inexplicably, I decided to stand on the line to defend my title and not duck the expected drubbing from the young Shaun Crossland, who was in terrific form. Indeed, he was a formidable opponent, wiry and tenacious – a double for Barry Manilow, and I wondered if my reputation was about to go the way of the Bermuda Triangle! He looked edgy and nervous at the start even though there was no need. I had won the Members' Cup on four consecutive occasions, and once by a five-minute margin. But this would be embarrassing: I finished in 22nd place, and 12-minutes behind Shaun. An onlooker snapped a photo of me clambering over the last style like an aging Billy Bunter escaping from a scrumping raid. On the plus-side, my display of humble futility was greeted warmly by the members in the club-house – or was it a sympathy vote. Shaun, writing in East Hull's newsletter said, *'I just wanted to correct one major misconception. In Pete Flatman's article he said I was a talented athlete, who did not need much training to get fit. Of course, this sounds complimentary for some to believe*

I was running well with very little training, but this was not so. I was running sixty miles a week and I don't think other club mates were doing much more. I think one hundred miles a week is a bit excessive.' He went on, *'I well remember Flatty turning up like Billy Bunter, but I was still convinced he would be competitive. His reputation was such that even if he was dressed as Santa Claus I would not have been convinced that I could beat him.'*

With the benefit of hind-sight opening a second shop the previous year was a mistake, but it gave my business more credibility and hitherto reluctant suppliers were now eager to do business. I started to watch Hull Kingston Rovers at Craven Park, and I was inspired by the skill, and never-say-die attitude of Roger Millward. Running again was never far away from my thoughts, and how I could recover from the bursitis. Trips to medics and physios were to no avail – I would have to find the answer myself. The pain in my hip joint was like toothache, and I only ran a short distance each day, which was painful and caused me to limp. When, I switched to grass the discomfort was less troublesome and within a few months, I was running free of pain.

Hence, I was now running about forty miles per week but carrying nearly a stone extra in body weight. By March 1979, I was running fifteen miles on Sundays with Peter Dearing and Derrick Pickering at an easy seven-minute pace, pleasant with the usual banter,

'Hi Pete, you're carrying a bit of weight,' Derrick said.

'Yes, I know, but I've lost nearly a stone since I was thrashed by Shaun Crossland.' I said.

'How do you plan to get fit?' Peter asked.

'Starting today, I'm back to my hundred mile a week schedule,' I said.

'Forty miles to a hundred, how does that work?' Derrick said with a smile.

'For a start, I plan another ten miles this afternoon – that's twenty-five on day one…'

In fact, the extra ten miles really took it out of me and I was forced to lay down on the living room floor which was hardly surprising as it had been nearly three years since I last ran twenty-five miles in a single day. With that statement of intent, I released three seasons of pent-up energy and was fresh for the challenge though I decided to give the club championships a miss. Instead, I decided to run the Maassluis Westland Marathon, along with three club mates on 21st April 1979. I bought a Ford Granada the previous autumn and drove to Dover and took a ferry to Ostend. We stayed with a Dutch family, which brought back memories of our time in Holland in the late sixties. I was very tired throughout the marathon, still absorbing the punishing mileage, and my finishing time was a fair representation of my fitness. **Results:** 1. Julien Grimon Belgium 2:19:24 2. Cor Vriend Netherlands 2:22:12. 3 Brian Tate England 2:24:51 … 9. Peter Flatman 2:29:56 … 15. Kevin Best – my RAF pal 2:32:43 I was really surprised with the reaction of East Hull members, who must have written me off, after such a long injury.

I did not realise, those extra seven pounds would be so obvious, but on a positive side my heavier body-weight would make my leg muscles stronger and the loss of the half a stone would make me faster! After three months, the bursitis cleared up, and I could run freely without pain, and my weight back to a trim nine stone seven pounds. A few weeks later, I met Peter Elletson on a swift nineteen-mile training run, he turned, and ran with me. Very soon, we were ticking off five-minute miles:

'You're cracking on Pete, what are you training for?' Elly asked.

'I'm aiming for the AFOS East Hull twenty next month,' I said.

'What do you think you could run in the marathon?' Elly asked.

'This may sound absurd, but if I could run 1:42 then 2:14,' I asserted.

'Bloody hell, Pete – that would be amazing,' Elly exclaimed.

'Of course, I'd have to stay fit, and run and least a hundred miles per week.' I said

'When do you leave for the States Peter?'

'Not till the autumn.' Elly said.

'So, how did you get to join an American college? I asked

'Yes, I got an athletics scholarship running for England junior men last year,' Elly said.

'Sounds too good to be true,' I said.

'It's not that simple, I'm on a degree course and need good grades,' Elly explained.

'That's not so easy serving academics and running at same time,' I said.

'How do you mean?' Elly said.

'If I'm preparing for a marathon, and shops, I have share my efforts equally,' I said.

'Well I hope I can run faster and study just as hard.' Elly said.

Peter went to the College of Southern Idaho at Twin Towers in 1979, then to the University of Nevada at Reno in 1980 and finally met up with Bob Coleman, who had lived in Hull in the seventies, at the Summer school of Berkeley in 1981, before Peter returned home at the end of 1982.

I was running twice a day, keeping to a hundred miles per week, but to train at or near race pace, which would give me confidence for the upcoming longer road races. The East Hull Summer League 10km would be my last race before AFOS East Hull Twenty. That morning, I ran five-mile acceleration run at 7am starting at seven-minute mile pace – reducing to five minutes on the last mile. Shaun Crossland was on top form, and ran a stunning 30:15, I ran 30:53, which was OK considering my heavy mileage, and Peter Elletson clocked 30:55.

With a week to go, I started a taper: Sunday 15 miles steady; Monday am 5 miles easy pm 8 miles steady; Tuesday am 5 miles easy, pm 5-miles fartlek; Wednesday am 3 miles easy pm 5 miles 4 x ½ mile reps; Thursday am 3 miles easy pm 3 miles (strides on grass); Friday am 5 miles easy; Saturday am 3 miles easy. Total mileage 60. Sunday 27th May 1979 duly arrived, and with it the moment of truth: My quest to win this race started in 1974 with 3rd place in 1:55:37; in 1975 with 3rd place in 1:49:24; in 1976 with 4th place in 1:45:26. I missed three years through injury and at 35 had my hour arrived? No training today: I showered and put on my battle-dress, navy EB light shorts with a micro-fibre liner, my red Ron Hill string racing vest, my thin seamless red ankle socks, and a pair of royal/yellow Adidas 80 racing shoes. My wife gave me my Adidas white/black, satin jacket, then a good-luck kiss and I set off for a very slow two-mile run to East Hull's recently opened club house. The sky was eighty per cent blue with a scattering of fluffy, white clouds, and a temperature rising to 65 – 70F, warm enough to need plenty to drink. When I arrived at the club, Shaun Crossland greeted me, and looked forlorn:

'What's up Shaun?' I asked.

'I don't know … it seems you run well in a couple of races …'

'Been there got the tee shirt, so do the lads think you can win the club 20?' I asked.

'Yeah, they reckon you're past it, Pete. Are you fit?'

'Best since I left the RAF in 1973 Shaun – how about you?'

'If I can't win I hope you do.'

'I'll have my hands full with the likes of Phil Romaine, Mike Hurd and Alasdair Kean.'

Runners were arriving from far and wide, and the excited banter was putting me on edge and ready for action. I decided to drink two pints of water before the start, so that I would not need to drink at the water stations. The extraordinary thing about this race, was the modest turn-out of eighty athletes, but what it lacked in numbers was more than made up with quality. I have often thought the winner of most races knows by instinct he will – it's more a feeling than something that can be logically defined, and this day, I had that feeling.

As the gun fired, I started my digital wristwatch, I was running within myself, and easily dealing with race-favourite Mike Hurd's surges, and making sure I remained in touch with the leader. The first mile was reached in 4:53, and I was a tad disappointed it wasn't quicker. Over the next mile the old Bridlington road snakes around the village of Ganstead, where Hurd put his foot down, only to ease off after a hundred metres, and when he tried the same tactic near Coniston, I lost patience. Something went ping and released my body now covered in goose bumps, and my head crammed with endorphins, yet I'd only raced two of the twenty miles! I never looked behind, and knew I was free when I could not hear the footfalls of the chasers, my race-pace training gave me the confidence to press on, and I reached the five-mile post in 24:47. So, what was I thinking: that everything had clicked into place; I hadn't run this race for three years and today I was putting distance on my lead with every stride and that I had put myself in a winning position with fifteen miles to go. I was surprised to see Shaun Crossland, who had to pull out of the race, but he gave me a wave from the rear of a pick-up vehicle. From another car, I saw Peter Elletson following the event as I raced through Skirlaugh and Long Riston on the A165, and turned left at White Cross towards Routh, and the ten-mile post where there were about twenty spectators. My time was 50:11, and the nearest challenger was Phil Romaine, (Holbeach) about a minute behind, but I would need to be wary.

My friend and former RAF team-mate, Ian Wilton-Jones came with his wife to see the race and warned me of Phil's presence while I concentrated on the next five miles on a twisting, rutted road through Meaux towards Wawne. Romaine began to fade and was being chased down by Alasdair Kean (Derby). To be fair, I was beginning to slow, but my lead was over a minute. I still had to concentrate with about four miles to the finish and turned left on to Noddle Hill Way – a meandering oval-shaped road around the northern edge of Bransholme, a huge council estate. Over the years, I had come to expect some ribald remarks from the younger residents and knew how to ignore them. When I turned onto Wawne Road, I began to anticipate the finish near East Hull's new pavilion. Near Sutton, I thought of my two favourite lines in Rudyard Kipling's *IF:*

> *If you can meet with Triumph and Disaster*
> *And treat those two imposters just the same*

The next day in the Hull Daily Mail this report was penned by Peter Dearing, '*Peter Flatman won the Afos 20-mile road race promoted by his own club East Hull Harriers yesterday with a superb display of front running. He had 400yd. to spare in a brilliant personal best time of 1hr 44min 50sec. Mike Hurd (Croydon) seeking his third consecutive victory finished fourth. Flatman astounded everyone with his return to form after a long absence through injury He surged clear at 2 ½ miles, and no one could match his scorching pace. At 35 years of age it was an amazing return to form.*' My win came off the back of a long hip injury, and a burning desire to finally win this great race – on another day any one of the first ten athletes could have won this event. The back slapping and plaudits are an illusion, because all of us are close to seeing that other, imposter. In the moment of victory, I was overcome with emotion, I barely spoke to anyone. I remembered walking around my daughter Sarah's school, Saltshouse Junior High, where the presentation was held, in a barely conscious state trying to take everything in. My body seemed to have added another layer to my aura as if to protect those seconds forever. **Results:** 1. P Flatman (East Hull) 1:44:50 2. A Kean (Derby) 1:46:09 3. P Romaine (Holbeach) 1:47:34 4. M Hurd (Croydon) 1:48:05 5. R

Group Captain Huxley presents me with a cup for athletics 1973.

Start of the Rotherham Marathon May 1976. I'm (127) and on my left
is Alan Domleo (Derby) and the uncle of my daughter-in law and wife of
my son Simon (1999).

Peter Elletson defeats in East Hull '6' 1977.

First loss, AKA Billy Bunter, by 12 minutes to Shaun Crossland
in East Hull XC 1978.

On Tenerife beach looking to the future.

Winning Cleveland Marathon
in 1979 (2:19:34).

Warm training Tenerife
February 1980.

L-R John Barker (Grimsby), Pete Flatman, Tim Johnson (Portsmouth) and Dave Allen (Manchester) at 15-miles – East Hull 20 1982.

Holding off John Barker near end of East Hull 20 1982.

Leading Hull to Grimsby Marathon across the Humber Bridge 1982.

Discussing the race (Humber Marathon at the finish)
with Dave Michaels 1983.

Humber Marathon 1984.

L-R George Reynolds, Dave Michaels and me at 16-miles.

L-R My daughters Sarah, Jayne and Clare 2014.

My four grown-up children Simon, Clare, Jayne and Sarah.

Harrison (Airedale) 1:48:39 6. M Palmer (Notts) 1:48:46 7. A Sladen (Salford) 1:48:54 8. C Nightingale (City of Hull) 1:49:17 9. M Exton (Holbeach) 1:49:37 10. J Barker (Grimsby) 1:49:46 11. S Clegg (Sal) 1:51:24 12. T Flory (M&C-V) 1: 51:54 13. P Blakeney (Sal) 1:52:04 14. K Breeze (Sal) 1:52:35 15 P Leach (Leics) 1:54:02 16. G Astill (Notts) 1:54:41 17. R Hepworth (Long) 1:54:50 18. K Binney (Barns) 1:55:02 19.T Hunter (E Hull-V) 1:55:02 20. R King (Unatt) 1:55:05 21. B Dale (M&C) 1:55:18 22. M Richardson (Dur C) 1:56:04 23. A Allen (Grims) 1:56:21 24. K Mayor (Bolton) 1:57:09 25. A Law (Camb H) 1:57:03 **Teams:** 1. Salford 2. East Hull 3. Notts AC 4. Middlesboro & C 5. Grimsby 6. Barnsley. **(Vets):** 1. T Flory 2. T Hunter 3. A Hughes ((Roch) 1:57:20 **(O/45):** Hughes **(O/50):** W Fielding (Leeds) 2:02:24.

Derrick Pickering (East Hull) came over to congratulate me,

'Now tell me, Peter, when did think you were going to win this afternoon?'

'That's easy, Derrick not this afternoon, but three weeks ago!' I said.

'OK, I see that's very funny, Peter.

I eventually struck a deal for the vacant shop at 175, Ferensway and I planned to open on Thursday the 5th of July 1979. The shop was small no more than two hundred square feet, but with a ceiling of ten feet. Yet my mind was still preoccupied with road-racing when I went down to East Hull to try and break the record for the Sproatley ten miles six hundred and sixty-yards race. I was surprised to see Peter Elletson who asked me,

'Are you running Flatty, and what kind of time are you expecting?'

'I will run inside fifty-one minutes thirty,' I said.

'Bloody hell, Pete that's way inside Brian Jones' record, Elly said.

The handicapper set us off last, and we were up to twenty minutes behind the slower runners. Elletson and I sprang off the line like greyhounds out of a trap, and quickly caught Shaun Crossland, who started 30-seconds earlier. Since 1977, Peter Elletson was the man to beat, and ran 10,000 metres in 29:39, a week earlier in a match for Hull select vs American Universities vs NCAAA at Costello. For me, I wondered if we would ever face each other on such excellent form, because Peter was due to fly to the States to take up an athletic scholarship at Southern Idaho. Picture the scene: the two of us running neck and neck along the quiet country roads of Holderness, the warm summer sun heading for the horizon, while we were concentrating on taking in huge gulps of oxygenated atmosphere and bouncing along the warm tarmac and enjoying the sensation of moving fast without fatigue. In the distance we saw a sign indicating the 5-mile point. With no other runners in sight, it did not feel like a road race more like a duel in the sun, and we were the only witnesses. We checked our watches, 24-minutes 20-seconds or put another way 4-minutes 52-seconds per mile:

'I can't believe that time,' Peter said.

'Not bad for a low-key summer league race,' I said, 'not bad for a vet-35?'

'By the time you finish you'll feel sixty-five!' Peter (Elly) said with a chuckle.

Now we were silent, apart from the sound of our foot-falls, and over-worked lungs. By the seventh mile, at Sproatley, we were passing small packs of backmarkers, who shouted encouragement, and realised the titanic struggle between us at the top of our form. As we neared Swiss Cottage roundabout we were trying to thread our way through a pack of slower runners with about a mile to the finish. Elly stole a lead but try as I might I could not pull him back, and he won by eight seconds. The final times for the 10-miles 660-yards race were extraordinary: Peter Elletson ran 50:35, and 2:25 inside Brian Jones' record that had stood for nine years. I had predicted 51:30, but ran 50:43, and 2:17 inside Brian's record. Shaun was also 12-seconds inside the record that had stood since 1970. If it had been an accurate ten-miles Elly's time would be 48:42 and mine 48:50. Yet neither of us could beat the handicapper, Peter was eighth and I was tenth. We had both obliterated the nine-year record of Brian Jones, and Peter Elletson's course record will never be beaten. In the club-house Peter looked whacked and said:

'Flatty you shattered me tonight.'

'That was one hell of a race, Peter, well done,' I said.

The East Hull 6.2-mile road race had become an obsession. I had held the record since 1974 and my best time stood from 1976 with 30:09. This time the race was handicapped, and I was the backmarker. In the last four hundred-metres I caught and overtook Derrick Pickering and have estimated I would have finished a further twelve seconds in front of him. In the melee at the finish there was a mix up of times and places. The revised, estimated finish was that I was just one second in front of Derrick, and if so I had already broken my obsessional thirty-minute barrier but could never prove it. I knew this might be my last chance to get a sub thirty clocking. Chris Vodden, a City of Hull athlete disagreed, *'Pete, you're injured, and you are three years older, you may have to accept that.'* But all I needed was a tiny improvement of ten seconds. To aid my pace judgement I went around the course and repainted all the mile marks. On the race night, the wind was a light south westerly, which I would face over the last two miles and I did not expect anyone to be with me to help me find those precious seconds to break thirty minutes. At two-miles my time was 9:26 I was ahead of my schedule; at three-miles I was still on target. By now I was straining every sinew and ignoring the pain and reached the mile to go post in 25:02. All I needed was a 4:57 or better and the record would be mine. Even the light headwind seemed exaggerated as I mentally

119

whipped my failing body but could not do any more and finished in 30:10. Chris was right, but if I had Peter Elletson for company, I would have done it.

Three years earlier, I ran the Freckleton half marathon a few weeks after my initial hip injury, but now I was fully recovered. Therefore, it seemed logical to try to win East Hull's Major Stone half marathon being held on 26th August 1979. In previous half-marathons, I tended to fade over the last three miles, and decided to run the East Hull course six days earlier on Monday evening. Furthermore, I thought I would try to run sixty-seven minutes or better, of course, that would be difficult if the weather was unfavourable. Indeed, the conditions were dreadful with gale-force winds, and a sullen sky. Still, I would do it. I put on my racing kit and jogged two-miles to the start. If anything, the storm was worse when I set off on Salts-house Road. I was annoyed with the howling wind for trying to spoil my half-marathon time-trial. Anyway, I fought the odds as the gale pushed and buffeted my body with brutal power. Consequently, by the finish my body felt as though it had been in a prize-fight with an invisible foe. My time was 68:11. In fact, I'd forgotten the golden rule about a time-trial – give yourself at least two weeks before an important race, in case things go wrong. On the day, the weather was sunny and benign. Dave Cannon (Gateshead) and Dave Allen (Manchester) got away leaving me to chase Colin Taylor (Airedale). Even if my trial had gone well I would have my hands full to win East Hull's race as Cannon's personal bests were 65:09 for the half-marathon and 2:11:22 for the marathon, and Colin Taylor's bests 63:42 and 2:15:15 respectively. **Results:** 1. D Cannon (Gateshead) 65:29 2. D Allen (Manchester) 65:40 3. C Taylor (Airedale) 67:04 4. P Flatman (East Hull) 67:25 5. R Belk (Airedale) 68:35 6. S Curran (Salford) 68:36 7. C Nightingale (CoH) 69:08 8. C Sweeting (Sunderland) 69:14 9. P V Connelly (Dark Peak) 69:55 10. J Trainor (Gateshead) 70:00 11. 11. S Clegg (Salford) 70:17 12. J Atkin (Airedale) 70:50 13. J Hunter (East Hull) 71:28 14. F Keily

(Altrincham) 71:38 15. J S Jones (Man) 74:07 **Team:** 1. Airedale 2. East Hull 3. Manchester H.

On Sunday September 9th1979, I won the Cleethorpes ten-mile in 51:00. Then followed that on Tuesday with a win in East Hull's road 5k in 14:52. I had read an Athletics Weekly profile on Greg Hannon after he'd won the AAA title in 2:13:06. Prior to that he ran a solo marathon trial in 2:21. As I was planning a marathon in a month's time it made perfect sense to run a solo marathon trial, but it had to be an accurate distance. The first twenty miles was the East Hull course, I'd raced many times, then East Hull's six mile which measured at 6.2 and only 30-yards short. I pushed the start button on my digital wrist watch in a pair of New Balance 420s with very soft mid-soles to reduce the impact of the hard road. However, I had not taken account of a marathon without an adrenaline rush and wondered if I could carry on for the full distance. My feet seemed to stay on the road a few nanoseconds longer on every stride in the super-soft shoes. I thought, I was running hard, but that was an illusion which was confirmed by my watch that read 27:30 for 5-miles. Despite the time, I thought the next five miles would be much better, perhaps 26:30, but the ten-mile was 54:45 – I thought I'd put my foot down but the result was a paltry 15-seconds faster or just 3-seconds per mile. Now, I was resigned to the pace and my fifteen-mile was 27:40. As previously arranged, Derrick Pickering was waiting to give me some company from twenty-mile (1:49:50) to the finish. Derrick started off very quickly, and it took me a mile to catch him up. Unfortunately, Derrick was now blowing, but he'd made me find another gear, which gave me a marathon time of 2:24:17. This marathon was the easiest I ever ran with an average mile pace of 5:30 and a bonus, I suffered no after effects and I was able to train normally the next day.

The emphasis, now switched to short, sharp repetitions of one or two minutes on ten-mile road runs so that, I could deal with sudden changes of pace on race day. I also wanted to keep my recoveries from the fast repetitions to at least sub-five-minute thirty pace, so I could endure racing under maximum pressure. Compared to most elite runners, who started at school, and had eight to ten years on the track sprinting, middle-distance for speed and cross country for strength, I started at 28 without that background, which meant I was always *Running to Catch Up*. Even though, I ran 800m and 1500m it could be embarrassing to race against athletes nurtured from young years, and only running further when that speed became second-nature. Charlie Spedding also had those years to perfect his speed as personal bests of a mile in 4:03 and 3000 metres in 7:54 would confirm. I wrote to Charlie's coach Lindsey Dunn, because I was getting dropped in longer road races. He wrote back, and said, I should run hard repetitions of five or ten minutes on road runs over ten-miles. Occasionally, I ran with Malcolm Prince, a 13:27 5000m performer, running at race pace over three, five and ten-mile circuits. These sessions were the next best thing to actual all-out competition.

Eleven days before the marathon, I drove to the capital to run an open 5000 metres, being held that evening, at the West London stadium. The other runners were all unknown to me, but that did not matter. I had come all this way, simply, to get a personal best. Within a few laps the fifteen athletes had narrowed down to two younger lads and myself. I felt great and I covered all their surges but try as they might, I would not let them break me. We finished almost in a line, but my watch confirmed my aim – a new personal best of 14:42.4. The other competitors asked me where I was from and why I came so far for this race, '*I'm from East Hull Harriers and I've run this to sharpen up before running the Cleveland Marathon*'. Suitably impressed, one said, '*I am sure you will win it!*' This was my final test and now, I could focus on the real examination at Middlesbrough. There was a lot of interest in the club house particularly by Peter Dearing and Dick Dobson. I just hoped I would not let anyone down. I did a modified version of the Spartan carbohydrate bleed-out diet, and by cutting my training down to a mere sixty miles, I did not suffer the headaches and loss of concentration caused by the full version of the diet. To be on the safe side, I went up to Middlesbrough and ran one lap of about thirteen miles at an easy pace to get a feel of the course. On the last Sunday before the race, I took my family to Luigi's restaurant in Hornsea for lunch, we all liked the food and Tricia loved the attention of the Italian waiters. Then I said something about running a marathon the next Sunday and wondered if they could serve us all at around 5pm after the race – happily they agreed.

Cleveland Marathon

I was so pleased all my family, Tricia, Jayne, Sarah, Simon and Clare came, on what I hoped would be a momentous day Sunday 14th October 1979. We headed to the Clareville Stadium in Middlesbrough, and it struck me the track had obviously been named after our one-year old Clare our beautiful baby. Nothing could possibly go wrong I hoped and even the weather was ideal – overcast with very little wind and a temperature of 50f. I double knotted my pair of Adidas royal and yellow Marathon 80 racing shoes, weighing 180 grams, with an extended heel designed to lessen the relentless pounding of road running. On the day, I wore my East Hull red vest, a pair of lined navy microfibre EB shorts and seamless red socks. For a change, I was at a race with time to spare. The renowned national marathon coach Alan Storey wished me well. Tricia was even more nervous than me. On paper, the previous year's winner Stafford's Malcolm Mountford posed the biggest threat, and I remembered he had reached twenty miles in 1:46:30, but my plan was to get there in 1:43:00.

The race started on the stadium tartan track, and I shuffled around in third place. The pace was very easy, and I was feeling good. Surely, the pace was too show, and I feared I'd be behind my target times. I continued to drift along until Mountford started to test the field with modest surges, which dropped a few runners, but soon irritated me – I wanted to feel I was in the race, and not a mere spectator. At three miles Malcolm broke away again, I went with him, and as he slowed, I speeded up. I had total inner-belief and ran the next two miles in 9:50

and reached five-miles in 25:45 which precisely matched my pre-race twenty-mile target. The wide-open road lay ahead, I had broken free, and reached 10-miles in 51:08 in reasonable comfort. I had taken a risk and was well clear of the field, but had I given the marathon due respect? Sure enough, I won the East Hull twenty leading from three-miles, but the marathon is six miles and three-hundred eighty-five yards longer. Perhaps, if I'd analysed the race, my age of 36, and the fact my personal best was 2:23:25, I might, or should have been more cautious. Instead, I was still running wild, and alone – still lapping up the joy of competing without fear. Fifteen-miles was reached in 77-minutes and the average mile pace would mean a 2:14:30 marathon, yet my focus was still on the next 5-miles instead of the next eleven miles. Meanwhile, I'm still in dreamland, and not the next fifteen thousand-strides I'd have to make to break the tape. My pace was metronomic, and my focus total and I felt euphoric when I reached twenty-miles in 1:43:18 and a personal best. At this pace I was still on for a finish time of 2:15:18 and would slash eight-minutes off my best. I started to slow, but GPS watches with their ability to give accurate feed-back per tenth of a mile were decades in the future, and I would have to rely on the 25-mile post to gauge my pace. In the distance, I could see Peter Dearing and Dickie Dobson:

'Hi Pete, your 25-mile time is 2-hours-eleven minutes-fifteen seconds,' Peter said.

'Thanks,' I said.

'You've got a lead of two minutes thirty seconds.'

Oh dear, I wished I'd not heard that. My body craved to be spared further punishment. The five miles split was 27:57 and my pace was now 5:35 per mile, but I had hit the wall. If, I had been able to maintain 5:35 pace, I would have finished the marathon in 2:17:57. Surely, I could have found the determination to run faster over the last mile? However, my subconscious had heard those sweet words, *'two and a half minutes clear,'* and saved my body from further unnecessary punishment. That last mile was excruciating, my head racked in exhaustion, and each stride felt like, I was lifting 100-kilogramme bar-bells. The Northern Echo photograph told all as I crossed the line: my hands, unclenched to save energy; my stride short; my right hand ready to stop the watch; my face twisted, and my teeth bared, and I did not have the strength for a victory wave. But I had won: it would be a life-time best of 2 hours 19 minutes and 34 seconds; it was a wonderful way to return from an injury that had lasted three years. All my lovely family were with me to share that special day. A few minutes later, I was shivering, as my body had been drained of every calorie of energy. I received a beautiful, embroidered sash, Winner of Cleveland Marathon 1979, and a crystal decanter and glasses. Then, as planned, I drove back to Luigi's restaurant in Hornsea as though nothing much had happened. **Results:** 1. P Flatman 2:19:34 2. A Kean (Derby) 2:21:05 3. D Dixon (Sunderland) 2:22:22... 15. Carl Nightingale (City of Hull) 2:29:21 16. C Vodden (CoH) 2:30:21 25. J Potter (EH) 2:37:00 33. D Pickering (EH) 2:41:30 35. T Hunter (EH) 2:41:52 49. D Longman (CoH) 2:48:47 98. B Child (EH) 3:04:36. **Teams:** 1. Sunderland 14 2. East Cheshire Harriers 46 3. East Hull 59.

When you achieve exactly what you set out to do, a vacuum sucks out your mind and body of inspiration, and determination. My sub 2:20 marathon had drained my being of vital nutrients, and my soul needed time to regain its equilibrium. A week or two of easy running, and sleep would be nature's restorer. Ten-mile races were my favourite events probably because of the Henlow Ten in 1972, when after only a year's training, I placed 3rd in 49:53. I decided to enter the Tipton Ten again with a personal best as my target. This was one of the biggest ten-mile races and attracting athletes from all over the UK.

In the seventies ten-mile races were more popular than any other road race, and the Tipton Ten, based in Birmingham, could draw runners from all parts of the Kingdom, and it was perfect challenge for me while I was still fit. For some the barrier was seventy minutes or sub seven minutes per mile; for others sixty minutes or sub six minutes per mile, while others, including myself the target would be under fifty minutes. In 1978, the first Tipton event, I was 27th in 52:30 and the only East Hull Harrier there. On this Sunday morning 18th November 1979, I took four team mates – all hoping to run personal best times:

'Nice to have company on such a long journey,' I said.

'Even though unfit Pete you ran 52:30,' Shaun Crossland said.

'I've been running well, and would love to break 55 minutes,' Steve Dobbs chipped in.

'It's bloody time, I ran a decent race,' opined Trevor Shields.

'You'd, better Trev, I'm ten years older, and I'll go sub 56,' Derrick Pickering said.

'What do you predict for yourself Pete, should be good?' Steve asked.

'If I can stay with the leaders till halfway, I think sub 50,' I said.

'What have you got on your feet, rockets,' Trevor said.

'Look it's a great time of year to race, cool and not much wind. You won't be intimidated, because local runners won't know you nor you them,' I said to lessen the pressure.

Tipton Harriers' clubhouse was beside the running track, about the size of an army billet and full of runners' banter. The wooden walls crammed with events and results dating back to the club's formation in 1910. We had arrived in good time, and the five of us went around one of the laps to warm-up before the start. We secured our paper numbers with four safety pins and lined up with every-one bouncing with bonhomie which made the atmosphere alive and electrifying. Not every runner could win, but all could strive for personal bests in one of the greatest British ten-miler road races set in the heart of Birmingham.

'Good luck lads, if the going gets tough, it means you're flat-out,' I said.

'That's right, Pete, and you lead by example,' Derrick said.

'Last word: you'll not be able to face the mirror, in the morning if you've not given this race everything,' Go for it lads.

The race started on the club track, the leaders went hell for leather. I knew I had to hold on to the front-runners, but also knew the pace would drop in the second mile. After a lap of three-miles, I was in eighth place, and I saw Grahame Ellis (Holmforth) battling for the lead with the amazing Andy Holden, one of Tipton Harriers' all-time greats. Over the next lap, I was slowly catching Tony Milovsorov aged 20, a rising star for Tipton, and being cheered on by groups of fans, but I prevailed to come 7th in a personal best of 48:43 – an improvement of nearly four minutes in the year. I watched Shaun finish 40th in 52:42, a time which would win most ten-mile races. I believe that quality races like the Tipton Ten provide a challenge and opportunity for athletes, who live in remote parts of the UK to reach a standard higher than they could have imagined if they only ran in local races.

Results: 1. G Ellis (Holmforth) 47:20 2. A Holden (Tipton) 47:23 3. J Wheway (W. Bilston) 47:29 4. G Helme (St Helens) 47:31 5. B Cole (Tip) 47:36 6. T Wright (W & B) 48:35 7. P Flatman (East Hull) 48:43 8. T Milovsorov (Tip) 48:47 9 R Cytlau (Tip) 48:55 10. P Heywood (Worc) 49:04 11. D Allen (Man) 49:23 12. Ian Stewart (Tip) 49:24 13. C Mattock 49:38 (W&B) 14. T Wright (Tip) 49:42 15. D Francis (West) 49:48 16. M Deegan (Old) 50:13 17. D Reeves (Dby) 50:23 18. J Bigham (RAF Cos) 50:36 19. K Angus (Sheff) 50:38 20. K Scott (W&B) 50:39 East Hull finishers: 40. S Crossland 52:42 48. S Dobbs 53:14 61. T Shields 54.17 72. D Pickering 54:45. **Women:** 1.J Smith (Lough) 54:47 2. S Hassan (Bir) 59:34 3. A Turland (Dav) 60:14.

My next race was the legendary13-mile 1000yd Morpeth to Newcastle road race, held on the 1st January 1980, and had been since the very first event in 1904. On the way north, I dropped off Tricia and the kids at her sister's house in Darlington and then drove to the centre of Newcastle, where I parked and caught the bus which took the athletes north to the market town of Morpeth. I had run this event twice before and it was always bitterly cold, which on New Year's Day gave a surreal atmosphere on this hilly road race of almost fourteen miles. The local population turned out in their thousands to see us eccentric souls run like Spartans to the Civic Centre in Newcastle.

Jim Alder was the local hero, who had won the event five times as well as the Commonwealth marathon gold. He recognised me on the bridge and turned to a group of Morpeth Harriers, '*This, is Peter Flatman,*' but he was interrupted by the club coach, '*Oh, we know all about him and the East Hull twenty!*' Reputations obviously stretched far and wide. The traffic was stopped, the gun fired, and we were on our way up the hill and out of town. Soon, I was in the leading group of eight, which included Jim Alder and race favourite Mike McLeod, who would go on to win a 10,000 metres Olympic silver medal in 1984. Mike was at the front of the group and looking a little nervous and kept checking to see how many of us were left. Jim was in his forties and had no chance of winning the race, he quipped, '*Its OK Micky boy, I'm still here!*' I was in very good company, but this day there would be no holding Mike, known as the *Elswick Express* as he struck out on his own at six miles up Blagdon Bank. The weather was closing in and my clothing inadequate, but I was pleased to be onto holding on to fifth place as we came to Gosforth, where we were greeted by hundreds of spectators, some outside public houses quaffing pints of beer. This really was bizarre, and getting darker by the minute, the cold had finally got to my legs and I lost a couple of places and came 7th in 67:28. This equated to a half marathon in 64:51 – the best of my career. The Morpeth to Newcastle New Year's Day race ceased in 2004, because of safety issues with increasing traffic could not be resolved. Mike won a few more times, but no one ever beat his performance of 63:25. **Results:** 1. M McLeod (Elswick) 1:03:25 2. S Irvine (Gateshead) 1:05:06 3. D Cannon 1:05:28 4. J Trainor (Gat) 1:06:53 5. G Grant (Army) 1:07:08 6. A Catley (Mor) 1:07:19 7. P Flatman (E Hull) 1:07:28 8. S McHale (Glouc) 1:08:03 9. S Markley (M&C) 1:08:12 10. R Lunnon (AF&D) 1:08:32 11. E Cameron (ESH) 1:08:39 12. A Keith (EAC) 1:08:46 13. D Robson (Els) 1:09:04 14. S Winter (Gat) 1:09:13 15. W Cain (Salt) 1:09:17. **Teams:** 1. Gateshead 9 2. Elswick 32 3. Morpeth 49.

When, I got home from work on Saturday 12th January 1980, I received this phone call,

'Hi Pete, it's Lindsay Dunn, Brendan Foster's coach, he cannot get to Belfast for an international meeting, his plane has been cancelled due to fog, and he wonders if he could have a run in the Ferriby 10?'

'Well I'll have to give Jim Kirkwood a ring, give me a call back in ten minutes.'

'Thanks, Pete. By the way, I got your evening number from your ad in Athletics Weekly.'

'Hi, can I speak to Jim please,' I said.

'Now then, Pete what's up?'

'Big Bren wants a run in the Ferriby 10 mile tomorrow.' I said enthusiastically.

'Bloody hell, never thought we would see him run here, but I'll have to sound out the committee.' Jim said.

'Thanks Jim, it'll be great publicity.' I enthused.

'I've had a word with the committee. Foster can run but *he* cannot win a prize!'

My adverts for Runnercare were always in *Athletics Weekly*, and my home number for after 6pm enquiries was never more useful. The

Ferriby 10, had a deserved reputation for appalling weather, but the race set off, at 11am, with sunny spells and light winds. Brendan, the Commonwealth 10,000 metre champion, cut a lonely figure as he strode up Westella Road. His image appeared on the front page of the Hull Daily Mail, with the caption, *Brendan Foster having a leisurely Sunday morning run!* In fact, the Gateshead athlete set a record of 48:01 on the hilly course that remains intact. Then he ran the course again! In the mid-nineties, I went to see him in 1984 regarding an energy supplement for his business in Newcastle. I was accompanied by Andy Ulrick, the supplier of the recovery drink. When Brendan saw me, there was only one thing on his mind,

'Hi Pete, tell me, do I still have the Ferriby 10 record?'

'It's yours for ever, Brendan,' I replied.

Results: 1. B Foster (Gateshead) 48:01 2. M Prince (CoH) 49:29 3. C Taylor (Airedale & SV) 49:34 4. D Allen (Man) 49:59 5. A Robertson (Harr) 50:03 6. J Atkin (A&SV) 50:22 7. A Kean (Derby) 50:26 8. J Ashworth (Bing) 50:28 9. W Domoney (Sheff) 50:45 10. P Lightfoot (CoH) 50:54 11. P Rawnsley (Sheff) 51:30 12. C Nightingale (CoH) 51:38 13. J Lunn (Leeds) 51:54 14. E MacKenzie (Barns) 52:06 15. C Vodden (CoH) 52:13 16. M Anderson (Grim) 52:20 17. P Moon (Bing) 52:23 18. D Weigel (Barns)52:57 19 T Wright (Long) 53:05 20. D Brown (Grim) 53:20 21. J Cook (Stain) 53:49 22. S Shallcross 53:26 23. P Connelly (Dark P) 53:29 24. R Hepworth(Long) 53:32 25. M Chorlton (Stain) 53:49 26. B Hilton (Leeds) 53:58 27. K Allen (Dark P) 54:07 J Turner (Holm) 54:13 29. J Chadwick (CoH) 54:16 30 K Robinson (Bing) 54:19. **Teams:** 1. City of Hull 2. Airedale & SV 3. Sheffield 4. Bingley 5. Leeds City 6. Grimsby. **(Vets)** E Chambers (E Hull 0/45 58:17.

I was encouraged with my performances and ran four hundred and twenty miles in January with some very good speed training especially over the longer repetitions. In hindsight, it was difficult to see how I could maintain this intensity for the Olympic marathon selection race at Milton Keynes in May. On 8th February, I went to Tenerife for some warm weather training and took some big books to read about the Great War. With no distractions, I threw myself into some heavy training and in the first week ran one hundred and twenty-one miles. On my morning run of twelve miles there was a downhill stretch with a concrete post marking each kilometre, which I ran in two minutes thirty-five seconds. On the final day, on the final long run I seemed to have an out of body experience. Over the last few miles my legs went flabby and I nearly stopped, it was as if my spirit had already left the island. I had missed our fifteenth wedding anniversary on the 20th. From wheels-down to wheels up over fourteen days I had run two hundred and fifty miles.

Two weeks later, I met Derrick Pickering at the club house who wanted a word,

'So, you're running the Swintex 25 km on Sunday morning.'

'Yes, I'm looking to race against the top boys!' I said.

'But you've got to run the club championship on Saturday afternoon.'

'Have a heart, 8-miles of plough – hours before racing Britain's best?'

'But you'll miss the chance to win a record fifth title, Pete.'

'You're crackers, Derrick!'

Nevertheless, here I was, wondering why I'm running this relatively unimportant club race, when I should have my feet up ahead of the real challenge, I would face at Bolton the next morning. I knew Tim Warrener would go all out to win the 1920 Member's Cup for the first time. He stayed in touch with me for the first half of the race, but now we were on deep rutted plough and I ran harder to make a decisive break but running over thick mud was never my forte and the clinging clay was pulling my hamstrings. Why had I given into Derrick's insane suggestion, ahead of the best road race I would ever compete in? The last half of the club-race seemed to take forever, but I won by about a minute.

Early the next morning, I drove to Bolton with time to spare. Then, I warmed up, and saw athletes, I'd only ever seen in Athletics Weekly. Bolton United Harriers vests were prominent, then I spotted Steve Kenyon and the memories flooded back to my first ever race at the Burton-wood Relays in 1971 and how he had won the first leg at a canter leaving others to stagger in as though they'd been shot. The great and good from England, Scotland, Wales, N Ireland and the Republic of Ireland were ready to do battle. My legs were still aching from yesterday's plough, but inside my head, I was ready to race. The roads were smooth and wide, the weather overcast, cold and windless, the waiting athletes tense and nervous. Squire Yarrow, 75 a pre-war European marathon medallist started the great race. From the off, I was in clean air and running freely. A Mark Shearman photo spoke volumes: I'm sharing foot-falls with the great Steve Kenyon with eyes like diamonds, while I'm transfixed in concentration, Keith Penny was on my right shoulder, and ex-RAF team-mate Ray Crabb on my left. My running dream was now complete. I'd witnessed such athletes as these scrapping for every yard, 9-years earlier, when I had no right to be there. Yet now, I was sharing strides with the running greats of Great Britain and Ireland. I was still leading and recorded 14:58 at 5 km. but as we started the long climb out of Lostock Village, the writing was writ large on the wall. How, I wished I'd not raced on the previous day. My time at 10 km was 30:18, but the mighty Kenyon was already 13-seconds ahead of me and proceeding to rip the field apart, and increased his lead by almost a minute in the next 6-km. His splits were extraordinary: 5 km 14:58, 10 km 30:07 15 km 44:44 – he went on to win by one minute, twenty seconds. In retrospect, I felt privileged to run in such a great race, which owed so much to my friend and organiser the late Vince Regan.

Results: 1. S Kenyon (Eng) 1:14:34 2. K Penny (Eng) 1:15:54 3. R Crabb (Bristol) 1:15:56 4. J McLoughlin (N Ire) 1:16:05 5. J Brown (CV) 1:16:11 6. P Eales (WS&E) 1:16:36 7. G Ellis (Eng) 1:17:02 8. J Dingwall (Scot) 1:17:09 9. M Longhorn (AS&SV) 1:17:19 10. G Laing (Scot) 1:17:36 11. Greg Hannon (N Ire) 1:17:53 12. W Domoney (Sheff) 1:18:03 13. P Flatman (E Hull) 1:18:05 14. M Lane (Wal) 1:18:08 15. J Robertshaw (Wal) 1:18:22 16: A Kean (Der) 1:18:32 17. K Best (Bol) 1:18:45 18. I Gilmore (W&B) 1:18:57 19. G Gregg (Dunc) 1:19:01 20. P Rivald (Horw) 1:19:08. **Teams:** 1. England 10 2. Scotland 39 3. N Ireland 46 4. Wales 69 5. Ireland 116. Vet40 1. L Carrol (Wirral) 1:20:57 2. H Kelly (E Ches) 1:23:21 3. G Vaux (M&C) 1:23:26 V45 D Lawson (Bing) 1:25:05 V50 E Kirkup (Barns) 1:28:58. **(Women)** 1. L Billington (Houns) 1:36:45 2. C Readdy (Stoke) 1:37:51 3. C Harkin (Bol) 1:40:37.

From the moment, Hull Kingston Rovers and Hull FC made the 1980 Rugby League Cup Final our three shops became magnets for both sets of fans. Rovers were based at Craven Park and their memorabilia shop was Runnercare situated on the same road, while our city centre shop was decked out with the Black and White of Hull FC. Bransholme, was where a lot of Hull fans lived after being rehoused from the Hessle road area, but there were still a fair proportion of Red and White fans who lived nearby. We were inundated with fans wanting to show their life-time allegiance. Soon we were stocking up on shirts, shorts, socks, scarves, bobble hats, sweatshirts, tee shirts, caps, banners, flags, mugs, key rings, and even dart flights. The city had never seen anything like it and when I received a new delivery of Adidas Rovers red and white shirts the news spread like wildfire and we sold the whole stock in a couple of days. The same happened with Hull FC's black and white irregular hooped shirts. I did an interview on Radio Humberside, which in turn promoted my three stores around the city. Our first shop on Holderness had queues out of the door, with everyone wanting a piece of memorabilia. In the last two weeks, I kept a record of the number of sales we had in our three outlets. The total was staggering, almost ten thousand or put another way, a twenty-fold increase on normal trade. Hardly surprising as it was the first and only time that these two giants of Rugby League would play each other at Wembley's Empire Stadium. Our shops were open as normal on 3rd May 1980, but a vast army of supporters left the city in virtual silence while on the last lamp post at the top of Boothferry Hill a fan left a sign, *'Would the last one out, turn off the lights!'* Steve Hubbard scored nine of Rover's ten points, but ended the match on crutches, while Hull scored five. Indeed, it was and will remain a unique day in the history of the city, because it was the one and only Wembley (Empire Stadium) Challenge Cup win for Rovers or Hull.

One of the hardest things to achieve as a runner is a persistent level of performance. I had made a dramatic return to top form in May 1979, which I sustained for eleven months, but it came to a grinding halt on the 13th April in the Cambridge ten-mile road race. My uncle Michael, who emigrated to America in the 50s, and became a USAF master sergeant came to watch me from nearby RAF Mildenhall with his wife Sarah,

'Hi Michael, lovely to see you both again.'

'Hi Peter, how far is the race, and how do you think you'll do?'

'Ten-miles is my favourite distance, and take me about fifty minutes,' I said.

'That's quick, Peter – I shuffle a couple of miles now and then,' Michael said.

'Peter, you look so fit,' Sarah said.

'We'll stick around and see you at the finish, good luck,' Michael said.

'Thank you, both – I'll see you soon.'

When I was warming up, I felt woozy, my limbs akimbo, and as though my body thought enough, no more. Meanwhile, my head was trying to focus, and rally my fatigued legs into one more battle. Four hundred of us lined up on a narrow country road on a warm spring day. Even amongst this throng I felt detached and alone, but I could not understand why there was no obvious start line or sense of urgency amongst the runners closest to me.

A dull thud in the distance startled me, I was right at the back facing the wrong way and four hundred athletes between me and the front of the race! The route was along a narrow country lane, I went berserk, like a footballer giving away a penalty in the dying seconds of the game and now the whole world would be laughing at me. How could I have been so stupid and have all that training wrecked by my idiotic inattention? My, desperation brought on a massive rush of adrenaline and instant source of energy for fight or flight and I needed the former to battle through the countless backmarkers being cursed, jostled and loathed in equal measure. If I was of sound mind, I might have thought I needed to take my time to get to the front, because this manic burst of effort would cause acute oxygen debt and limbs scorched by lactic acid. But I was still part blinded by the red mist and then amazed to be on the shoulder of Tony Simmons, the European 10,000 metres silver medallist, at the mile post in four-minutes-forty.

Of course, it was incredible that I had reached the front, but these boys had not started their racing yet and how would I cope when they did? They pushed on, but I could not respond, Tony won in 49:10 and I finished crestfallen in tenth in fifty-one minutes thirty-six seconds. But the damage was done, and this debacle would revisit me many times in early morning nightmares.

'Hi Peter, you did well,' Michael said.

'I lined up at the wrong end of the race and had to fight my way to the front.'

'You came tenth, Peter, that's brilliant,' how could I ever explain my despair to them?

'Thanks, for coming, wish I could have run better,' I said wearing a worn smile.

The AAA marathon and Olympic selection race, 3rd May 1980, coincided with the most frenetic period of trade for my shops, because of the Hull rugby league final. An amazing coincidence that they both occurred on the same first Saturday in May. I had gone through all the motions, reducing the miles to almost zero and piling on the carbohydrates. Then, I received a card from East Hull Harriers, which was very thoughtful and kind, but this, for me, merely compounded the pressure. Of course, in any calm assessment I was still supremely fit, but no longer could I demand total obedience from my body – it was likely to go on strike at any time. The club well-wishers would not know this and even if I had told them they may not have been able to understand. The marathon course was around cycle paths of the sprawling new town of Milton Keynes and the weather cool with a north-east breeze. I was in a large group of about twenty that stayed together for the first ten kilometres reached in 31:28. Unseen by most of the group, two athletes were poleaxed by concrete bollards, only in place to keep joy-riders off the cycle paths. Thereafter, every time we reached bollards the leading runner would shout, and to our great amusement, *Bollards!* I started to get blisters or was this my body's way of working to rule as a precedent to an all-out strike! My body's engine started to shut down, and as I cracked the whip, my feeble organism started to crumble, and my blisters became unbearable. It was the first race I dropped out of, but that blemish would cast a negative attitude in some of my later races.

My immediate reaction was a feeling of shame, and that my moral weakness and perhaps I needed to rest. However, in one week, I was determined to show who was master my head or my body and set about a gruelling week of one hundred and fifty-two miles. I followed this with one hundred and twelve miles. Then I won the East Hull twenty race by nearly three minutes in one hour forty-six and three seconds. There was another complaint from the shop floor and my body refused to take further punishment. This battle continued unabated and I tried another massive week of one hundred thirty-one miles and I faced a crisis. On a lovely sunny morning, I had a fuzzy headache, but went for a run, to Raywell, a hamlet-seven-miles north-west of Hull, and I took the bridleway. Within a few minutes, I felt stifled, limp, and out of sorts. I tried to run but couldn't. It seemed I had exhausted my body – there is a limit to mind over matter, and that day, I found it.

CHAPTER 14

Time for a Change

Iwondered what my future would be at East Hull Harriers, I had been a member for nearly seven years. Initially, there was a good response from some members, like the late Tom Hunter and Johnny Crawford, to make the club more competitive, and thanks to Peter Dearing, a tireless secretary, who coached and cajoled youngsters like Peter Elletson, Tim Warrener and Geoff Clarkson, who seemed certain to make the grade. Elletson did so in spectacular fashion, when he gained a world junior men cross-country team gold medal for England at Glasgow in 1978. Then, Shaun Crossland joined and within a short period, he achieved a club record by placing 70th in the 1979 National cross-country championships. I had returned to form after a long injury and at last it looked like we would have the makings of a good team, but first Peter Elletson won a prestigious scholarship in America and then Shaun Crossland was side-lined with injuries. I knew they would have given me tough competition, which I welcomed, but alas it was not to be. With that in mind, and with great regret, I decided I needed a new challenge, and hoped City of Hull, could provide it before the end of my competitive running career.

I joined East Hull Harriers in 1973 aged 30, and eight years later the club still lacked enough decent runners to make an impact in out of town road races, area or national events, which required teams of six, nine or twelve to compete. As a former club captain, I knew trying to get nine runners on the line for the English National cross-country is often a forlorn task, and a dire result can be demoralising. When I joined East Hull, Peter Dearing suggested the club might not be suitable for me. In some ways, he was correct as my two-season track career came to an end. East Hull did not have a track team or Hull have a tartan track. In the Forces, I was competing for the RAF and Combined Services alongside athletes of national and international standard. After a serious hip-injury I returned to run well in long distance road races, but still hankered for another go on the track. I resigned from East Hull Harriers – not knowing the furore it would evoke. Apparently, I would have to serve a nine-month suspension from team competition. This would rule me out of area and national road relays and the National XC. I felt the suspension was petty and unfair and took no account of my needs as a serious athlete, or the seven seasons I ran for East Hull, nor the fact I'd soon be a veteran runner. My solicitor could not understand how an amateur athletics club, which does not pay me to compete could impose such rules and he reckoned, I would have a good case in front of the Equal Opportunities Commission. On reflection, there would be little point in proceeding, because a judgement would be unlikely within the nine months suspension period.

I joined City of Hull in 1981, who had some very good athletes on their books, like Malcolm Prince (5000m personal best of 13:27) Stuart Shallcross, Martin Farrall, Steve Rennie, Chris Vodden and Gavin Dalton – who could all give me a run for my money. So, I was not surprised at the speed of 12 x 200 metres track-session in around 30 seconds with minimal recovery. However, my new club mates were surprised an ageing marathon runner could live with them. Unfortunately, I soon realised that my new club mates were, like East Hull Harriers, not over keen in running road relays, cross country, or high-profile events such as the Tipton Ten. At the time, my club had a retrospective newsletter which came out once or twice a year and I knew I had to launch, write and distribute an information-leaflet every month to enthuse my new club's members to seek better races out-of-town. I came up with *Distance News* as a title but did not imagine the amount of time needed to produce the newsletter. In for a penny in for a pound, and it made sense to volunteer to become the next club captain.

I stared at an advertisement in the Hull Daily Mail, *'Portable Video Recorder' It lets you film and playback on your TV! – £1100'*. The concept was unknown to me at the time. I spoke to lots of my friends, who thought it seemed too far-fetched to be true, it was only when I went to the shop on Princes Avenue that I finally believed in the impossible. The video tape recorder was in a case with a shoulder strap and weighed twenty pounds. The camera was also substantial and a hefty twelve pounds. I would now be able to make films, which hitherto had only been possible at huge expense and with a crew. This invention was so far ahead of public imagination that for several years I was still trying to convince friends, and family that what I was filming could be seen right away. Even after I had explained it in methodical detail some would say, 'When will you get the film back from the processors?' The equipment was so bulky, that most people assumed it was for television.

My Ferensway shop required a new manager and I took on Colin Martin, who had sports retail experience at Allsports. I wanted to video the Major Stone East Hull ½ Marathon, and asked Colin if he could drive the Runnercare van while I filmed through the opened back doors. We parked to film the whole field pass the one-mile mark – giving all the competitors a chance to see themselves in the club-house after the event. Best of all it was a cracking race. Peter Elletson on holiday from his American College was tanned, fit and by two-miles had a 100-yard lead. The chasing group included Bill Cain, Kevin Best, Des Austin and Paul Lightfoot. At six, miles Kevin made a break, although Elletson was now ahead by 200-yards. Just after 7-miles I filmed Peter, who was puffed and looking tired, while Best had reduced his lead to 80 yards. At 8-miles Kevin Best took the lead while the rest of the group started to pass the early leader too. By 11-miles there was some more drama as Des Austin was closing in on Best. I am running every step with my RAF pal with this commentary:

'Kevin has sensed the threat, he's digging in, he's digging in. He's running hard. He's pulled another fifteen yards. Is this the victory strike? This is impressive running by Kevin Best,' I continued,

'Des Austin is making a determined effort to get back on terms.'

Kevin won in 65:30 pressed by Des all the way to the tape, also under 66-minutes. My first of many videos and commentaries, and an exciting race to watch – as it happened.

I never made any allowances or sought any excuses in my business life or athletic career. To me that would be a sign of weakness, and if I once gave in I might lose my determination to keep trying. This was an inflexible principle, but one I had strived to live by. To maintain this regime, I had to consider myself invincible. One shop, then two and then three, I thought no problem, and the only thing stopping me running a two-hours twelve-minutes marathon was the right balance of training and racing. This policy had a lot going for it, never giving in, always being positive and to quote the Olympic motto, *'Faster, Higher, Stronger.'* But was it possible to climb two mountain tops at once – I had thought so the previous year when everything clicked into place, or was this just my own self-indulgent delusion? My training was on a perpetual day to day basis, and more arduous than many professional sports people, my business needed constant attention with staffing, buying and selling issues and the ever-present problem of external or internal theft occupied my mind.

I once heard a fruit farmer describe what it takes to get an optimum crop from his apple trees, *'They, need a winter of sustained, cold weather to conserve energy and rebuild strength. This means that when the season arrives they are strong and eager enough to capitalise on all that energy with a bumper crop of apples.'* This analogy works with all living things under the sun and that includes myself. In 1979, my body was ready for something special, and I held this intensity for nearly a year before the rot set in. Living on the edge, living in the fast lane had its pluses, but also a constant risk of spiralling out of control.

My training and racing had hit the buffers, but it seemed I was out to punish my body by racing 10-miles, marathon, 10-miles, marathon weeks in consecutive weeks. First was the York ten in 14th in 51:38; then the Harlow marathon in 18th in 2:27:30; followed by Tipton ten in 18th in 50:39 and finally a very poor Barnsley marathon, on 30th November in 17th in 2:32.45. As a comparison, just one year earlier I had run the Tipton ten 48:43, the Cleveland marathon in 2:19:34, but I noticed a common theme amongst other runners with illness and poor training leading to erratic performances. At my new Club, City of Hull, I had competition from several runners, who were better than I was especially at the shorter distances, and this should provide me with the focus to regain my form.

Then, I found an immediate target to get me training again. The first London Marathon and was the brainchild of Chris Brasher and John Disley and first held on 29th March 1981 and I was determined to try and set a new personal best. This, of course, meant triple digit miles per week, with lots of speed work. I set a best time on my nine-mile circuit in forty-five minutes and felt I had recovered my best form. The day before, I set off by train to Kings Cross and booked into the Strand Hotel in the heart of the West End. There was an exhibition in the Hotel's basement which I visited out of curiosity. I was asked at one stall if I would like my blood pressure taken. Then the alarm bells, I was told my blood pressure was high, but I felt well, and I ignored their warning. But within thirty minutes, I could not speak – struck down with laryngitis and although I was shocked nothing would stop me from running the first London Marathon and confirmed my total insanity.

I was feeling quite light headed next day and shivery, when I made my way to the start. The weather was cool and overcast as the gun went. If I was going to race I would give it everything I had and was in the leading group of about ten athletes till around ten miles. Even if I was forced to stop now it would not be so bad, but although I was slowing I was still moving alright. I was running with no one in sight and no one behind and at about seventeen miles a DJ from Capital radio idled up to me on a motorcycle,

'What's, your name, where do you come from and how are you?' This was a new experience, I thought, my running world would never be quite the same again.

'Peter Flatman, East Hull Harriers, and I'm not feeling too good,' I said wishing I had heeded the doctor's advice.

The motor cycling DJ had got his sound bite and he disappeared to get another. Now, I was struggling and barely putting one foot in front of the other. My experience had not included hitting the wall at 19-miles in the largest marathon the UK had ever seen. Friends tried to egg me on, but to no avail as other runners passed me. Every mile, seemed to take an hour, I felt humiliated as I trudged towards the Mall. My running became ever more laboured and lots of runners passed me as I struggled to keep moving. Never would I long so much for the finish, which would not be a personal best. My club-mate, Brian Jones beat me to the line in one of his best races in 2:25:20. Given the circumstances a performance of 2:25:22 was not too shabby, and I was pleased to finish a race I should never have started. I went back to my room and for the first time heard the BBC's theme music, 'The Trap', by Ron Goodwin from the 1966 film of the same name starring Oliver Reed. Given the unique event in London's history, my own struggles to finish, and then that cathartic theme music, I couldn't stop a tear. **Results:** 1.eq I Simonsen (Norway) & D Beardsley (US)

2:11:48 3. T Wright 2:12:53 4. M Kearns 2:13:37 5. G Laing 2:13:59
6. B Cole 2:14:01 7. J Dingwall 2:14:54 8. K Penny 2:15:31 9. P Eales
2:15:55 10. D Faircloth 2:16:36 ... 65. B Jones (E Hull) 2:25:18 66.
P Flatman (E Hull) 2:25:22. * Note (I failed to re-register on the day,
along with others)

I knew I had not done myself justice and entered the Westland
marathon on 9th April 1981 just thirteen days later. This is considered
suicidal for a serious runner, because of the trauma the body goes
through in the latter stages of the twenty-six-mile event, the optimal
time between marathons is at least six months, yet again, I had stuck
my neck out. Jayne, now fifteen and Simon nine came with me on
the Norland ferry from Hull to Rotterdam arriving at eight on the
morning of the race. While it would have been better to have travelled
the day before, I felt very well and raring to go. We stayed with Henk
and Coby Valstar in a typically immaculate Dutch house in Maassluis.
The Westland Marathon was also the Dutch national championships,
a high-quality event and I felt great to be running again, although, I
was not fit enough to go with the leaders.

At about thirteen miles I had an urgent call of nature which was
probably exacerbated by the overnight ferry crossing. However, this
was in the middle of the pan-flat Dutch landscape and not a toilet in
sight. Only one thing for it, and I clambered into a thirty-foot-deep
dyke just above the water line – then to my horror when I looked up,
there was a crowd who were following the race from a bridge, but
now watching me with my shorts around my ankles. By far, the most
embarrassing moment of my life. I probably lost one or two minutes,
but I was back and running well. With around three miles to go, I
could see a runner slowing and I knew I would soon pass him. He
was Turkish and there was a car load of fanatical supporters cheering
him on and waving flags. But all to no avail as he had hit the dreaded
wall and could not respond. I left him to face the last miles alone

and empty. Although it was not my best time it was a marathon that gave me some much-needed boost to my confidence. We all enjoyed a lovely social and prize giving party at the local football club and our Dutch hosts made us very welcome. I invited them to our home in Hull and they accepted, and Henk and Coby arrived on their cycles and then toured Yorkshire. **Results:** 1. Cor Vriend (Ned) 2:17:06 2. Barry Kneppers (Ned) 2:17:20 3. Gerald Mentink (Ned) 2:18:44 4. Colin Youngson (Sco) 2:18:54 5. Bram Wassener (Ned) 2:22:38 6. Peter Flatman (Eng) 2:22:54 7. Achmed Altin (Tur) 2:23:06 … 10. R Roath (Eng) 2:25:46 11. Evan Cameron (Sco) 2:27:48 … 18 G Milne (Sco) 2:32:22.

The last Sunday in May and the East Hull twenty. Although, I was not particularly fit, I wanted to compete, and it became a trying race. The winner was a guest runner, Andy Robertson from Harrogate, who was on great form, and I had to settle in to try and come second. I seemed to run the whole race, as if in a bubble, but in the last five miles I came under pressure from Robert Harbisher (Holmforth) and if he knew how shattered I was he could have easily beaten me for second place. In the end, I hung on with one hour forty-nine minutes and twelve-seconds and maintained my decent record. Andy Robertson an army PT instructor entered on the day and won by an incredible seven minutes. Later, I learned, he finished in 5th place in the Inter-Services representing the Army against the RAF and Navy three months earlier. **Result:** 1. Andy Robertson (Army) 1:41:53 (course record) 2. P Flatman(CoH) 1:49:12 3. R. Harbisher (Longwood) 1:49:31 4. J. Cook (Stainforth) 1:50:15 5. D. Gaskell (Airedale) 1:50:34.6. L. Smith (Ealing) 1:51:14 **Vet40-44:** 1. T Parr (Bolton) 1:59:16 2. P Dolan (Bolton) 1:59:58 3. C Davison 2:04:06 **Vet45-49:** 1. P Whittaker (Longwood) 1:56:31 2. H Gamble-Thompson (Middlesboro) 2:13:48 3. H Cooper (CoH) 2:20:38 (CoH) 2:20:38 **VetsO/50:** 1.S Pailer (Burn R) 2:12:56 2. J Caddy (Middleboro) 2:13:48 **Teams:** 1. Bolton 6:03:43 2. Middlesboro 6:03:39 3. East Hull Harriers 6:22:56.

The Humber Bridge, the World's largest single span suspension bridge, was opened by Her Majesty Queen Elizabeth on Friday 17th July 1981, and I thought a wonderful venue for a road race across the bridge and back. I checked a possible route for a ten-mile event, and sought the expertise of East Hull Harriers, to assist with the organisation and the race was fixed for 27th September 1981. The ten-mile race and 4-mile fun-run attracted nearly two thousand entries. Rob Stones, a cyclist with *Hull Thursday* helped with the measurement, and Rob suggested a prize for the first runner across the bridge. The early pace was set by Chris Woodhouse, Graeme Ellis and Ian Gilmore, but the participants were shocked by the ferocity of a near-gale-force south-westerly. Roger Hackney, triple Olympic Steeplechaser, and RAF Medical Officer was first across the bridge then a steady climb to Barton roundabout, but by five-miles in 25:29 Ray Smedley and Malcolm Prince were being left behind by the relentless surges of Woodhouse. John Clark of Grimsby was moving through and eventually came in fifth, less than a minute behind the winner. A steep climb on the return to the Humber Bridge weakened the resolve of Ellis and Gilmore. The race was now between the experienced road racer Chris Woodhouse and the still fresh-looking Roger Hackney running his first ever 10-miler. Chris tried everything to wear down his younger opponent, but Roger timed his sprint to perfection. The Bridge-master Malcolm Stockwell was really pleased the event passed off so well and due to the competent organisation of East Hull Harriers he approved the race for the following year. I believe this event could have reached national status, but it was not to be, because it was decided after the 1982 race that East Hull Harriers could no longer commit to the extensive organisation. **Results:** 1. Roger Hackney (Aldershot F&D) 49:51 2. C Woodhouse (Derby) 49:55 3. G Ellis (Holmfirth) 50:22 4. I Gilmore (W&B) 50:31 5. J Clark (Grim) 50:44 6. K McDonald (Bing) 51:05 7. M Prince (CoH) 51:11 8. R Smedley (Bir) 51:19 9. C Moore (Bing) 51:26 10. D Topham (Long) 51:38 11. P Moon

(Bing) 52:08 12. P Blakeney (Dark P) 52:20 13. D Allen (Man) 52:24 14. D Brennan (Warr) 52:29 15. A Jones (Sutt) 52:31 16. P Flatman (CoH) 52:34 17. J Temperton (A&SV) 52:39 18 T. Byrne (Sal) 52:42 19 D. Gaskell (A&SV 53:04 20 S Bushell (Salt) 53:19. 21. T Fieldsend (Sheff) 53:31 22. R Pearson (Dark P) 53:32 23. D. Weigel (Stain) 53:34 24. N. Jobson (Blaydon) 53:34 25. S Shallcross (CoH) 53:35 26. A Boast (C&C) 53:39 27. M Martin (Sheff) 53:41 28. S O'Callaghan (WYP) 53:48 29. D Quinlan (Bing) 53:54 30. D Jackson (B'burn) 53:55 31. P Rawnsley (Sheff) 53:59 32. J Cook (Stain) 54:14 33. G Anderson (Grim) 54:19 34. A Parkinson (A&SV) 54:39 35. M Henderson (Hallam) 54:47 36. P Howdle (East H) 54:48 37. C Nightingale (CoH) 54:49 38. T Wright (Long) 54:52 39. B Jones (E Hull) 54:55 40. E McKenzie (Barn) 54:58. **Teams:** 1 CoH 69 2 A&SV 70 3 Sheffield 79. Bingley finished 1st but were disqualified as Kim McDonald & Peter Moon were not wearing club colours. **Vets** 1. J Nettleton (Rown.) 55:15 2. K Scurr (East H) 55:30 3. A Hughes O/50 (Roch-O/50V) 56:10 **(Women)** 1 J Pearson (Sheff) 60:20 2 J Lochhead (A&SV) 61:28 3 E Adams (S in A) 62:57.

I went back to run the Cleveland Marathon on 11th October 1981, which had ended in my victory two years earlier. There was a good field including Ray Smedley, a former Olympian on the track, who was hoping to be selected at this event for the Commonwealth Marathon. But hopes of personal bests were blown away by a ferocious gale with gusts up to sixty miles per hour. No one wanted to take the lead or, no pun intended, blow their chances. The result was a dawdle of a race, which in the end Smedley won in two hours twenty-five while I placed fifth in two hours twenty-eight dead. On a good day, I had hoped for something close to two twenty, but it was not to be. Just seven days later, I lined up for the first Hull to Grimsby Marathon and I entered for no better reason that it was on my doorstep, and I would have been doing a long training run anyway. The public went crazy for this,

148

'*Ultimate challenge*', which had its origin in 490 BC, when a soldier, called Pheidippides ran from Marathon to Athens to announce victory over the Persians and promptly died. Then a surreal moment as we waited for the roller skaters to start before we could mirror the ancient Greek's challenge. At five miles, I was in the leading group of six, which was soon whittled down to four and included an East German, Andreas Jost, who was hoping to defect to the UK. From about twenty miles I slowed, as the impact of the marathon of the previous Sunday took its toll. Even the amazing scenes of the last three miles failed to revive me. Each side of the route was lined three or four-deep with spectators, and it had to be experienced to be believed. **Results** 1. A Jost (Germany) 2:25:30 2. J Barker (Grimsby) 2:25:55 3. W Eldridge (East Hull) 2:29:37 4. P Flatman (CoH) 2:30:56 5. G Kay (Barnsley) 2:33:25 6. T Shields (E Hull) 2:34:31 7. M Anderson (Grim) 2:35:04 8 L Bonner (Grim) 2:37:20 9. T Tebbutt (Sheff) 2:39:27 10. J Haines (Grim) 2:40:37.

For a fourth consecutive time, I left home early on a Sunday morning to take part in the Tipton ten miles-race starting at eleven am, 15th November 1981. This race had gained a great reputation for good competition from every part of the United Kingdom, and this day was no exception. It was like a who's who of the nation's distance runners, and year after year I would run out of my skin and finish ahead famed athletes I had only read about with awe in running magazines. I was not on great form, and I still had two hard marathons in my legs, yet again I was inspired by the buzz of this great race and ran forty-nine minutes and forty seconds. My former team mate, Trevor Shields was 64th in fifty-three minutes and seven seconds. It was not a bad way to sign off the year 1981. **Results:** 1. C Mattock (W'ton) 48:16 2. M Hazlewood (R Marines) 48:17 3. J King (Solihull) 48:18 4. R O'Hara (Sparkhill) 48:22 5. R Cytlav (Tipton) 48:33 6. J O'Hara (Tipton) 48:52 7. C Kirkham (Coventry G) 48:53 8. M Poutney (Tipton) 49:04 9. P Bank (Coventry G) 49:16 10. N Gray Solihull) 49:18 11. M

Densify (B'field) 49:20 12. K Angus (Sheff) 49:21 13. D Allen (Man) 49:33 14. J Atkins (Wor) 49:35 15. P Flatman (CoH) 49:40 16. M Phillips (B'field) 49:52 17. S Brown (Cheltenham) 49:58 18. S Jackson (Bedford) 50:06 19. L Pearson (Derby) 50:10 20. N Spiers (Sheff) 50:11 21. P Griffiths (Tipton) 50:14 22. D Smith (C Godiva) 50:17 23. J Wagstaff (Tipton) 50:18 24. H Leeming (R Royce) 50:19 25. M Martin (Sheff) 50:41 26. A Bill (Halesowen) 50:59 27, M Davies (Worcs) 51:00 28. D Pratt (Sheff) 51:02 29. P Miller (C Godiva) 51:20 30. J Wright (Tipton) 51:36. **(Women)** 1. Joyce Smith (Barnet) 54:00 2. C Gould (Barnet) 57:45 3. K Williams Swansea 59:00 4. T Grumbley (Cov G) 59:06 5. A Kirkham (Cov G) 59:21. So much for a slow Sunday morning run!

The world was spinning ever faster; doors opening and closing; schools, shops, houses and cars came and went like the phases of the moon. This life was frenetic, there was barely time to catch breath, or savour a moment. Even Christmas could not assuage the on-going tension of the ever-spinning clock. Christmas celebration was cut down to just two days; the twenty seventh of December became the busiest day of the year; Sunday trading was considered essential to maintain or boost turnover. Was this a sensible way to live and why was I driven in all aspects of my life, when all that really mattered lived in the same four walls? Our kids were growing up as fast as May flies; Clare had already been at nursery for six months and had her third birthday there; Jayne almost sixteen would need to make a decision, A levels or work; Sarah was still coming to terms of being taught by the sisters of St Augustine at Rise Hall and discovering her Catholic heritage; Simon, who had just been parachuted into Dad's dream that prophesised he would be taught at Ampleforth College, although at first he was apprehensive, he now had to grow up faster than he could have ever imagined.

Since, I had recovered from my hip injury in 1979 nearly all my training was on the road, and my races ten-miles and above. At nearly 38 years of age, I wanted to train specifically for the 1982 English National on 6th March at Leeds. I felt I had lost a lot of leg strength and started to train on Spout Hill on the Yorkshire Wolds. The climb is half-mile with an initial gradient of 14%. The first time I ran the hill it was like I was being kicked in the lower back by a wild animal, and my calf muscles were screeching in agony. My target was to complete six but could only manage three. Four days later, I started to time my efforts, so I could measure my improvement. Soon, I was running six repetitions, and within twelve sessions was averaging under four-minutes. After this training, I would have no fear of Hill 60 at Roundhay Park. On the day, the course was wet, muddy and hilly. My training would help, but true to form, I charged to the front and had no right being in the first fifty at a mile. On every hill and turn were club supporters bellowing support and giving me a headache. My limb muscles were not used to mud, and I began to falter in the increasing quagmire at the foot of the hills. Nevertheless, I was still running my best National ever at the age of 38 and my place of 151st proved I could have been a better cross-country runner with specific training and racing. **Results:** 1. D Clarke (Hercules Wimbledon) 42:19 2. H Jones (Ranelagh) 42:33 3. M McLeod (Elswick) 4. D Moorcroft (Coventry) 42:56 5. R Hackney (Aldershot F&D) 43:09 6. S Kenyon (Salford) 43:10 7. B Knight (Westbury) 43:13 8 J Woods (Liverpool) 43:26 9. N Muir (Shettleston) 43:36 10. P Standing (W S&E) 43:37. **Teams:** 1. Tipton 24. M Kearns 26. J Wild 48. A Holden 60. A Rushmere 61. R Westwood **pts 263.** 2. Coventry pts 304 3. Aldershot F&D **pts 308** …48. City of Hull – 151. P Flatman 254 S Rennie 302. C Vodden 577. G Dalton 603. K Bartlam 759. P Jones **pts 2646**

The amazing success of the London Marathon led to a boom in marathon races around the country and good club athletes were soon picking up cash prizes of several thousand pounds for relatively modest winning times. Indeed, mass events were springing up at other distances such as ten kilometres and half marathons. A half-marathon at York caught my eye and, I decided to see what time I could run, especially on the flat roads around the city. There were several thousand participants on a sunny day on the 28th March and over a hundred quality club runners at the sharp end. As the race developed in the cool spring conditions the pace was very hot. I reached five miles in less than twenty-five minutes and I felt assured of a personal best. Every mile was marked so I could gauge my effort and at twelve miles my time was precisely one hour. Even though I tired at the end, I recorded a personal best of sixty-five minutes fifty-two seconds. **Results:** 1. R Smedley (Birchfield) 62:08 2. G Ellis (Holmfirth) 63:05 3. C Spedding (Gateshead) 63:18 4. J Clark (Grim) 63:59 5. I Gilmore (W&B) 64:17 6. D Wilson (B'burn) 64:34 7. C Hallimond (Sun) 64:54 8. C Taylor (A&SV) 65:25 9. P Knight (Rown) 65:28 10. M White (Yk.U) 65:34 11. D Mayho (A&SV) 65:38 12. W Domoney (Sheff) 65:50 13. P Flatman (CoH) 65:52 14. S Winter (Gate) 66:07.

CHAPTER 15

Free Fall

On the 18th April 1982, Peter Moon, East Hull, John Barker, Grimsby and myself represented Humberside in the Inter-Counties 20 mile at Finchley. Prior to this, Humberside had never won anything at senior county level. I finished 15th (1:47:32) John Barker came 21st (1:48:36) and our final scorer was Peter Moon 23rd (1:48:49) which gave us a creditable 4th prize, and a certificate from Humberside County AAA. **Results:** 1. M Gratton (Invicta/Kent) 1:42:44 2. D Faircloth (Croydon/Surrey) 1:43:09 3. R Sinclair (Sheffield/Yk) 1:43:14 4. D Clark (Ver/Herts) 1:43:29 5. J Offord (Leic/Leics) 1:44:31 6. J Ashworth (Bing/Yk) 1:44:57 7. K Best (Bol/Lancs) 1:45:01 8. S Markley (M&C/Yk) 1:45:31 9. G Staunton (Lon. I/Mx) 1:45:41 10. N Brawn (Inv/Kt) 1:45:48. **Int/counties:** 1. Yorks 17 2. Kent 23 3. Lancs 36 4. Humberside 52 5. Surrey 55 6. Staffs 69 7. Leics 73 8. Essex 74. 9. Middlesex 77 10. Glamorgan. Note: Mike Grattan placed 3rd in London Marathon three weeks later.

I entered the East Hull twenty held on 23rd May 1982, which would be for the final time before the club declared it a closed event for East Hull members only. The event had become the race I was most associated with and this would be the seventh time I would compete. The day was around sixty degrees with occasional cloud cover. Andy Robertson had returned and despite my optimism he was the favourite, but you never know, and I decided that I would give him a run for his money. Within a mile, the two of us started to pull away from the field, which as usual contained some good quality athletes. My tactic was quite risky, because if I failed to match his pace I would be cut adrift in no-man's land. I kept with Andy till seven or eight miles but was forced to let him go. No matter, I thought, I have a lead of a hundred metres on the chasing group. For the next five-miles, I was aware of them working together to reel me in like cyclists do in the Tour de France. I needed to be wily and eke out my strength: I needed to slow, but only slightly, but most of all I needed to lull my chasers into a false sense of security. They would catch me when I decided I was good and ready and even then, I had to know what to expect. That was my plan and one, which I hoped, I could play out to perfection. I told myself, *If, they were as good as me, they would have challenged Robertson, which they did not, so I will remain confident.* By this time, I had been running alone for seven miles and had to be aware that the four runners would want to go passed me and leave me for dead – in other words *they would take no prisoners.*

Now I could hear their foot-falls but kept my pace even and took a deep breath. In the group was Olympic marathon runner, Tim Johnston, Manchester's Dave Allen, and my local protagonist Grimsby's John Barker. I gathered myself to fight the onslaught as they tried to break me straight away, if this was to be my last twenty then letting these guys spoil my swansong was not going to happen. They seemed to be running fast, but I told myself this will only last for about a minute. But their surge ended in thirty seconds, and I was soon running comfortably in the group. Now for part two of my plan, and for the next few miles, I needed to be patient. With two miles to go, I was surprised when Barker and not Tim Johnston, tried to make a run for home. That's good, because now it was just me and John my younger adversary. We quickly forged a gap, but I had only one thing in mind and that was to finish in second place. I was not fit enough to just take him on in a long run for home, so it would have to be a sprint, which I never had to do in my six previous East Hull 20s. Consequently, on Saltshouse Road just before the Golf Club, I surged, but didn't break John, now my spirit came to my rescue, and I sprinted again and came home with a second to spare in one hour forty-seven minutes forty seconds. Moreover, I had run six Hull 20s in less than 1 hour fifty, but I knew John was upset to lose to me in a sprint, and one week later, he turned the tables on me in the East Park five. **Results:** 1. Andy Robertson (Army) 1:43:30 2. Peter Flatman (CoH) 1:47:40 3. John Barker (Grimsby) 1:47:41 4. Tim Johnston (Portsmouth AC) 1:49:08 5. Dave Allen (Man H) 1:50:24 6. Jack Cook (Stainforth) 1:50:54 7. Peter Elletson (East Hull) 1:51:14 8. G R Naylor (Rockingham) 1:52:51 9. Lance Kirlew (East Hull) 1:52:54 10. Brian Jones (East Hull) 1:53:14 11. Martin Anderson (Grimsby) 1:53:42 12. P Whittaker (Longwood) 1:53:43 13. R Hepworth (Longwood) 1:54:14 14. P Gledhill (Barnsley) 1:54:42 15. John Potter (East Hull) 1:55:10. **Teams:** 1. East Hull 2. Barnsley 3. Longwood 4. S Shields

The second and final running of the Humber Bridge ten-mile was held on 12th September 1982, a race that united both sides of the river, starting and finishing on the north bank. This year it would be organised by East Hull Harriers, which made sense, because I had left East Hull Harriers the previous year, and joined City of Hull AC. The previous year's race was the first across the bridge and only three months after its official opening. This time the entries topped three thousand for the ten-mile race event and four-mile fun run, which twice crossed the then longest single span bridge in the world and a magnet for athletes far and wide. Colin Martin, one of my managers filmed on equipment that was rudimentary and temperamental. After the race, I provided commentary and apt music. Despite the difficulties, it remains a vivid and entertaining record of a great day in the history of the area and athletics. The 10-mile race was started at 1pm from Heads Lane Hessle and provided a stunning sight as over 1200-hundred swarmed towards the Humber Bridge. An early leader was the then seventeen-year old, Darran Bilton showing the kind of form that would, in later years, make him a great athlete. But for now, he had to let the big guns go, firstly Ray Smedley, a three-minutes fifty-seven second miler trying to make his name at the marathon and Chris Woodhouse, a tough, Derby refuse collector. Crowds lined the bridge to exhort the runners and create an unforgettable atmosphere. There was a group of about eight runners in the front as the race reached the first tower. I switched the music from Vangelis' *'Chariots of Fire'* theme to Elvis Presley's, *'I slipped, I stumbled, I fell!'* At the very moment that Bingley's John Atkinson hit the hard tarmac of the bridge, seven sets of eyes turned to witness his mishap. He got up quickly, but his chances of winning were left on the road he had just struck. Such a famous bridge deserved a prize for the first across and a grand scrap ensued between Derby team mates Chris Woodhouse and Nicky Lees, and the latter prevailed by a whisker.

Spotting his chance, when both were winded by the sprint, Ray Smedley stole a march on them as he powered towards the Barton roundabout, but he hadn't reckoned with the determination of Woodhouse, Lees and Holmfirth's Graeme Ellis. Through the town, the four of them looked like a sheriff's posse committed to ride the hoodlums out of town, to the sound of Elvis singing, *'Mess of the Blues'.* Even the full power of a force eight westerly could not stem their resolve, but now the two marshals, Smedley and Woodhouse went on ahead, up a mighty canyon, locally known as Gravel Pit Road. This would now be a fight to the death, and which one would get the glory, in this deadly duel, with the elements.

The returning athletes are rewarded with an epic vision of the mighty Humber Bridge supported by two spine-like, 500-feet towers and the carriageways stabilised by 44,000-miles of steel cables. The music was Rick Nelson's *'Travelling Man,'* and the speedsters were in perfect harmony and as they reached the bridge a group of spectators cross the road and watch in awe. As the leaders were virtually flying it seemed appropriate that *'Wings'* provided the accompaniment with, *'A Little Luck,'* but still not a cigarette paper between them yet I sensed Woodhall's chance as he fought for the lead in the final mile. At first it was just a few inches, yet almost imperceptibly it grew to a foot, then two and finally a yard. Both athletes were at maximum effort and with nothing left to give, Derby's Chris Woodhouse crossed the line his right index finger raised in a hard-won victory. Then the soundtrack changes to a tuneless depiction of waste, desert and defeat as the hordes create their own memories – exhausted, yet proud of their achievements. I wrote the report that appeared in Athletics Weekly, and I quote from the final paragraph: *The Humber Bridge is exactly 10-miles and will yield much faster times in better conditions – even sub 48-minutes. The Bridge-master, Malcom Stockwell was well pleased with the competent organisation of East Hull Harriers and hoped it might become an annual event. Furthermore, it is my belief this great race over the world's largest suspension bridge could rival the Great North Run. However, it was not to be, which remains a shame for our sport and for the area of Hull and Grimsby.* **Results:** 1. C Woodhouse (Derby) 50:10 2. R Smedley (Birchfield) 50:16 3. N Lees (Der) 51:02 4. A Jones (Sutt) 51:40 5. G Ellis (Holm) 52:02 6. J Atkin (A&SV) 52:30 7. J Clark (Grim) 52:34 8. P Moon (Bing) 52:39 9. I Gilmore (W&B) 52:54 10. A Jones (Roth) 53:01 11. D Mayho (A&SV) 53:02 12. P Flatman (CoH) 53:09 13. T Byrne (Sal) 53:23 14. B Jones (E Hull) 53:33 15. W Eldridge (E Hull) 53:46 16. L Kirlew (E Hull) 54:20 17. R Heathcote (Sheff) 54:21 18. J Temperton (A&SV) 54:25 19. C Nightingale (CoH) 54:47 20. C Vodden (CoH) 54:48 **Teams:** 1. Airedale & SV 35 2. E Hull 45 3. City of Hull 4. Sheffield 66 5. Grimsby 112 6. Rotherham 113 7. Bingley 115 8. Worksop 128. 70 3. Sheffield 79. 4. Grimsby 83 5. Longwood 94. **(Vets):** 1. K Darby (Wigan-V) 54:58 2. G Entwhistle (Man-V) 56:21 3. M Rawson (Hallam) 56:48 4. D Anderson (Bing) 56:50 5. K Scurr (E Hull) 57:03 6. R Dimbleby (Linc W) 57:17 7. E Kirkup (Roth-V) 58:16 8.

T Hunter (E Hull) 59:06 9. M Simpson (Works-V/45) 10. S Wild (Hall-O/50) 60:05 11. J Stones (E Hull-O/45) 61:16 12. R Mackay (Holm-O/45) 61:30. (**Women**): 1. J Lochhead ((A&SV-V) 61:21 2. J Pearson (Sheff) 62:07 3. S Catford ((T&S) 64:36 4. S Robinson (Linc W) 64:40 5. B Brown (Grim) 65:13 6. C Hirst (Long) 65:59 7. D Harris (C'field-V) 66:51 8. C Rigby (Leigh) 67:29 9. L Richardson (LOAC) 68:19 10 C Borrill (E Hull-V) 69:16. **Teams:** 1. Grimsby 49 2. Hallamshire 68 3. Rockingham 83.

I was busy setting up a new shop in Hull city centre near my main rival and completing the purchase of our art-deco bungalow in Hessle. Coincidentally, my new shop was 27 Jameson Street and our bungalow named, Jameson Villa! Indeed, we'd made an amazing transformation in ten years: from a second-floor Bridlington holiday let, to our lovely home near the Humber Bridge, and my shop on a prime site in the middle of Kingston upon Hull. When I opened my first shop at 334, Holderness Road in 1976, locals insisted it was doomed to failure. Management and staff of other local-based sports outfitters came and stared at our double-fronted windows and made ribald comments about the sparsity of stock – and predicted our swift demise. In 1974 we were told by Guardian Building Society, who I'd saved with for six years that we had insufficient status to offer a mortgage to buy a house on Belvedere Drive Bilton, but then we were offered a mortgage by Beverley Building Society. I was told when I opened my second shop at Bransholme shopping centre to ditch all my sports goods and fill the shop with fishing gear and live bait! When we completed the purchase of Jameson Villa in 1983 the owner was shocked we put in an offer as she thought we were mere time wasters.

Of course, I was very busy with my important new shop lease and the purchase of our bungalow which meant I had to reduce my training mileage. However, I saw a third marathon race, south of Lincoln, was being held on the 27th February 1983, and fancied a run out. But when

I got there, I was shocked to see three thousand souls limbering up on a large sports field wearing expensive trainers, and flash running kits. I felt unnerved, and out of place, when I changed into my dreary purple, club vest, a pair of minimalist black shorts, and lightweight racing shoes I'd worn in thirty races. After twelve-years a runner, I felt this could be my ultimate humiliation and I'd be buried by this new generation of trendy athletes, who at the start dashed off like sprinters rather than distance runners. After ten-minutes, I reckoned I was in the first fifty. At halfway I had latched onto the leading pack of eight runners and started to feel comfortable. The first runner to drop off the space was former RAF team runner, Pete Hurt and the only other runner I knew was Derrick Pratt of Sheffield, who won East Hull's twenty in 1973 in one hour forty-three minutes. We ran together, pushing the pace along, gradually leaving the two of us to fight for the win. I have no idea why I waited for the last hundred metres to sprint, because it had never been my strong point, but kick I did, and came home with a dozen metres to spare in forty-four minutes twenty-four seconds. An unexpected win, that gave my confidence quite a boost in the year I would become a veteran.

Now, I had to be single minded, but still thought I could burn the candle at both ends, and in the middle if necessary. Was it not enough that we were opening a large city centre store on Good Friday; that we were moving from east Hull to Hessle; that we now had three children in private education; that I needed to find time and energy to run one hundred and sixty kilometres every week; but I chose this time to become club captain of City of Hull and wrote and produced a monthly newsletter called, *Distance News*. The next Saturday, and only six days after I had won the Lincoln third marathon I drove my team to Luton for the National cross-country championships over nine miles of muddy fields. I had hoped that our star man, Malcolm Prince might compete, but an injury ruled him out. Still we had a nucleus of good club athletes, including Steve Rennie, Martin Farrall, Gavin Dalton,

Pat McLagan and George Baker and they packed well, and City of Hull had a fifty-four per cent improvement in points. I was out of salts and could not get going, and thus felt I had let my team-mates down.

I sold the lease of my Bransholme shop, which had served its purpose in the early days of Runnercare, but my new aim was a bigger shop in the centre of Hull. Finally, I found the perfect shop situated at 27, Jameson Street close to the centre of Hull. The premises consisted of a basement, ground floor, (clothing and equipment) first floor (sports footwear), and second floor (storage and exercise equipment). I used the cash from the sale of the Bransholme shop lease to fit the shop out and set a tight schedule to open on 1st April (Good Friday). I bought several dozen daffodils to display around the shop to match Runnercare's new logo. This was my fourth shop and would be the most profitable in my 30 years of trading.

I was now training for the Hull to Grimsby marathon and thought this could be my last chance to win it. I was running twenty-three-miles on a hot Sunday morning in June over the bridge and around Barton and Barrow. Unfortunately, I became dehydrated and was pleased to get back home. Then I rehydrated with tea and decided to clear an eight-foot high mezzanine shelf of clutter in the garage. In fact, I needed an extending ladder and not the freestanding, paint-splattered steps, I used around the bungalow and neither a ladder two-feet short of the shelf. Anyway, I clambered up and cleared the mezzanine of miscellaneous bric-a-brac and I felt good I'd finally cleared the eyesore. Now, I needed to come down and sat on the edge of the mezzanine using my feet to locate the free-standing steps, then nanoseconds of abject terror – the sound of the aluminium ladder crashing on the concrete floor seemed to confirm my fate. I was disorientated, yet certain I would be the next object to hit the concrete. In a split second, I knew my head must not hit the floor and my legs must be spared – I would have to do a belly-flop and crossed my arms to protect my skull. My body hit the floor, broke my watch, my knees and arms were bleeding and the shock made me motionless. Then I shook like a jelly. My wife found me, called a doctor and put me to bed. My rib-cage took the brunt of the fall and I was sure some of my ribs were fractured. So, why did I think it necessary to clear that shelf after a hot and exhausting 23-mile run. I should have asked my wife or one of my daughters to steady the ladder, but no, it was my idea, so I took a risk that could have taken my life. In fact, I'd defied the odds with no broken bones, even though my heavily bruised ribs felt fractured.

I'd taken a foolish risk and yet my recurring thought was how could I compete in the Selby Marathon the following Sunday. I wondered if it would be possible to take my normal eight-mile run to my shop. Then, I brought the route to my mind's eye: the start at the top of Swanland Road, and towards Darley's, turning left onto Beverley Road heading to Anlaby and Haltemprice Sports Centre – two-miles at 6-minutes a mile average. When necessary, I would stop my watch at busy intersections to avoid accidents. Gorton Road took me to Kingston Road, a dual carriageway which I would need to cross. So far, the roads were lined with trees, as noted by Queen Elizabeth on a recent visit to Kingston upon Hull. Just passed Springhead Golf Club my route turned left onto Hotham Road South named after Sir John Hotham, Governor of Hull, who in 1642 refused, in person, to allow King Charles 1 entry to the town. This led to the Siege of Hull and signalled the start of the English Civil War. My route crossed Priory Road and over railway bridge across the Hull to Bridlington line and a smooth path passed sports fields before I took the northern part of Hotham Road to Cottingham Road where Hull University was founded in 1927. In the eighties, I would see the red-bricked campus hundreds of times, but never imagined I would be studying there in my seventies. In the eighties Cottingham Road was smooth, tree lined and where, I often thought, running would be easier than walking. The last part of the route was on Beverley road with heavy traffic of vehicles and people. I would complete the eight-mile run, on average, in forty seven minutes.

Yet, how would I fare after the disastrous eight-foot fall the previous day? In fact, even slow walking reminded me of every bruise and every breath creaked my rib-cage and convinced me that I could not compete in the marathon on Sunday. Instead, the run which usually took forty-seven minutes now took me almost two hours. The next day, I completed the painful exercise in ninety minutes. The next morning my race number arrived – surely going to Selby would be unthinkable? My last walk/run was on Thursday was a bit quicker. Until now, I thought the whole idea of running at Selby was ridiculous, however, as I was trying to run further on Sunday perhaps I could run the first lap. Consequently, I drove to Selby on Sunday 26th June 1983 another hot day with wall to wall sunshine and not an ideal day to run a marathon. I stood right at the back of the start line – no heroics nor interest in finishing the race let alone running a decent time. For the first mile I jogged along the road and hoped I could make the halfway point. Anyway, with every stride I seemed a little more comfortable. Although, I was still a good distance behind the leaders I passed runners which in turn brought an adrenaline rush and masked the pain from my ribs. Within five minutes, I could see the leader who was out on his own. Then I caught him up but did not pass him as I was feeling twinges from my rib-cage. Later I learned he was Peter Morris from Wigan, who ran the London Marathon in April in 2:19:34 the same as my PB! Nevertheless, I was having difficulty breathing, and was still intent on dropping out when we reached thirteen miles. Then I saw a hundred spectators, waiting to cheer us on and I was faced with a dilemma: do I drop out while sharing the lead and spend years regretting my weakness, or carry on in pain for another half-marathon? As we got nearer the cheering got louder and in the space of ten-seconds, I decided to carry on to the bitter end. The cheering dulled the aches in my body, Peter Morris opened a gap which was more to do with me having to slow down than my rival speeding up. By fifteen miles my ribs were very sore, and I was gasping for breath.

When I looked behind there was not another runner in sight. Towards the end, I felt disconnected from my body – moving ever slower and the finish line growing ever more distant. My body was in motion but my senses almost obliterated. Finally, I saw the finish on a sports-field, I came second in two hours twenty-nine minutes and twenty-seven seconds. No waves to spectators, no quickening of pace, I just collapsed on the grass and was eventually elated, to have finished another marathon, I should have not started. **Results:** 1 Peter Morris (Wigan) 2:25:37 2 P Flatman (CoH) 2:29:27 3 Paul Venables (Roth) 2:33:16 4. R Dalby (Glouc) 2:33:21 5. J Nettleton (Rown) 2:35:27 6. A Spence (Bing) 2:35:47 7. J Dalby (Leeds) 2:36:00 8. G Kay (Stone) 2:36:27 9. H Bates (Sky) 2:37:35 10. J Haines 2:37:46 11. N Weeks (Bing) 2:39:04 12. A Sedman (E Hull) 2:39:56 13. P Taylor (Sky) 2:41:09 14. M Peake (LRRC) 2:41:28 15. R Train (E Hull) 2:41:34.

The first three-months takings at our new shop at 27, Jameson Street were slow and disappointing, which enabled me to take up another project, a half marathon over the Humber Bridge, starting on Pickering Road and finishing at Hull Marina. I asked my wages clerk to take the entries and let me know if we have a big-name entrant. She rang me one day and said,

'I have an entry from a H Jones from Ranelagh Harriers, is he any good?'

'You bet, Christine, Hugh won the London Marathon last year, that's all!'

This made for a good story for the local paper and by the closing date we had over twelve hundred entries. I remember going around the full course at 6am, on the day of the race with Graeme Brummitt and George Slater checking the distance and placing the mile markers.

The finish was slightly awkward with the changing and finishing being about a mile from the start, but all was well when we lined up on Pickering Road for the Humber Bridge Half-Marathon at 1 pm on Sunday 4th September 1983.

Apart from a gale force wind it was good weather, but not too warm. In the early stages, runners were driven by a brisk backwind. Just after two miles Hugh Jones forged ahead, which I followed till it would have been foolish to continue, as he had run a half-marathon in sixty-one minutes thirty-three seconds – more than three minutes better than my best. The wind was ferocious on the bridge and I deliberately slowed to get some shelter. John Clark, a Lincolnshire farmer, came passed me and I latched onto him for a couple of five-minute miles. This created a decent gap to Bob Sinclair and John Barker, while Aberdeen's George Reynolds was just behind us. George then came past both of us and I hitched a ride with him till around the eleven-mile mark, when I got a stitch and George stole his moment and second place. Meanwhile, Jones was winning in a creditable time on a windy day of sixty- five minutes fourteen seconds, Reynolds second in sixty-six minutes forty-four seconds and I was very satisfied with third place in sixty-six minutes and fifty-eight seconds a month short of my fortieth birthday. Sinclair was about to get his GB vest in the Chicago Marathon, but then giving me a vest at my age would not make any sense. **Results:** 1. H Jones (Ranelagh) 65:14 2. G Reynolds (Aberdeen) 66:44 3. P Flatman (CoH) 66:58 4. R Sinclair (Sheffield) 67:18 5. J Clark (Grimsby) 67:36 6. J Barker (Grimsby) 67:48 7. P Clarke (Grimsby) 70:10 8. R Aconley V40 71:09 9. G Baker (CoH) 71:23 10. C Vodden (CoH) 71:28 11. B Jones (EH) 71:36 12. J Fisher (Staff Moorlands) 72:02 13. M Cox (Leeds City) 72:13 14. D Lancaster (Rowntrees) 72:32 15. G Dalton (CoH) 72:54 16. P Muddleman (Leamington) 73:07 17. R Eccles (Bingley) 73:11 18. W Eldridge (EH) 73:15 19. D Butts (Grimsby) 73:39 20. S Rennie (CoH) 74:23 21. D Pickering 74:31 22. A Peet (Wigan) 74:38. **Teams:** 1.

City of Hull 57 2. Grimsby 79 3. East Hull 108 **(Vets):** 1. R Aconley 2. D Pickering (E Hull O/45) 74:31 3. A Sedman (E Hull O/45 76:36 4. E Owst (O/50 79:17) **Women:** 1. K Smith (Grimsby) 80:37 2. K Pyrah (CoH) 80:44 3. M Jefferson (Unat) 91:22 952 finished.

I was coming into form at the right time for the Hull to Grimsby Marathon on 25th September 1983, and I felt confident of a victory at last. I knew all the main contenders including the winner from the previous year, Dave Michaels. Just four days from the event, I received a call from Colin Kirkham who asked me,

'Hi Pete, are you running the Marathon at the weekend?'

'Hi Colin, I haven't seen you since the AAA's marathon at Rotherham in 1976,' I said.

'Yes, that was a bad run – my feet were skinned to the bone.'

'I know Colin – your feet were a bloody mess.'

'Anyway Pete, about the Humber Marathon on Sunday, what's the field like?' Colin asked.

'Colin if you run, it will between us,' I said, regretting my remark.

'Oh, well may the best man win.'

If I'd thought about it, I wouldn't have made it sound so inviting. Colin was a tough cookie. He had competed at the Olympic marathon in 1972. Served me right for not keeping up with marathon running, I later learned Colin had won the Harlow in 2:15:33 in 1981 and had a stunning victory in the Bermuda marathon in 1982, when he clawed back a three-minute deficit to win in 2:17:28. When I saw Colin after the Rotherham marathon with the blood pouring from his feet, I was shocked and yet part of me understood his gritty determination – to prevail at any cost.

If I was going to win against an Olympics Game's athlete, and winner of twelve marathons it would, on my part, take a mighty effort and a little bit of luck. Colin put in several efforts and eventually by half way it was just as I had predicted a race between us. We ran together for the first seventeen miles and I was beginning to feel confident. When I heard him breathing heavily on a hill, I seized my chance. Afterwards he told reporters, *'I thought Pete had got me when he got a lead of fifty metres,'* meanwhile, my wife was with Colin Martin, one of my shop-managers, who was filming at eighteen miles. Colin asked her,

'Can you see who's in front?'

My wife was almost too frightened to believe her eyes and spluttered,

'Pete's leading … Pete's leading …'

Colin started to peg me back, as he had, when he won the Bermuda marathon. We went through twenty miles together in 1:47:20, but I was under pressure, and my adversary must have sensed this. He came home a worthy winner in a new course record of 2:20:57 while I was second and inside the old record in 2:22:50. Dave Michaels came third in 2:25:40 and said,

'Kirkham was in a class of his own, but Pete gave him a run for his money.'

I had first met Dave Michaels when I ran for the RAF against Borough Road College in 1972. Later he joined the RAF as a parachute instructor. I ran against him in 1981 and then in 1983, he always had a good word for everybody – several months later I was shocked to learn he died when his parachute failed to open over Cyprus.

I always found it tiresome walking downstairs for several days after a marathon and this was no exception. But I needed to be on my mettle as captain of City of Hull when I left my Jameson Street shop and ran a couple of miles to pick up a mini bus to drive my team to the Northern Six Stage relay in Middlesbrough. I sorted out the running order for each stage – a lap of four miles and decided to run the first leg. My nerves got the better of me as I warmed up just six days after the marathon and the added pressure of still nursing sore legs. Indeed,

I needed to give City of Hull a decent start but was still shaking when the gun fired. However, I scorched round in 19:14 leaving City of Hull in seventh place. Even Peter Elletson (East Hull Harriers) was only a second ahead and asked me if I was taking drugs! Unfortunately, our team lost eight places on the five remaining legs. City of Hull had some potentially fine athletes, but they rarely performed at their best in relays. **Results:** 1. Gateshead 1: 55:10 2. Stretford 1:55:57 3. Liverpool 1:56:14 4. Derby 1:56:26 5. Bingley 1:56:50 6. Holmfirth 1:58:03 7. Airedale & SV 1:58:12 8. Elswick 1:58:22 9. St Helens 1:58:25 10. 1:58:45 11. Salford 1:59:31 12. Morpeth 1:59:38 13. Bolton 2:00:27 14. Rotherham 2:01:03 15. City of Hull 2:01:17 … 24. East Hull 2:04:57. **Fastest:** 1. B Smith 18:26 2. S Cram 18:27 3. M McLeod 18:31.

CHAPTER 16

Veteran

Pat McLagan came to Hull University as a lecturer, he was also a sub-two-twenty marathon runner from Victoria Park running club, He rang me, one evening,

'Hi Pete, Jim Dingwall is moving to Hull next month.'

'That's great, Pat. I met him at the Swintex 25k in 1980.'

'He's a research chemist and will work at BP at Salt End.'

'Jim ran a great time in the London Marathon – 2:11:44,' I said.

'As you are the club captain I'll get him to give you a ring,' Pat said.

'Of course, he should be a great asset to local athletics in Hull.'

A new era was about to be born, for me, as I was entering veteran athletics. Not only was Jim Dingwall a great athlete but would be a good ambassador for athletics on Humberside. A couple of days later the *Governor* as Jim was affectionately known in Scotland called me:

'Hi Pete, it's Jim Dingwall. I'm coming to Hull and need a new club to join.'

'It's nice to talk to you – Where are you hoping to live?' I said

'Cottage Drive, Kirkella – I see you have a decent team at City of Hull,' Jim said.

'Come and meet the lads on Tuesday 7-pm sharp,' I said, 'or you'll miss them.'

'That's fine I'll see you there,' Jim said.

'City do OK, but with your input – I'm sure they can do better…'

I had met Jim at a couple of races and he came across as a very accomplished athlete, but more importantly an even better human being, and he soon became a very good friend. On Sunday 9th October, I ran the Rowntrees (York) ten-mile race on a new course and it turned out to be an excellent race in ideal conditions. It was like a who's who of British distance running and one of my last races as a non-veteran, so to finish in 10th in forty-nine minutes fifty-three seconds showed that my form was intact.

I was now looking forward to my last race as a non-Veteran in a new half-marathon at Bridlington on 23rd October 1983, and a perfect build-up for my first outing as a Veteran in the Dublin Marathon on 31st October 1983. My new shop on Jameson Street was doing well, so I needed a manager for my original store on Holderness Road and interviewed Geoff Richardson, a Scot, and ultra-distance runner to manage the shop. Previously, Geoff, 33 had worked in the States and competed in a Six Day Race at Pennsauken, Philadelphia. Then, he came to England and was instrumental in organising Six Day Races in Nottingham in the early eighties. Geoff was a charismatic being, who lived to run, and I thought he would be suitable to manage my shop. Quite soon, it became apparent that ultra-distance running dominated Geoff's life and his timekeeping left a lot to be desired. Nevertheless, he was punctual when he came to manage Runnercare's stall in Bridlington's Spa before, during and after the races. We spent an hour setting up our stall and we were selling straight away, however, it was not a surprise as over two thousand had entered to compete in the half-marathon and fun run around the streets of Bridlington. The Spa was capable of seating 1700 or 3800 people standing, and so ideal for my trade stall. Then, I left the stall to get changed for the half-marathon, but when I returned Geoff had disappeared! Consequently, no transactions were taking place and the stock-laden tables were open for anyone to help themselves. I was infuriated when, I discovered he went to do the fun-run which meant I could not warm-up for the thirteen-mile race, I hoped to win. Eventually, Geoff returned, and I barely had time to reach the start-line let alone warm-up. Consequently, I started too quickly and got into oxygen debt, which gave me lactic-legs and a gap to the leaders. Anyway, I gradually recovered my momentum, and passed Ian Gilmore but there was no way back to Peter Moon, Dave Allen or Duncan Gaskell. Obviously, I was disappointed with my run, on the other hand, I consoled myself that the runners in front of me were five to ten years younger. **Results:** 1. D Allen (Manchester) 66:01 2. D Gaskell (Wakefield) 66:30 3. P Moon (Bingley) 66:39 4. P Flatman (CoH) 66:56 5. I Gilmour (M&C) 67:05 6. D Weigal (Barnsley) 67:29 7. N Jobson (Blay) 68:33 8. G Baker (CoH) 69:15 9. S O'Callaghan (WYP) 69:20 10. C Nightingale (Sheff) 69:29 11. P Elletson (EH) 70:18 12. C Haynes (WYP-V) 70:21 13. W Wilkinson (Rown) 71:04 14. P Urwin (Newc) 71:10 15. W Eldridge (E Hull) 71:17 16, B Jones (E Hull) 71:36 17. S Hunt (Ask) 71:38 18. M Cox 71:59 (Leeds) 71:59 19. S Dooley (Hull S) 72:03 20. Ron Hill (Clay-V O/45) 72:04 **(Vets):** 1. Haynes 2. Hill 3. K Scurr (E Hull) 73:09 4. A Sedman (E Hull) 75:15 **(O/45)** 1. Hill 2. D Pickering (E Hull) 75:43 3. J Daniels (Low-O/50) 75:47 **(Women):** 1. D Baker (CoH) 82:53 2. C Borrill (CoH-V)) 85:50 3. T Smith (Newc) 88:37 4. M Jefferson 88:27 5. J Smith 92:22 6. B Danby 92:46.

My wife and I, flew to Ireland via Manchester for the Dublin City Marathon on 31st October 1983. We booked into a nice hotel opposite the famous Guinness factory on the banks of the River Liffey. Like most tourists, we believed the myth about the stout using the Liffey water, when in fact it was piped in from the Wicklow Mountains. There was a big entry of over ten thousand, but I was on good form, although another marathon just four weeks later might be too soon. The race got away at ten-am and I was running quite easily in the lead group as we went through Phoenix Park, which I had last visited as a fourteen-year old boy scout in 1958. Then we went through a sprawling housing estate and over numerous bridges.

The race was being televised live, and it would be the time many of my distant Irish cousins would see me for the first time. I was running in the colours of City of Hull AC and getting numerous name-checks from the race commentator. This was a long time, before social media invaded our lives and my Irish cousins were watching me running through the streets of Dublin in my first race as a veteran. I started to get stomach cramps after fifteen miles and lost touch with the leaders. Eventually, I was forced to stop at a loo, but managed to get going again. When I reached the docks, I started to feel cold and the extra marathon was now taking its revenge. Still I came eighteenth in two hours twenty-five minutes and twenty-two seconds. I had hoped to win the veteran's prize, but the outstanding Irish international, Danny McDaid won the O/40V 5th place in 2:19:29. Then the shivering started in earnest and I was suffering from severe hypothermia. Tricia took me back to the hotel and even though it was heated, and I buried myself under the duvet I was still shaking. We went down to the bar and Tricia bought me a large brandy, which instantly stopped the hypothermia. We went out for a walk later, but became lost, and I asked a driver crossing a bridge over the river Liffey the way back to the hotel. Irish hospitality must be experienced to be believed, as he drove us back to our hotel! **Results: 1**. R Agten 2:14:19 2. G O'Rourke 2:14:31 3. M Deane 2:19:16 4. S Doherty 2:19:20 5. D McDaid 2:19:29 O/40V 6. N Cusack 2:19:36 7. M Shields 2:19:43 8. J McGlaughlin 2:19:46 9. T Ryan 2:20:21 10. J Kiernan 2:20:26 11.G Hannon 2:20:35 12. J Griffin 2:21:41 13. A Daly 2:22:52 14. B Leddicoat 2:23:55 15 M Crowell 2:24:30 16. A Hartigan 2:24:32 17. B Murphy 2:24:47 18. P Flatman 2:25:22 O/40V 19, N McEentegart 2:25:23 20. G O'Neill 2:25:26.

I was rather disappointed with my run, but sometimes I needed to remember my body was not a machine and that any tiny change in fitness or health can alter an average performance to a great one or vice-versa. Still I had one of my favourite races coming up the perennial Tipton Ten being held on 20th November 1983. And this year I would face an awesome challenge from the Governor, as Jim was known in Scotland, in his first race in City of Hull's purple colours. Nearly five hundred runners faced the starter on this three-lap classic. I lost sight of Jim as he vied for the lead, but then, I did not believe I had a realistic chance of beating him. However, Jim proved he was mortal, like all of us, as he was stationary by the side of the road and clutching his right hamstring but being the gentleman that he was he turned to cheer me on. The race pace demanded a flat-out effort from start to finish and like many events, below half marathon, if you were still surviving at three miles that position will not alter much. I was feeling very pleased to be running sub-five-minute miles after a below par marathon. Although, the places did not change much the pressure was keeping me focussed. I had quite a battle on the last lap with Bob O'Hara of Sparkhill and he prevailed and beat me to the finish line. Inexplicably, I was convinced Bob was a veteran, and gutted he'd stolen my first win in the over 40-category and asked, *'Are you a veteran?'* O'Hara glared at me, *'No I'm f****** not, I'm only twenty-six!'* On the contrary, I had won the first veteran prize by a margin of over two minutes and recorded a time of forty-nine minutes and two seconds in 9th place only nineteen-seconds shy of my all-time best. Although I had beaten Jim Dingwall by a technical knock-out I had to accept that it may never happen again, but I would live in hope. **Results** 1. P. Davies-Hale (Cannock) 46:58 2. G Ribbons (Epsom) 47:10 3. A Holden (Tipton) 47:22 4. P Magner (E&E) 48:27 5. M Fromont (North) 48:39 6. N Lees (Der) 48:46 7. C Murray (Inv) 48:49 8. B O'Hara (Spark) 48:53 9. P Flatman (CoH-V) 49:02 10. S Brown (Chelt) 49:07 11.C Mattocks (W&B) 49:21 12. C Bell (Telford) 49:32 13. M Davies (Worc) 49:46 14. M

Pountney (Tip) 49:50 15. J Wheway (Tip) 49:55 16. R Cytlau (Tip) 50:01 17. R Piotrowski (Warl) 50:05 18. K Davies (N Lon) 50:07 19. J Wagstaff (Tip) 50:09 20. I Atkins (Worc) 50:22 **(Further Vets):** 2. M Bardsley (Bir-V) 51:05 3. D Fownes (Tip-V) 51:33 4. D Cooper (Worc-V) 52:09 5. J Lansbury (Alt-V) 52:25 6. G Bagnall (Newc) 52:40 **(Women):** 1. T Bateman (Bir) 57:33 2. A Kirkham (Cov) 60:12 3. S Lappage (Bir) 60:55. NOTE – Local runners, I drove to the race from Hull 34. G Baker (CoH) 51:55 53. S Dooley (Hull S) 52:47 95. D Pickering O/45 (EH) 54:42.

On 1ˢᵗ January 1984, I ran the Morpeth to Newcastle for the first time since the race had been extended to 14.25-miles from 13.37 miles. I remember being disappointed with my run even though I won the veteran prize by nearly three minutes. Nonetheless, my Tipton 10 times of 49:02 and the 1:14:00 at Morpeth were noted in a world-wide veteran's athletics magazine at the time. **Results:** 1. A Hutton (Edin/S) 1:09:06 2. K Forster (Gate) 1:09:53 3. F Clyne (Aber) 1:10:00 4. P Campbell (Bol) 1:10:07 5. P Cuskin (J&H) 1:10:44 6. C Spedding (Gate) 1:10:48 7. K Penny (Camb H) 1:10:53 8. C Bucknall (Stret) 1:11:33 9. K Hunter (US) 1:11:36 10. I Gilmour (M&C) 11. J Merryfield (Corn) 1:11:43 12. D Gaskell (A&SV) 1:11:57 13. R Smedley (Bir) 1:12:01 14. D Hill (Sun)1:12:05 15. – 1:12:06 16. D Robson (Els) 1:12:10 17. W Cain (Salt) 1:12:29 18. A Daly (Bella) 1:12:30 19. J Dingwall (CoH) 1:12:34 20. P Faulds (FVH) 1:12:37 21. J Harper (Mor) 1:12:42 22. P Leddicoat (Gate) 1:12:46 23. L Robertson (EAC) 1:12:49 24. D Ellis (Bir) 1:12:51 25. K Johnson (Els) 1:13:0 26. J Atkin (A&SV) 1:13:10 27. D Wilkinson (A&SV) 1:13:18 28. S Markley (M&C) 1:13:23 29. S Irvine (Gate) 2:13:29 30. I Elliot (ESH) 1:13:35 31. S Beattie (Mor) 1:13:51 32. P Flatman (CoH-V) 1:14:00 33. P Whittle (Els) 1:14:03 34. J Caine (Gate) 1:14:05 35. C Chandler (Sale) 1:14:18 36. A Kean (Der) (Der) 1:14:24 37. M Brown (Darl) 1:14:27 38. S Donnelly (Els) 39. J Larkin

(Gate) 1:14:44 40. J Maitland (Leeds) 74:55. **Teams:** 1. Gateshead 57 2. Airedale & SV 65 3. Elswick 74 4 Middlesboro & D. 83. **(Vets):** 1. P Flatman 2. A Ritchie 1:16:38. **(Women):** 1. A Tooby (Car) 1:19:44 2. G Penny (Camb H) 1:23:04 3. K Lock (Car) 1:24:15 4. L Irving (Bord) 1:24:38 5. G Burley (LOAC) 1:25:42 6. M Hurst 1:27:18.

My next race was the Woking ten being held on 26th February 1984. I had not run this since 1976 and wanted to see if I could get near my time when I was thirty-two and take Bill Venus's over forty's record of fifty minutes fifteen seconds, which had stood for three years. It was a very cold day and I struggled to know what to wear. In retrospect, I should have worn gloves and a long sleeve top. The race pace was ferocious as I strained to stay close to the leaders, but at about four miles, I was forced to ease off, because my heart was fibrillating, exacerbated by the freezing weather. Then I remembered in the 1976 Ferriby ten, in similar weather suffering from the same symptoms, I was frightened and thought my race, or even my life might be in danger. The route turned away from the biting east wind and my heart returned to normal rhythm and not like an old car with a misfiring piston. I had lost some time, but not my determination, to take Bill Venus's record. From the mile-posts I knew I was close to my target, which had become my fixation and then in a blur it was all over. I had broken the veteran's record with forty-nine minutes fifty-six seconds to eclipse Bill Venus's time and despite the trauma and passage of time I was only thirteen seconds slower than 1976. Martin Duff wrote the AW report, and this excerpt was a great morale booster: *The leading pack of eight were some 50m clear from a further 15 runners, including Pete Flatman from City of Hull, who has run some super-fast times as a first year Vet, and was here testing himself against southern runners, after having gone to both the North East, and the West Midlands to establish how he rates in Vet circles. The course record of 47:49 remained intact, though not so the Vets record of 50:15 held since 1981 by Bill Venus. Flatman confirmed his superb form by placing 13th in 49:56, and must be one of, if not, the best Vet in the country. Eight years ago, he ran 49:43 on the same course!*

Results: 1. N Sirs (Windsor S&E) 48:20 2. J Boyes (Bournemouth) 48:43 3. K McDonald (Hillingdon) 48:44 4. A Douglas (Craw) 48:53 5. P Jones (Camb H) 49:05 6. J Hooper (Car) 49:11 7. C Hensby (Wok) 49:20 8. P Eales (WS&E) 49:48 9. P Sanderson (Wok) 49:50 10. M McGeoch (Les C) 49:53 11. T Crossman (Wok) 49:55 12. M Page (Om) 49:56 13. P Flatman (CoH-V) 49:56 14. P Ross-Davies (HW) 50:09 15. K Clifford (Ilf) 50:10 16. S Collingridge (Rane) 50:11 17. C Moxsom (Har) 50:27 18. R Ede (Barn) 50:31 19. S Brace (Bridge) 50:52 20. J Peel (AF&D) 50:53 **Teams:** 1. Windsor S&E 36 2. Woking 59 3. Aldershot F&D 82 **(Vets)** 1. P Flatman 49:56 (rec) 2. B Smith (Bourn) 51:45 3. J O'Bryan (BridgeV45) 52:26 **(0/50):** 1. R Coxon (W Gn) 56:14 2. A Ferguson (High) 57:38 3. L Forster (Dac) 57:46. **(Women)** 1. G Burley (LOAC) 57:27 2. L Watson (LOAC) 58:08 3. S Foster (Wok) 59:22. **Team:** London Olympiades.

My wife and I went to Gran Canaria in March 1984, and stayed in some self-catering apartments near the beach, and what was fast becoming an annual pilgrimage. I needed to have a break, to escape, briefly, the long, northern winter, a rest, and the joy of running fast in vest and shorts. The sun was heading for the horizon, and all was good in my world. In the distance, I saw a runner and decided to lift my pace and catch him. Initially, I was making little impact, and needed to up my tempo several times to close the gap. As I got closer, I noticed his cadence was quite slow, though he had a raking stride that ate up the ground. Finally, I drew up alongside, and managed to find enough breath:

'Hello, you're running well.' I said, trying to hide the effort it had taken me to catch him.

'Buenos tardis, me llamo es Jose Abascal,' It's not every day you catch up the Spanish 1500 metres record-holder and representative for the forthcoming Olympics in Los Angeles. He continued,

'Voy a batir, Sebastian Coe, Steve Ovett y Steve Cram en los Juegos Olímpicos!' he said in a manner that was very convincing, but surely unlikely he could beat such athletes. We ran along the edge of a fairway, when a tourist playing golf yelled,

'*Goddam joggers – get your arses off the golf course!*' said as though he belonged to a master-race, and we were mere flies. How could this arrogant buffoon be so insulting and ignorant to warrant a response, but he got one all the same,

'This guy will be leading the 1500 metres final at LA in the summer and you may just be lucky to see him on TV winning a medal!' I said.

We continued speaking the few words we knew of each other's languages till the end of our run and bade our farewells. I never saw him again but watched the final of the Olympic 1500 metres on 11th August 1984 at Los Angeles with rapt attention. Steve Ovett fell ill with heat exhaustion and only just made the final. Meanwhile, Seb Coe was seeking a second gold, and the younger Steve Cram seemed to offer him the sternest challenge. Jose Abascal took the lead on the third lap with his long, loping stride. Could Cram, Coe and Ovett win team GB, an unprecedented clean sweep of the medals, but it was not to be as Ovett left the track and collapsed with heat exhaustion. At the bell, Abascal was leading, but with a half a lap to go, and in unison Coe and Cram swept past Jose, and Seb Coe, at his imperious best, kicked for home, and took his second 1500m gold by seven metres. **Results:** 1. Sebastian Coe 3:32.53 (Olympic record) 2. Steve Cram 3:33.40 3. Jose Abascal 33.34.30. Six months earlier Jose Manuel Abascal told me he could beat the British superstars and was the lead athlete for most of the race. I don't know if the rude American golfer remembered our encounter or had misgivings for his outburst, but I think Jose's bronze medal was a fitting reward for a fine athlete. In December 1984, Abascal was voted Spanish Sportsman of the year, and in 1986 ran his best 1500 metres in 3:31.13.

My wife, came with me to run the Ballycotton, ten-mile road race in Ireland on 11th March 1984. We flew from Manchester to Dublin and another flight to Cork, where John Walshe the race promoter was waiting to greet us and take us back to our destination in Ballycotton, a fishing port to the east of Cork. The village consists of a couple of shops, a village hall, a lighthouse and six bars. For the race, the local population would be tripled with almost a thousand runners. The rural countryside was perfectly highlighted by white-washed cottages and wonderful views across the bay and a small island with a lighthouse. Balleycotton was a friendly place and it seemed all the villagers knew you within a few hours. Race-day was sunny with variable cloud and quite a stiff breeze. I had to be at the sharp end and soon lost sight of my wife, who had never run more than a few miles before and I hoped she would take it easy. The start was chaotic with runners going hell for leather as if no one realised ten-miles was a long-distance race. By three miles, I had dropped out of the leading group and was around sixteenth. From there, I clawed back a few places to finish tenth overall in fifty minutes and thirty-two seconds. This was a record that stood for over ten years until broken by Liam O'Brien in 1995. To my amazement, Liam is the only person to have run faster in the over forty-section in the history of Balleycotton ten-mile races. My wife completed the course in ninety-three minutes and thirty seconds and placed eight hundred and second. We both had a grand evening in one of the bars and watched videos of the race and enjoyed the wonderful craic of our hosts. I was impressed by Tricia's ten-miles completed at nine minutes eighteen seconds per mile – it was, and would remain, the one and only event that we competed in together. **Results:** 1. T O'Leary (Leevale) 48:22 2. L O'Brien (Midleton) 48:28 3. J Griffin (St John's) 48:42 4. T Ryan (Dungarvan) 48:47 5. R Treacy (Deise) 49:27 6. S Griffin (St John's) 49:34 7. R Burke (St Finbarr's) 49:47 8. P White (Midleton) 49:52 9. S Faulkner (Kilcoole) 50:00 10. P Flatman (CoH) 50:32. **(Vets):** 1. P Flatman (CoH) 50:32 2. T O'Loughlin (Clonmel) 53:29 3 D Hodgins (Leevale) 53:42.

On the first Saturday in April, I captained City of Hull AC in the Northern twelve stage relay at Heaton Park, Manchester. There was great excitement, because Jarrow's arrow, Steve Cram would be trying to help his team strike the bull's eye for a golden win. Surely, I was taking on too much, but my sense of responsibility overcame my common sense. For the past six months I had been here, there and everywhere to gain national recognition as the best new veteran on the block, I was trying to improve my business, and eventually make it a national chain. Nevertheless, here I was taking another busy Saturday away from my business to captain my team in a four-hour event, which we had virtually no chance of qualifying for the national final at Sutton Park. I wondered if similar thoughts went through Steve Cram's head, when on lap four he was handed the baton way behind the leading teams. Of course, he gave it his best shot, cutting through the field like a ballistic missile from a lowly twenty ninth to an extraordinary third on the fourth stage, but it was all to no avail as the rest of his team-mates were not superstars, and finished way down the field. Obviously, these thoughts affected my run, and try as I might, I was at least a minute slower than expected. Dave Lamont, the Hull Daily Mail's athletics correspondent headlined our debacle thus, *City Muscled Out of the Finals*. In fact, we finished a lowly twentieth and my former club East Hull were thirty ninth.

The next week there was a large article about my friend, Jim Dingwall's attempt to beat his performance from the previous year in the 'London Marathon' where he came fifth in two hours eleven minutes and forty-four seconds. I had been running with him and I knew it was difficult for Jim to do all the training and have time for his church and singing for the, *Hull Choral Union*. He told me he thought he could run two hours ten but thought the 1984 London would be his last realistic chance. I also thought his move to Hull must have had a detrimental effect on his routine and reminded how difficult it was for me when I left the RAF and came to Hull. Whether, he liked it or not, there would be a huge weight of expectation from Scotland and now England. Jim's plan was to get to half way in around sixty-five minutes as comfortable as possible, which he did, but a mile later the eventual winner Kevin Forster quickened his pace and Jim's marathon target diminished with every passing mile. Meanwhile, I had made a good start, but got stomach cramp at fourteen miles and meant I needed a toilet and quick. Eventually, I had to push through spectators lining the road and found a public convenience down a steep stairway, which cost me two to three minutes and any chance of getting the first veteran prize. Apart from that I was running reasonably but amazed to see Jim coming bank to me along the embankment, I was upset to see my pal reduced to a jog. I tried to say something cheerful as I went by and quipped, '*Hi Jim, I'll see you in the Top House in Hessle on Tuesday!*' We shared the same sardonic humour and instantly Jim replied, '*Yes, Pete, but not for a run!*' I got around in 2:26:22, and in a way felt, it was a turning point in both of our careers. Jim decided to run less and support his club, but never sought to run such a fast marathon again. As I was six years older it was also becoming apparent that I should wind down too. Charlie Spedding won in 2:09:57 and went on to win an unexpected bronze medal at the Los Angeles Olympics in 2:09:58. **Results:** 1. C Spedding (Gateshead) 2:09:57 2. K Forster (Gate) 2:11:41 3. D Fowles (Cardiff) 2:12:12 4. Oyvind Dahl (Norway) 2:12:17 5. J Lauenborg (Denmark) 2:12:20 6. J Ikangaa (Tanzania) 2:12:33 7. J Ashworth (Bingley) 2:13:49 8. M East (Ranelagh) 2:14:01 9. C Bunyan (South.E) 2:14:03 10. S Kristensen (Denmark) 2:14:22… 150. P Flatman (CoH-V) 2:26:22 223. J Dingwall (CoH) 2:29:28.

I have known Peter Elletson since his teenage days, when he was being coached by Peter Dearing, who would wax lyrically about his talent and appetite for hard training. Soon he was dominating, and not just at local level, but also for his country and represented England in the Junior Men's World Cross Country at Glasgow in 1978. He went on to place twenty-fourth, which helped England secure the team gold medals, but despite this Peter has always been modest about his success. **Results:** 1. England (1, 13, 15, 24) **53pts** 2. Canada (2, 8, 14, 29) **53pts** England win as final counter (Elletson) was ahead of Canada's 4th place. 3 Spain (3,4,16,31) **54pts.**

Peter first met Jim in a local hostelry when he was in his early twenties. After some opening pleasantries, there was the usual banter, but Pete's opening statement set himself up as the fall guy,

'Jim, I hope you can inspire us all to run faster!' The *'Guv'nor'*, as he was known in Scotland could not pass up this chance,

'Peter, I hope I drag you up and you don't drag me down.' Yet away from this banter they held each other in enormous respect. Peter was a competitive animal and wanted to beat Jim in a proper race, but Jim, ten years his senior would have been mortified to lose to this young whippersnapper. Jim had beaten Elletson at the Runnercare eight-mile race, held a fortnight earlier and in another ale house Jim spiked their rivalry to a new level,

'I'll tell you what, Peter here is a challenge: I will drink a pint before you finish the Cottingham five!' I heard it too and was stunned by such bravado, and Elletson took it all in, but could he make Jim Dingwall eat his words?

On a cloudy Wednesday evening the cameras rolled as did the runners. Peter Dearing was the vivid commentator about this duel between his best coached athlete, Pete Elletson and Jim Dingwall the pride of Scotland. As the field charged down South Street, Peter entertained us with, *'Here's comes Jim Dingwall – he's the one with the beard on!'* Meanwhile, I went with the duo even though I did not expect to win. Sure, enough at three miles I had to let them go. The film crew caught up with them on Southwood Road a half a mile from the finish and Peter commentated, *'These two have fought a terrific battle. Peter and Jim*

Dingwall are having a ding dong scrap all the way to the finish' As Jim Dingwall hit the tape in front of the *'Duke of Cumberland'* was packed with spectators. The landlord gave him a pint and those who did not know of the bet must have been amazed, when Dr Dingwall won in 21:16, then quaffed his pint before second-placed Peter Elletson finished in 21:30, I was third in 21:50, and Steve Rennie fourth in 21:58. Jim's bravado, and the humbling of East Hull's Peter Elletson brought condemnation from his club's president Grahame Brummitt – who never forgave the Scotsman's sense of humour!

I was still competing better than most runners up to half my age in road races and now the focus was on trying to adapt to track races of five and ten thousand metres and explained my dilemma to the, Hull Daily Mail's athletic correspondent Dave Lamont, *'The track five thousand metres is like twelve races and the ten thousand metres is like twenty-five. There is more dodging about. It is difficult to relax, and you worry about getting boxed in or running into the guy in front and every hundred metres there's a hundred and eighty-degree bend. In addition, if forced wide it can add an extra three or four metres per lap. It is a bit like horses for courses and I am much better on the road, which I think becomes more marked when you age. Even in mass fields there was always enough space to get with the leaders and no obstructions to a smooth rhythm making it easier to keep up.'* So, I ran the track with no great enthusiasm, although I won the Northern veteran championships at five and ten thousand metres. Then, I went with my son Simon to Edinburgh for the National championships where we stayed with Margaret, Jim Dingwall's mother. She was a wonderful host and showed us the sites of *'Auld Reekie'* with enthusiasm and pride. We soon learnt why Edinburgh has the title of, *'The Athens of the North'*. Meadowbank Stadium was the venue for the championships and I ran a very unimpressive sixth place in the five thousand metres but ran a better ten thousand against Tim Johnston and Martin Duff, but I had to settle for silver.

Now all Veteran's eyes focussed on Brighton the venue for the European Athletics championships from the 20th to 25th August 1984. I set off with Tricia, Sarah, Simon and Clare for the long journey south, but our car broke down near RAF Wittering and had to be towed back to a garage at nearby Stamford. Perhaps that was an omen and we should have diverted to Skegness for a week while our car was fixed. In the event, I hired another car and drove through some very heavy holiday traffic before arriving at a house we had rented for a week in Brighton. Including the breakdown, we had been on the road for over eight hours. I did the dad thing and insisted the kids needed to muck in to keep the house ship-shape, but with little success. The championships attracted over three thousand entries across all age groups and my races were scheduled for a track in Crawley. The first day was hot and humid and my event the five thousand metres was scheduled for 2 pm by which time the temperature was eighty-four degrees. I only managed sixth place, and even a season's best of fifteen minutes thirteen seconds could not console me. In another interview I told Dave Lamont, *The East Europeans will be there, but they are not very good. They have a de-training scheme for their Veterans, which gradually takes them off competition, whereas we want to go on for ever.'* Two days later I ran the ten thousand metres and thankfully it was cloudy, with lower temperatures. This time I was on the pace at half way in close to fifteen minutes, however, the eventual winner Alan Rushmere eased away and broke the European record by over a minute with thirty minutes and eleven seconds. I had a much better run and broke the European record with thirty-one minutes, but still just sixth. However, I had beaten Rushmere by over three minutes four years earlier in the Tipton ten, but there's no accounting for form. **Results:** Men's Events **40-44 5000:** 1. L ROBERTS 14:53.6 2. G Mielke (FRG) 14:54.08 3. A RUSHMER 15:04.5 4. H Jansen (Bel) 15:07.6 5. L Overskov (Den) 15:12.6 6. P FLATMAN 15:13.0 7. H Jonsson (Swe) 15:25.1 8. S WARZEE 15:29.8 **10,000:** 1. A RUSHMER 30:11.1 2. L

ROBERTS 30:21.1 3. G Mielke 30:47.4 4. H Jonsson 30:53.2 5. T JOHNSTON 30:55.0 6. P FLATMAN 31:00.6 ... 9. G OGDEN 31:17.4 10. D SPARKS 31:27.3.

We had a break until Sunday's event, the marathon and had a mini holiday visiting the Brighton Pavilion built for the Prince Regent and the later King George 4th. The Pavilion is a lavish and opulent building and completely out of place in an English seaside resort, yet also an amazing copy of an Indian palace. I also wanted to visit my great aunt Peggy, who I had not seen since she lived in Fulham in the late-fifties. With a little local help, I eventually tracked her down to a suburb near the town centre. One of her grand kids came to the door and I said, '*Tell Peggy, there is someone to see her,*' she ran to tell grandma, who must be telepathic, because thirty years had passed since we last met, yet she opened the door and said in her inimitable Irish accent,

'Peter, I knew it was you!'

Marathons tear the athlete apart, devouring muscle tissue trying to maintain energy and at any age must be treated with extreme caution. I had already run the 5000 metres and 10,000 metres in very hot weather, and on Sunday morning travelled to Barnes Green to run the European veterans-marathon, but my heart wasn't in it. The heat-wave had got to me, and I thought the Humber Bridge marathon was more important, in three weeks-time. Something about a bird in the hand is worth more than two in the bush should have sprung to mind.

However, it was another hot day. Within a few miles, I was running with Tim Johnston, who had competed in the Mexico Olympics, but on the road, I usually prevailed. In my mind, I was still in turmoil, and this would have been another occasion when a coach would have been invaluable. Even if I had not already run the five and ten kilometres the marathon I was now undertaking would be daunting enough, but I was not in my comfort zone, and my mind was set on winning the Humber Marathon. Tim was not stretching me, although psychologically I would be happy to drop out and I wished I hadn't started the marathon, and just wanted to go home. Besides, I never came to terms with Veteran-races, and preferred to run in races open to all-comers even though I would have less chance of winning. When we reached the sixteen-mile mark, I dropped out, even though, I was virtually guaranteed a silver or gold medal. I was persuaded to get back in the race and soon caught Tim up, but my heart and soul said no more and I finally dropped out a mile later. In retrospect, this was catastrophic psychological setback for which I would pay dearly. Tim won with ease in two hours twenty-seven minutes, while I contemplated my embarrassing feebleness of mind, which had left me without a medal. Another interview I did was printed in the press, when asked about running the World Veteran Championships in Rome the following year, *'Ultimately, Veteran's athletics will be even bigger than mainstream athletics where, every event is a race – even if it's a ninety-eight-year old running the fifty metres'*. **Mar:** 1. T JOHNSTON 2:27:44 2. Overskov (Bel) 2:28:37 3. J Shrader (FRG) 2:28:49 4. P Grief (FRG) 2:29:34 5. J DAVIES 2:31:06.

Chastened by the experience I started to prepare for the Humber Marathon, for which I had thrown away a European medal. I had some shoes called '2:08', but they had so little support that the liners crept out of my shoes by twenty miles as I threw caution to the wind in a race I had yet to win. Unfortunately, I was not in the right mental state to tackle a marathon, as I punished my body over the last six miles, I lost two places in the process to come home in two hours twenty-nine minutes and forty-six seconds for fifth place. Ironically, had I won it I would have been a free trip the next month to run, 'The New York Marathon'. My feet were in shreds, and the next day, I went to London for a shoe exhibition at the Savoy Hotel. As I reached the door to the trade show a young lady said:

'Here's your free raffle ticket and if you are lucky you'll get a free flight and entry to run the New York Marathon.' I was flabbergasted and still walking like I had just got off a horse and spluttered,

'I don't believe it, I can barely walk after running the Humber Marathon I tried to win for the same prize and now you tell me I can win it with a raffle ticket!' The winning ticket went to a middle-aged yuppie for a wannabe brand of sports fashion shops. His response to winning a prize to run a marathon in New York was that of a man who'd never consider running for a bus.

Two days later, back in my main shop I received a surprise call from the very same lady I had spoken to at the Savoy,

'Is that Peter Flatman, I remember you telling about how you had tried to win the Humber Marathon and a trip to New York and how disappointed you were that someone could win it in a raffle. We would like to offer an all expenses trip to New York Marathon.' Of course, I was excited, but added a caveat,

'Sure, as long as I can take my wife!' I wasn't sure about my marathon form, but this was a marvellous opportunity to visit a few of my relations who lived in nearby Yonkers.

We flew on a Air Lingus to John F Kennedy airport. Along the way to the baggage hall we saw dozens of celebrity-backed posters informing us that, *New York Loves You,* on the contrary, the brusque manner of the border police suggested the exact opposite. Our hotel on 42nd Street was close to Times Square where drug-dealers and prostitutes operate. Nearby, was a 24-hour supermarket where we bought some food and beer and waited at the cash point. An elderly woman did not have enough money for her shop but had difficulty in deciding the items she did not want. After what seemed an age, but only a minute or so, a young woman, brown hair, and thick make-up went ballistic,

'For fucks sake, how many dimes you need?' she raged.

'You OK – don't worry it'll soon be sorted,' my wife said kindly.

'I've been on a film set all goddam day,' she bawled.

'What kind of film?' my wife enquired.

'It's called, *Desperately Seeking Susan*,' she yelled.

As I was aware of skin-flick booths in the vicinity and the film title seemed to suggest it was a pornographic film, yet it occurred to me this excitable woman could have been the young Madonna. Later, I learned that *Desperately Seeking Susan* was being shot in Manhattan at the time. Short of asking Madonna about the incident, I had no definitive way of proving or disproving our unexpected meeting with a soon to be global, super-star.

The next day, we packed a bag and took the subway to Grand Central Station – its all-seeing clock reflecting humankind's need for a vacation, a new start in life, or, simply, to go home. We bought our tickets and proceeded to track one-zero-nine. Our two Irish cousins waited for us at Yonkers. They took us to Nancy's 1930s house on a leafy drive made more dramatic with the colours and falling leaves of autumn.

Finally, the day arrived for the New York Marathon on Sunday 28th October 1984, after three hectic days of sightseeing and visiting my extended family in Yonkers. I took a bus to the start on the Staten side of the Verrazano-Narrows Bridge, which superseded the Golden Gate as the world's longest single span bridge in 1964 and held the title till overtaken by the Humber Bridge in 1981. As soon as I arrived I found a place near the front, where I could see lines and lines of portable loos, and long queues, but my biggest concern was the heat and humidity. As we waited for the Mayor's gun, I got talking to Dave Lem, a prolific road runner from Leicester and we were both worried about the rising temperature and humidity. Nonetheless we got a decent start and I noted the slope to the middle of the bridge to be much steeper than the Humber Bridge, and I was already sweating profusely. However, the sweat could not evaporate in the moisture saturated air. Consequently, as my body temperature rose the nervous system feigned fatigue, the breathing became harder and my heart rate raced. Apparently, the effect can decrease energy levels by up to 12%.

Put another way running in these extreme conditions felt, to me, like I was wearing a heavy wet blanket. At ten miles, I was still thinking of a time around two hours thirty, but the temperature was rising to 79 degrees and humidity to 96%. This would be my worst marathon, when my pace dropped to seven-minute miles as I crossed the Queensboro Bridge. I saw my wife at 16-miles, and she urged me on towards First Avenue Manhattan. As I approached 19-miles, I started to get severe cramp, and had to stop for a few minutes to unknot my legs, while about fifty runners passed me. After my stop, I felt full of energy and was soon passing dozens of runners, but this was short lived as the cramps came back with a vengeance. Meanwhile, spectators were urging me to get back in the race with the constant cry of, *You can do it!*' At 20 miles, I jogged over the Willis Avenue Bridge for a short trip through the Bronx on Fifth Avenue till I reached Central Park with a few hills that brought further cramps. Finally, I crossed the line in 1512th place in a personal worst time of 3-hours 20-minutes and 54-seconds, indeed it was game, set and match to the Big Apple Marathon! Further, if I had run my best time I would have placed 12th and my worst marathon 91st. I was so far off my predicted time that no-one stayed to greet me in the reunion enclosure, so I was faced with a two or three-mile jog to our hotel. My pathetic performance knocked me sideways, yet it was impossible to convey to Nancy's family the depths of my despair. Instead, they kept saying, *You, kept going and you finished,* while all I could think was, the marathon had finished me. **Results:** 1. Orlando Pizzolato 2:14:53 2. David Murphy 2:15:36 3. Herbert Steffney 2:16:22 … **Women** 1. Grete Waitz (Nor) 2:29:30 2. Veronique Marot (GBR) 2:33:58 3. Laura Fogli (ITA) 2:37:35.

Meanwhile, I was still smarting at my recent results from Brighton and the Humber marathons and was determined to do everything in my power to try and beat Jim Dingwall in the club track ten thousand metres. If I could have beaten him with the power of my thought process then Jim would stand no chance, but who was I kidding? I followed Jim like a greyhound chases the electric hare with the same relentless monotony. Slowly, he started to edge away while I was counting down the twenty-five laps and the hundred corners on a dark night with poor lighting. Most of the participants were there to run a personal best and not to get lapped too many times. Meanwhile, I was working my socks to make Jim feel he had been in a race. My plan was coming unstuck, yet I was still in touch at halfway, but Jim's younger limbs and superior talent allowed him to gradually edge away and win by half a minute. Dave Lamont an observant sports journalist wrote, *It was an impressive display by veteran Flatman to beat useful club mates, Steve Rennie and George Baker by a half and one and half minutes respectively.'* I could not beat Jim, but I needed to remind myself that I was a 41-year old Veteran. Anyway, my next race massaged my flagging spirit when I ran the York Ten in forty-nine minutes thirty-four seconds, and my third sub-fifty since turning a Vet.

Before the disastrous marathon at New York, I entered the Tipton 10 to defend my Vets title from 1983. Martin Duff wrote an interesting article on Veteran athletics and his first year as a first year V40 in which Martin observed that maintaining form as a Veteran becomes increasingly difficult to maintain. Specifically, Duff quoted my road form when I was first Vet in the Tipton Ten, first in Morpeth to Newcastle and first in the Woking Ten in a record time and how I had failed to take that form to the UK and European Veteran track events. My personal view was that in each of those road-races, I was running against all comers. Besides, I had little idea who the veterans were in any given race, so much so that when Bob O'Hara (Sparkhill) overtook me at the end of the Tipton Ten, I asked him if he was a Vet. Bob, still in his twenties was not best pleased! Additionally, I was never at ease on the track, due in part, to taking up running in my late twenties.

'Are, yes, very nice.' I said then leant back with a sense of oneness and pleasure, because all my family were still together on Christmas Day.

'I wish you a Happy Christmas, Happy Christmas to you all.' My wife said at her most ebullient as she touched all our glasses with a clink.

After Christmas and the January sales, the turnover in my shops, dropped to the lowest ebb and would not recover before Easter. The weather in late March was particularly cold with day time frosts and a biting easterly wind. I had bought all my stocks six months earlier in the hope of good weather and having sufficient cash-flow to pay for the merchandise at the end of April. Plus, a further hindrance which I had to learn to cope with: there had been a national recession for four years, with unemployment of three million into 1985, the highest since the thirties. Accordingly, I needed to be frugal when it came to buying merchandise but still realised I needed to stock the best sellers. I had to remind myself that eighty per cent of my business's sales came from just twenty per cent of my stock. Of course, that twenty per cent shifted season to season, but emphasised the volatility, I had to overcome to have a viable business in straightened times.

I always had an edge on the other sports retailers, who relied on local walk-in trade, because of my mail order service I had provided since 1976. Anyway, this would really take off if I could buy out a complete inventory of, for example, top quality Adidas running shoes at up to half the normal cost price then I would have cornered the market and would be able to sell up to two thousand pairs through mail order and local trade. Besides, the offers never failed to boost trade and kept my staff busy when they might have been bored. A further spin-off from mail order specials was the number of customers, who visited from far and wide. My near constant presence in my Jameson Street also ensured that runners of all abilities were treated with respect and honesty.

Jim Dingwall and I decided to raise a team to run the Balleycotton 10-mile race near Cork and gathered at my bungalow at 9 am on a foggy day on 8th March 1985. Well at least some of us. First to arrive was Dave Ainsworth ex-paratrooper and his co-conspirator and maritime historian Rob Robinson, who brought Dave Ford. Dave Ainsworth stared at his watch,

'It's nine seventeen and we're still waiting for Jim Dingwall!' Dave said taking on the hat of a regimental sergeant major.

'We know Jim is a slow starter, but didn't realise he was this slow', chips in Rob.

'I blame my elderly next-door neighbour for not waking me up,' Dave Lamont, Hull Daily Mail athletics correspondent joked.

'We thought you were filing late copy', said Rob, who was over dressed in bright, coloured winter wear and a striped two-yard long, patchwork scarf.

'Here's Jim, looking like he's just woke up by the looks of him!' Ainsworth castigated Scotland's fastest distance runner for his tardiness.

My dad, Allan George Flatman emerged from our fog shrouded house, hands in pockets and looking forward to a trip to Southern Ireland – his favourite destination. We gathered for the departure photos and our motley crew. We then studied the maps to Holyhead and agreed to meet at the Valley Inn five miles from the port.

'Let's get this show on the road', I said optimistically.

It was a close-run thing as we boarded the Holyhead ferry with minutes to spare. I joined Rob and Dave out on deck and enjoyed the views as the boat slipped out of the harbour to a pan-flat Irish sea at three pm on Friday.

'How are things going Dave?' I asked light heartedly.

'Pretty good, except for Rob's organisation, but we can blame Jim for that. He was late this morning and when we got to the pub he had to have an extra pint more than us. We only just made it! Think we are going have to start to wake Jim up a bit!' Dave said pithily.

'Now then Rob, as joint organiser of this jaunt, what do you think so far?' I said and laughed.

'Not too bad now we are on board and have sorted out where all the bars are!' Rob said.

'What time do you think you'll run, Rob?' I asked.

'I would like to run fifty-six minutes but will be pleased to get under the hour,' Rob said.

We returned to an upper deck lounge, where Dave bought a round of Smethwick's, a red Kilkenny beer from Ireland's oldest brewery. The rest of the team was not on the beer and resting or sleeping. However, that did not stop Rob who wandered about the cabin asking our team members to predict their time for Saturday's race. When he reached Jim, he was fast asleep with not a hint of rapid eye movement.

'Jim what time do you think you'll do in the Balleycotton ten miles on Sunday?' Rob's question had fell on deaf ears and he was about to move on.

'Forty-eight minutes and seventeen seconds,' said a reedy voice from Jim's prostrate body. Jim was accurate to the second, but would he be able to deliver?

We disembarked in our two cars and headed for Carlow and the 'Seven Oaks Hotel' in the centre of the town, which then had a population of thirteen thousand. Michael Keogh was the manager and a cousin of mine and we were given VIP treatment. We enjoyed a grand night, particularly in the intimate atmosphere of a local pub with a ceilidh band. Dad and I went to Michael's house the next morning and swapped our families' news. Then we gathered at the hotel and departed to the sound of penny whistles played beautifully by Michael's two sons.

The City of Hull's captain, Jim Dingwall beat the challenge from Irish international Dick Hooper to win the Balleycotton Ten from a field of six hundred and forty-eight finishers with a time of forty-eight minutes and five seconds – the fifth fastest since the race was first held in 1978. With a two-mile, downhill stretch at the start of the race, Dingwall was concerned to find he was trailing the leading pair, despite a four thirty-five first mile and clocking nine minutes ten seconds for two miles. This breakneck pace inevitably slowed down, and Jim gradually stamped his authority on the race, but he had company of Dick Hooper, who was fifth in the Olympic Steeplechase final the previous autumn. At the eight-mile mark, Jim put on a spurt and created a fifty-metre gap he held to the finish. My dad was sitting on a wall watching Jim near the finish and said, *'I nearly fell off when I saw Jim winning!'* I was second home for City of Hull, and I held on to my veteran's title – in 25th with 53:39 – 3:07 slower than the previous year. **Results:** 1. Jim Dingwall (CoH) 48:05 2. D Hooper (Raheny Shamrock AC) 48:16 3. R Costello (Burgerland/Limerick) 48:36 … 25. P Flatman (CoH-O/40V) 53:39 43. D Ford (CoH) 55:15 68. R Robinson (CoH) 57:58 89. D Lamont (EH) 59:11 154. D Ainsworth (CoH) 62:11. Total finishers 646.

As you could imagine we now needed to celebrate and this would require copious amounts of Murphy's stout to loosen our tongues and celebrate our success. Rob started his post-race interviews in the crowded pub.

'Now then Pete, you'll be disappointed with your run, but I'm sure you'll be flying again soon,' Rob was being kind, but I could not resist this reply.

'Yes, Rob, seven four seven preferably!'

Despite the heady night, we were up and away at five am the next morning on the N11 east coast route. We had the roads entirely to ourselves until the outskirts of Dublin and the only living things we saw were murders of rooks perched in the middle of the road and only took to the air seconds before we might have murdered them! We were a quiet and subdued team and feeling the effects of such a busy weekend. Dave, my navigator was keeping me awake as I drove towards Manchester.

'I don't like the sound from the engine. Reckon that's the big ends going,' I said, concerned we might break down a long way from home.

'There you are Pete, you can't hear it anymore!' said Dave as he turned the radio up to full volume!

CHAPTER 17

Heart Scare

The Monday before Easter 1985 was a stressful day. I had employed extra staff to try and reduce shop-lifting, but when I looked at the security camera I saw two thieves stealing expensive Adidas clothing. Luckily, I was still wearing my running shoes and charged down the stairs after them, but they were already down the street. Now, my years of training had a practical use and I was determined to chase them down. Then I turned thief as I stole the breath from their lungs, so much so, they laid exhausted in an alley, begging for mercy. They never bothered to steal from me again. I also had to deal with a succession of reps, eager to sell to me, when all I wanted to do was concentrate on selling to my customers. Despite my poor form the previous winter I had upped my mileage of the previous week to a hundred plus. By the end of the day I was looking to add my second eight-mile on the way back home.

At closing time, I stripped off my business wear and donned shoes, shorts and vest ready for my intake of diesel fumes and carbon monoxide. Prospect street was jammed with huddled people-traffic trying to escape the bitter weather, courteously supplied by an easterly blast from Siberia. I was shivering, dodging and weaving, and running hard to keep warm. On Beverley Road, I glanced at an insurance building and a neon sign informed me the temperature was zero-Centigrade. I ran faster, but something was not right. My heart fluttered like a butterfly and my body felt limp. I tried harder to pick up the pace but couldn't hide from the unspoken fear of dying alone on the pavement. Now I was shuffling like a dole-queue, and a foreboding shadow passed over me. On Cottingham Road, I sought refuge in a home for orphans of sea-farers. A kind carer then called my wife, who set off to collect me. I was given a blanket and had only one thought, *If, it's my turn to die, please God let me get home first.* My wife gathered me up and stared at me in a compassionate way, then she put me to bed, and rang a family friend Dr Monsoor to examine me. The GP thought I might have suffered a heart attack and arranged my admission to Hull Royal Infirmary. The junior house doctor carried out a range of tests and put me on a heparin drip to thin my blood as a precaution. Meanwhile, I felt fit as a fiddle and wanted to get back to my business and running! On the second day, I needed to go to the loo, but couldn't stand the ignominy of sitting on a bed-pan, especially as I still had a heparin drip stuck in my arm! Next, I removed the drip from my arm and went to the loo. Consequently, the doctor confirmed me fit and well and let me go home.

If ever there was a wake-up call this was it even though I'd not had a heart attack, there were three incidents giving genuine concern. The first happened in the Ferriby-10 in January 1976, when in a snowstorm, I suffered atrial fibrillation anyway I finished the race in 51-minutes. The fast, irregular heart-beat lasted throughout the night then returned to normal the next morning. A second incident occurred in February 1984, when I was determined to break Bill Venus' record of 50:15 in the Woking 10-mile race. At 4-miles running into a bitter wind, I felt the return of the same heart irregularity I'd suffered in 1976, I eased off, till my heart became regular and finished strongly to break Bill's record by twenty seconds. After the latest scare, I was forced to take stock. I was nearly 42 with three children dependant on me, and a flourishing sports retail business, so why would I chase veteran's records that could endanger my life? From then on, I kept fit with daily runs, and occasional races.

In October 1976 I opened my shop, Runnercare to serve runners in the store and by mail-order, but also hoped I could help my club, East Hull Harriers to be more competitive. When I joined in 1973 the club was at a low point with very few active runners and but for one man may have ceased to exist. Peter Dearing had a dream and spent hours training kids to be good athletes, but that would take time, so he set about transforming the East Hull Summer League and producing lists of records and even ranking lists of every performance over the years. This created a great deal of interest in Hull and across the East Riding. I was a willing participant and inspired to break the records for the four courses of six, eight and ten miles. In 1977, I decided to sponsor East Hull's Summer League and hoped this would help the club's finances. Next, I advertised in the runner's bible, 'Athletics Weekly', placed adverts for the series and we began to attract talented athletes from other towns. Initially, runners were coming to race from Sheffield and West Yorkshire which created a more competitive league.

Hull was even more out on a limb then and it was exciting that better athletes found their way to our little club. I jogged down to the start of the six-miles event on a sunny evening in 1981 and was staggered to see Barry Smith, who had just won the World 5000m championship warming up to go around the Runnercare Six. In football terms, it was like Pele turning out for Hull City. I had held the course record with thirty minutes and nine seconds on a course almost spot on ten kilometres. Then, Peter Elletson broke my record with twenty-nine minutes forty seconds. Just to make the race even more competitive, Malcolm Prince turned up, but all that did was ignite Barry as he smashed the record with twenty-eight minutes, twenty-five seconds. By now, I was running for City of Hull and would never be forgiven for leaving East Hull for the enemy on the other side of the river. Everything Mike Hurd had said to me, in 1973, about the bitter rivalry amongst the Hull clubs was now coming home to roost. A couple of years earlier the club made a retrograde step by closing the East

Hull twenty-mile to club members only which resulted in a lack-lustre race with the loss of decades of tradition and quality performances. Even today it has not regained its place as one of the North's great road races, but from another view-point the race has never been more popular and is oversubscribed every year and an important stepping stone for those running the London Marathon. So, it was with a sad heart, when I found out that East Hull, and probably quite rightly, turned down my sponsorship.

I bought a large clear-out line of men's running shoes from Adidas called Denver and sold a lot through mail order. A favourite western of mine was, *'Big Deal in Dodge City'* and it inspired this one liner for my mail order advert, *'Big Deal in Denver!'* Then the shoes started to sell well as a cool urban shoe, but the only trouble was I starting to get returns, because of the sole leaving the upper. I had hundreds of pairs left and contacted Adidas, because I might have to stop selling them and send them all back. This rang alarm bells at Adidas UK and they asked me what price, did I think I could sell them for and I said £19.50. I settled for a credit note on the remaining pairs and put them in my sale at less than half price. It was an absolute winner, with customers queuing up to buy and, perversely, I had no more faulty returns.

After the troubles with my existing Ford Granada I decided to order the Granada Scorpio from Ford Crystal in Hull for delivery on 1st August 1985. The car has since won plaudits as the second ugliest car ever made, but my son didn't think so and would sit in it for hours after it was delivered. The car was diamond white, automatic, air-conditioned and went like the wind. A year later I and my family were still suffering the trauma of Elizabeth, Clare's school friend, losing both her parents in a road traffic accident near Blackpool. Eventually Elizabeth moved away and consequently, we took Clare out on little adventures. One of her favourite places was a local dale at Welton on the edge of the Wolds, which became our magical valley, where imagination was better than reality.

'Do you want to go to Welton dale today?' I said to Clare.

'Yes, please are we going to catch a rabbit?' Clare asked with a smile.

'Sure, I have got the right size box today,' I said teasingly.

'Dad, you said that last week!' Clare said, still smiling.

'Clare, I know, but we need some carrots!' I said and hoped we'd catch one.

'Dad, I know let's pick some plants with storks,' Clare said.

'Sure, we will we just need to keep trying, Clare,' I said.

This went on all summer, without success of course, yet the memory of the care-free nature of those languid days always cheered me up.

My heart scare at Easter convinced me to slow down, and most of the races, I did we were local with no pressure. That year, the only notable race, I ran was the York (Rowntrees) '10' on 12th October 1985, and my performance showed my lack of fitness. **Results:** 1. P Howdle (East Hull) 50:07 2. R Woods (Durham City) 50:27 3. D Allen (A&SV) 50:29 4. M Martin (Sheff-V) 51:17 5. G Baker (CoH) 51:21 6. W Cain (Salt) 51:30 7. P Rawnsley (Sheff) 51:40 8. G Heatherington (Dur. C) 9. A Connelly (S'fields) 51:53 10. B Eden (Vall) 51:44 11. R Pearson (Dark P) 51:46 12. M Bailey (Leeds) 51:48 13. K Singleton (Wake) 51:50 14. R Padgett (Spen) 51:52 15. H McEwan (Vall) 51:56 16. C Hallimond (Sun) 52:00 17. R Smith (A&SV) 52:05 18. D Littlewood (Crook-V) 52:23 19.B Sargent (Grim) 52:34 20. A Trigg (Leeds P) 52:35 21. J Goodman (Crook) 52:37 22. A Gregory (Hallam) 52:42 23. K Hesketh (S'fields) 52:50 24. P Matchett) (Long) 52:53. 25. M Nice ((Rown) 52:55 26. J Coulson (Rown) 52:56 27. **P Flatman (CoH-V) 53:00** 28. I Gilmour (M&C) 53:06 29. N Smith (Leeds) 53:09 30. D Lawson (Bing-V O/50) 53:13. **Teams:** 1. City of Hull 81 2. E Hull 95 3. Bingley 106 4. Rowntree

114 5. Elswick 130 6. Sheffield 131 7. Wakefield 139 8. Valley S 191. **(Women):** 1. S Catford (Thirsk & S) 59:47 2. J Pearson (Sheff) 61:39 3. P McFarland (Claremont-V) 62:00 4. K Palmer (Grim) 62:23 5. J Wakeman (Barns) 63:19 6. J Allison (Brid) 64:03 7. B Brown (Grim) 65:36 8. S Duffy (Spen) 66:24. **Teams:** 1. Grimsby 1491 2. Barnsley 1758 3. Bridlington 1847. **Vets** – 1. McFarland 2. R Miller 67:11 3. S Barron (Clare) 68:16 4. S Kirkup (Dur C).

After nine years trading, I had opened four shops, 334, Holderness Road, Bransholme Shopping Centre, 175 Ferensway and 27 Jameson Street. I decided to consolidate and closed Bransholme and Ferensway. Meanwhile, my Jameson Street shop was doing very well and adverts in Athletics Weekly was bringing in customers from other towns across Yorkshire. One Saturday a group of athletes from Sheffield visited my shop including Carol Wild, who joined East Hull Harriers in 1978, but later settled in Sheffield,

'This is a great shop, Pete,' Carol said.

'Glad you like it,' I said.

'It's a real runners' shop especially with race videos on the telly,' Carol said.

'We've been filming races since 1980 everyone likes to see themselves,' I said.

'So, Pete when are you opening a shop in Sheffield?' She said.

'Well, I've had an offer on my Holderness Road shop,' I said, 'So, I might be tempted.'

The manager of my first shop offered £10,000 plus stock which would realise nearly £20,000. Sheffield was 65 miles from Hull and would be my most ambitious plan to date. Finding a site, at a price, I could afford was relatively easy. The position was next to Sheffield's busiest McDonalds, and 20-yards from the Moor – a popular shopping district. The ground floor was about 200-square-feet and an upper floor of 700-square-feet and ideal as a footwear department. However, the landlords were McDonalds and tenancy negotiations expensive and long-winded. Just as well because I needed to consider the day to day management of a distant location, therefore, I ordered two fax machines for customer orders, stock-takes and sales reports. Furthermore, I needed some control over shop-thefts external and internal, and purchased a computerised stock-control system to identify shortages and reduce shrinkage. Kevin Tolchard worked part-time at Jameson Street while at Hull University and I offered him the job to manage the Sheffield store. He was a good athlete, popular with staff and customers, and broke four minutes for a mile on a treadmill and he had an ability with languages such as French, German and Geordie English! The following year, he was head-hunted by Nike, who gave him a promotions job for Nike Europe. The Brooks footwear rep rang me,

'Hi Pete, I've just had a call from Mel Batty, my boss, who drove onto the M25 hard-shoulder just to tell me about your state of the art fax machines,' he said.

Mel Batty was a running legend, but he needed to know all about my fax-machines. He won the 1964 and 1965 National XC title and set a world 10-miles record on a cinder track of 47:26.8 or put another way 71-second laps!

My Sheffield shop opened in July 1987, and I became a part-time athlete. Never mind, my business was booming, and my family had a comfortable life-style. I still ran most days but not attracted to the idea of trying to become a super-vet. One Sunday morning, I ran across the Humber Bridge to compete in a 10k around the streets of Barton and was surprised to win in 33-minutes – my 99th and final race win. Though, I won a few more Veteran category wins over the next few years – one that gave me the most pleasure was Vet45 win in the 1989 Ferriby 10. **Results:** 1. R Keeney (Telford) 49:44 2. A Hill (CoH)

50:21 3. C Nightingale (Sheff) 50:45 4. V40 M Martin(Sheff-V40) 50:58 5. M Lake (CoH) 51:14 6. B Ward (CoH) 51:27 7. R Smith (Keigh) 51:28 8. J Dingwall 52:18 9. B Sargent (Grim) 52:25 10. A Keen (Derby-V40) 52:27. 11.T Wright (Longwood) 52:29 12. J Barker (Grimsby) 53:02 13. J Hood (CoH) 14. C Ayres (Doncaster P) 53:30 15. S Rennie 53:45 16. I Grewer (East Hull) 53:50 17. P Flatman (CoH-V45) 53:53 18. D Tune (CoH) 53:53 19. A Gregory (Roth) 53:58 20. R Jones (Mansfield) 54:01 21. P Groves (CoH-V40) 54:16 22. K Robinson (Bingley) 54:18 23. J Clarkson (East Hull) 54:20 24. S Spooner (Bridlington) 54:28 25. A Bagley (Stockport) 54:31 26. A Morley (Hornsea) 54:47 27. J Matthews (CoH-V40) 54:51 28. I Chidwick (Grimsby) 54:53 29. P Rawnsley (Sheff-V40) 54:59 30. M Jackson (Spartan) 55:01.

CHAPTER 18

Bankruptcy

My shops' sales in 1990 hit a new record, in fact, twenty times my first year of trading. However, the middle-east crisis led to a three-fold increase in the oil price and caused a recession, high interest rates, and increased unemployment of 3 million. In fact, the downturn caused my business to lose a quarter of its cash-flow and left me with a high inventory of dated stock. Meanwhile, large sports shops, such as JJB Sports and Sports Soccer (later named Sports Direct) were finding ways to sell direct from Far-East factories for lower prices and bigger profits. Unfortunately, the high rate of unemployment led to disturbances in some cities, and in Hull and shops, like mine, being targeted by ram raids, consequently, I would dread the phone ringing in the early hours. If this was not enough, the big brands like Adidas and Nike decided to sell exclusive merchandise to the large outlets and to leave traditional sports shops the crumbs of dated-stock. The independent sports retailers, the backbone of the sports trade, would soon be decimated. Given the circumstances, I decided to take a trade stand at the London Marathon Exhibition to sell souvenir wear and runners clothing, shoes and equipment. To minimise costs, I hired a ten-ton truck, which I drove to London and my manager drove Luton van for back-up. The first year was very good and in four days we sold £50,000 of shoes and merchandise, but the security was so poor we had to have our staff manning the stands through the night. Similarly, we had other sales venues such as Bath and Bedford to maintain cash-flow.

Because of this financial turmoil, my business finally succumbed to the relentless recession of the nineties which caused 200,000 business failures. Therefore, I declared myself bankrupt in front of a judge in 1999, aged 55 and then went to the job centre in Essex House to sign on for job-seekers allowance and joined a long queue. Then, I noticed a notorious shop lifter staring at me,

'For fuck's sake, what are you doing here?' he said, as he continued to eyeball me.

'I've lost everything now I'm signing on just like you,' I explained.

'Well if you're in here mate, they might as well bury us!' he said.

'Thank you and good luck,' I said to my unexpected, new friend.

The bank repossessed our house to pay creditors, and we sought somewhere quiet and remote to live in Welton. My wife got a job at Hull Royal Infirmary, and within a few months we started to drift apart. She made new friends at the hospital, and often stayed over with them – while I was managing a runner's shop in Hessle.

I called the new shop, Humber Runner situated on Darley's roundabout, which, I ran for five years. We had already lost our beautiful house to the bank and now I was losing my wife of thirty-seven years and I felt the need to keep busy. Unknown to me at the time, my wife had started to see someone. I could not really blame her and with the benefit of hindsight, I realised she was totally devastated by the loss of our family home.

I was head-hunted by the Hull Rotary Club in 1998 to help launch a half-marathon race across the Humber Bridge, because I had organised the first race over the bridge in 1981, and a half-marathon in 1983. The first event was held on 14th June 1999 with over 1500 finishers. 1. Steve Bateson (East Hull) 71:45 2. Jonathon Frost (East Hull) 72:57. 3. Gregan Clarkson (Kingston AC) 74:32 Women 1. Amanda Crundall (Doncaster) 87:07 2. Dawn Broon 0/45 (Holmfirth) 91:52 3. Laura Holmes City of Hull) 92:57. Since then over 25,000 runners have competed the half marathon, raising a million for good causes.

Coaching Scorpions…

When I thought about it, I'd advised and coached runners since 1972, and helped the RAF Valley team win the Henlow 10, the Training Command Cross-Country, and an unprecedented third place in the RAF Cross-Country in 1973. While at Valley I formed a group of athletes and called them *SCORPIONS* and gave each member a sand-coloured shirt with the slogan, *Sting in the Tail.* When I left the RAF, I occasionally coached at East Hull Harriers, City of Hull AC, and advised training sessions for hundreds of runners, who came into my stores. When I opened my final shop on Boothferry Road, Hessle, I realised the location was perfect for track training at Costello, a 14% hill called Spout at Brantingham and Stretford (Manchester) running track for serious racing ninety minutes away.

Tim Wright came into my shop in March 2000, looking for running shoes. He looked very fit and was a mid-field footballer aged 28 and soon we were talking about running,

'I'm looking to see what you've got in running shoes – just to keep fit for football,' Tim said.

'I was the same age as you *and* also a footballer,' I said.

'I ran a six-mile fun run over the Bridge and won in 38-minutes,' Tim said.

'That's pretty good without proper training.' I said, suitably impressed.

'My dad was a runner and said as much,' Tim said, 'What sort of training?'

'For a start you'll need to run every day and do fifty miles a week,'

'I run thirty miles now, and often run an eight-mile circuit,' Tim said.

'OK, then you'll need some track/hill training,' I said.

'So, what do you think, I could achieve at 10k?' Tim asked.

'I'm sure, you'll run under thirty-three minutes next year,' I assured him.

'I'll have some of that!' Tim exclaimed, smiling ear to ear.

Soon, Tim was impressing me by running eight miles at 5:30 pace per mile. His track training was improving every week and his hill training excellent. Next, I needed to form a group, I would call Scorpions the name of my running group at RAF Valley. About two months later, Tim rang to say he had placed 2nd in the Grimsby 10k in 32:57. I was speechless, Tim had beaten my prediction in just a few weeks, I was ecstatic and wondered how many other Tim Wrights were out there waiting to be discovered? After a while, Stuart Carmichael also a non-club runner came into my shop like a fly to my web. He was 29, and had run 10k in 38 minutes, and he listened to my proposal to coach him, but seemed unconvinced. I was disappointed but knew without Stuart's 100% commitment and inner-belief, my coaching would fall on stony ground. A week later, he rang me,

'Now, tell me again about your coaching?'

'I'm forming a group of runners who would like to run thirty minutes for 10k,' I said, 'And I feel you have the potential.'

'How can you be so sure?' Stuart asked.

'Well, Stuart when I started running I was far less fit than you are now yet went on to run sub-thirty. All I need from you, to reduce your 10k by six minutes, is your complete inner-belief. Likewise, all you need from me Stuart, is the training and my total conviction to make it happen,' I pronounced.

'Still seems a bit far-fetched, Pete,' Stuart said.

'Well, Stuart for a start, you are already running six-minute miles, you'll be training with like-minded athletes and I'll tell you how to train, and the races to sharpen your form,'

'OK, Pete I guess I've got nothing to lose.'

'That's great, Stuart see you on the track at Costello tomorrow at 6:30 pm.'

An important part of my coaching was to get my protegees to test themselves at Stretford track at 800m 1500m and 3000 metres against competitive athletes. I had made the journey from Anglesey to Stretford in 1973, ran in an open 5000 metres and reduced my personal best to 14:45. Within a few weeks, I had recruited Gary Slater, Jim Crisp, Matt Turner and last, but not least Andy Swearman to my new Scorpion group and I met them at the track and listened to their banter,

'Hi lads, two new faces, Matt Turner from York and Andy Swearman from Kirkella,' I enthused.

'So, these are the famous Scorpions,' Andy said.

'You'd better believe it, this is no place for the faint-hearted,' warned Stuart.

'Hi, Tim heard about your great race 10k at Grimsby in 32:57,' said Matt.

'I can't imagine running that fast yet,' said Gary.

'You'll all get there, believe you me,' I said

'I've not done many races, but I run a lot of miles,' Andy said.

'By the time Pete's finished you'll be running like a greyhound,' Jim said.

'I can vouch for that my dad is pleased I've joined the group,' Tim said.

'OK lads, tonight's session: 200m x 2, 400m x 2, 800m x 2, 400m x 2, 200m x 2. Let's do it!'

'I like this session – piece of cake,' Gary said.

'You would, Gary, speed-merchant, Slater,' Stuart quipped.

The 200s and 400s went OK, but the 800s showed who was fit. By the end of the session the stress of the training was shown on the faces of the newcomers. The power of group training then comes into its own, through support for each other, and competitive individuals, who do not want to let the group or themselves down, and in consequence everyone gets fitter and faster.

'How did you find tonight's session Matt and Andy? I asked.

'Really hard, especially the last few reps,' Matt said.

'I found the 200s the most difficult,' Andy said.

'Next time, the sessions will be harder, but you'll be running faster,' I assured them.

By the autumn, the sessions became progressively longer but I would never divulge the night's training to the group until they arrived. Then, I announced the killer-session,

'OK, lads, we have a great session tonight: ten x 1 kilometre in 3-minutes with 90-second recovery,' I said. This caused a chorus of moans and growns.

'Listen up, this is the key session give it all you've got, it'll make the Leeds Abbey Dash 10K feel like a walk in the park,' I asserted.

'Aye up lads, Pete's trying to kill us. Ten x 1k– he'll have us all in A & E!' Stuart said.

'Yeah Stu, reckon he wants us dead all right. After this session, we'll be like zombies drifting through the night!' Gary quipped.

The runners are completing their sixth kilometre and showing signs of terminal fatigue. I noticed Gary was flagging, when he usually sprints to the front at the end of each rep,

'Gary are you feeling OK?' I said quietly. Gary turned to Stuart:

'Do you know what Stu, Pete just bollocked me!'

'That's very funny Gary – if I wasn't so knackered I'd be in stiches.'

Despite the banter, I felt the lads, representing City of Hull AC would do well in the Northern 6 stage relay at Sefton Park Liverpool on 30th September 2000. The course was four miles over undulating pathways of the Park. Stuart was on the first leg, which he completed in 20:28 for 15th from eighty teams. Gary was next in 21:58 dropping our team to 38th. Chris Smales ran 20:56 taking City of Hull to 31st place. Andy Hughes, former Welsh guardsman, really got amongst them with 19:48 taking us to 21st. On the penultimate lap Tim Wright scorched earth recorded 19:22, an amazing feat after only six months a runner and lifted our team to 15th. The performance was remarkable as the area's top runner Darran Bilton was 17 seconds slower in 19:39. City of Hull AC finished 13th, and already my group were making their mark.

At Brantingham, eight miles west of Hull is an awesome four hundred feet hill, a half a mile from bottom to top. The gradient is up to 14%, and the torture would linger in the limbs and lungs of my Scorpions for days.

'Look at me lads. I'll never ask you to do anything I haven't done myself, but this was my toughest session. I promise you'll ache all over for days, but embrace the pain, because when you recover it will be the pain your opponents, will suffer, when they try to live with you,' I said positively.

'I'll need a new pair of pins, I've just walked up part of Spout and I'm knackered,' Jim Crisp said with a grin.

'Ha ha, very droll Jim. Imagine if we could manage seventy-five, before the next track session then you'll have exceeded the altitude of Everest – excuse the pun, and by then you'll be at the peak of fitness,' I said hoping for a laugh.

'Bloody hell coach, it's bad enough being tortured on Spout without your terrible jokes!' Stu quipped, 'Anyway if we survive it'll be a sodding miracle.'

'I promise to attend your funerals. Let's be having you, and remember there's no gain without pain,' I said fearing a mass walk-out.

'Coach you're all heart,' Gary said.

I walked up the hill to my timing position for the first ascent thinking about a great set of lads: *who would have thought, most of my athletes had little experience of hard training or have been members of athletic clubs. But there is a spirit and unity of purpose as they can sense their goal of thirty minutes for ten kilometres.*

'Come on lads, dig deep for the last rep. Don't worry if you're sick, or your back feels it has been trampled over by a wild buffalo. It's all grist to the mill,' I said with gusto.

I wanted my athletes to test themselves against the UK's best 10k competition, and the Leeds Abbey Dash ticked all the boxes. The route is westwards from Leeds city centre to Kirkstall Abbey situated on north bank of river Aire. The Abbey was founded in 1152, by French Cistercian monks, and was prosperous until 1534, then dissolved under King Henry V111's reign and is the 5k turning point for the Abbey Dash. The course is virtually flat and the only climb of 22 feet was near the finish at Leeds Town Hall. Over two thousand runners had entered for the event on 3rd December 2000, which in later years would be restricted to ten thousand entries. I prepared my group with some under distance time-trials at race pace, so they could get the feel of the effort needed to post a personal best. On the day, my athletes did not disappoint: Andy Swearman was 38th in 32:11, Stuart Carmichael 55th in 33:08, Gary Slater (who ran 40:00 at Harrogate in July) 56th in 33:10, and Andy Hughes 57th in 33:12. They all ran personal bests, but we had only just begun and I was already planning training and racing for 2001, unaware of how my life was about to change forever.

'Pete, I never thought I'd be running a thirty-three-minutes this soon!' Stu said.

'What kept you Stu – you're a minute behind me?' Andy jibed.

'Don't worry Andy lad – I'll get you next time!' Stu said.

'I took seven minutes off my last 10k – bloody amazing,' Gary gushed.

'Fuck, fucking hell, what a fucking result,' Andy Hughes said.

'Andy – you have a lovely way with words,' Gary chided.

'It's comes with being a fucking Welsh guardsman!' Andy said laughing.

Now, I was coaching six to eight athletes with an average age of about thirty to follow the same level of training that worked for me. The winter months were about running high mileage and I would often be asked to suggest 70, 80, 90 or 100-miles per week, because I reasoned that the individuals would find their own level and felt like it should be their decision and not one imposed by their coach,

'We'll be returning to Spout Hill soon,' I said.

'Oh no, how did I get roped into that torture again?' Stu said.

'I know it's tough lads but if you want…' Matt said.

'… an early death,' Gary mouthed.

'Any way I'm up for it coach,' Jim said, 'I've got a paint-spray gun if you want?'

'Where did you get it?' I asked.

'Found it on the side of a road,' Jim said looking pleased with himself.

'It's for marking the road, electric blue and indelible, Pete,' Jim said.

'Let's hope it will electrify our hill-work,' I said jokingly.

'Hey, coach, when are you going to ditch that terrible joke-book?' Stu said.

'When you win the Leeds Abbey Dash!' I said.

Jim gave me gun-like container of quick-drying resin paint, and thermo-plastic to bind to any road surface. I put it on the back seat of my new Citroen Saxo and drove towards Spout Hill to mark the start and finish line on the hill. The afternoon was quite warm, and I was wearing vest and shorts. I was startled by a noise like a hand grenade exploding, hissing like a steam locomotive and belching out electric blue paint with brute force. Then, the gun gyrated like a huge Catherine wheel and the quick-drying thermo-plastic paint flew everywhere, and I was forced to despatch this unwanted intruder. I pushed the seat back, grabbed the barrel of the paint gun and I was immediately sprayed by another dose of indelible, sticky paint.

I was livid. The goo was sticking and solidifying in seconds. The slightest movement ripped my body hairs from their follicles. Ouch, so much for Jim's freebie paint. I managed to despatch it to a road-side ditch. The beast was still alive, but only just!

I drove back to my flat above Humber Runner in a car, I barely recognised. Every part of my Saxo was disfigured with congealed resin road paint. Walking to the flat was excruciating, the hardened resin paint more efficient than body waxing. The mirror revealed the impact of my dance with the paint-gun, on my resin splattered body. I needed help, and rang my recently divorced wife,

'I've just lost a battle with an exploding paint container – can you get some turpentine to get it off my body?'

'OK, I'll see you later…'

'So, tell me how this happened?'

'Jim gave me this roadside paint gun, which went off like an Exocet missile,' I said, 'I used to have a green car, but it's now splattered with bright blue paint – like an exhibit in the Tate Gallery!'

'Ha ha, stop it before I wet myself, anyway how did you get splattered all over your body?' she asked.

'Maybe, I was hoping to make News at Ten,' I said.

'You're such a cry baby. I had four of your kids. This is nought. Here's a sip of meths.'

'Anyway, shouldn't you be looking after your husband?' I asked.

'What he doesn't know won't hurt him,' she said with a grin.

Whereas, I removed most of the offending road paint, it was impossible to remove all the electric-blue gunge from the inside of my once lovely, emerald-green Saxo. I bought some non-exploding paint for Spout Hill sessions. Anyway, Spout was still there, ever defiant, and could not be broken by the lads. Regardless, after six gruelling weeks my group were battle-hardened for the long track repetitions. When we returned to Costello, there was conflict in the air. My group were warming up for the session, but Andy was agitated, in six months he improved dramatically and was our best endurance athlete. However, he lacked humility and looked down on my other athletes, Stu came across to see me,

'Can I have a quiet word about Andy?' Stu asked.

'What about?' I said.

'He reckons he's the fastest runner in the group,' Stu said.

'Well Andy can't stay with you or Gary on shorter reps,' I said.

'I know he can't sprint and thinks we're trying to send him up.'

'It's a shame, because you're all good runners,' I said.

'He's a loner, what's his problem?' Stu asked.

'I'll have a word, away from the track – there's more to this than meets the eye,' I said

This was a difficult situation. Andy had only been with the group for a few months, and he was running over one hundred miles a week. He was intent on proving his worth and was already the best 10k runner in the district and ran a personal best 3000 metres in 8:39.21, at Stretford. Next, I took Andy to Wythenshawe for a British Milers Club meeting for his first race over 5000 metres. Although, I did not expect him to win this race, I was confident he would run under fifteen minutes. Even so, I was alarmed as he was extremely nervous, and urinating throughout his warm up and close to the race start. He got a good start and was running close to the leader for the first few laps, I gave him his split time at 3000 metres – an excellent 8:45, and at even pace would give him a 14:35 finish time. Andy slowed slightly and placed 6th in 14:40.80. He was in his mid-20s, and with any luck he would be running under fourteen minutes within a couple of years, but his temperament let him down. He never ran a faster 5000 metres, even though he trained in Kenya for six weeks and later joined Birchfield Harriers.

Gary Slater was primarily an 800/1500 metre specialist, who had lived under the shadow of his dad, George, and his exploits at 800 metres. On Saturday 20th May 2001 at Costello athletics stadium, Gary lined up for his first 800 metres. He was in lane eight, so he could not see his competition, but no matter he ran hard and was marginally ahead at the bell. Then the whole field made for the nearside lane, and Gary was still in contention for the lead. Was this the same lad who months earlier ran outside 40-minutes in the Harrogate 10k? Would he finally prove to his dad, George, who was the family king of the track? I watched as he held his form and my stopwatch confirmed his sporting elevation in the Slater household when he crossed the line in 1:57.69.

I had been a member of City of Hull since 1981, when Kingston upon Hull AC was formed in 1990 to revive track and field athletics in the area. Meanwhile, my former club was more interested in keeping the tradition of low-key running events and the burgeoning veteran's ranks happy, than using their experience to encourage youngsters to take up athletics. Several of us joined the new club, including Jim Dingwall, Mike Baggott and Steve Rennie to pass on our knowledge to younger athletes. We raised a team for the Northern Counties 12-stage relay in April 2001 at Leeds, which included four athletes from my group and four from Andy Lyon's squad. Andy was a nationally ranked track athlete with PBs of 3000m 7:59.85 5000m 13:44.49 and 10000m 29:04.03 and has owned my former shop, Humber Runner since 2005. Hull clubs found it difficult to raise teams, and the best result I remember was when City of Hull placed 23rd in the eighties – so to place 6th was an amazing achievement.

We travelled further afield to Sunderland in October to run the Northern Counties 6 stage x 4-mile relay with an excellent team: Andy Swearman (9) 20:00 Darren Bilton (3) 20:03 Stuart Carmichael (5) 21:15 Chris Smale (6) 21:39 Gary Slater (6) 21:20 Andy Lyons (6) 20:48. We placed 6th and ahead of Derby & County, Sale Harriers and Sunderland. In 2002 Kingston upon Hull placed 10th in the 12-stage relay at Stockport, and 17th at Sefton Park. In 2002, my wife of 37 years and mother to our four children divorced me, and it was no surprise, I was at my lowest ebb.

CHAPTER 19

Winning Scorpions

Kingston upon Hull athletes were gathered around their coach on a bright, cold winter's day. The PA announcer was Bud Badaro UK national distance coach adding another layer of gravitas to the Leeds Abbey Dash on Sunday 2nd December 2001.

'Hi lads at last the time has come. Seize the day, and leave everything on the road,' I said.

'Bloody hell you don't want much, coach,' Stuart Carmichael said.

'I know – I'm too kind. Just blood, sweat and tears – that's all!' I said with a smile.

'He'll have us fighting on the beaches next,' quipped Jim Crisp.

'Give Crispy a pitchfork,' I said, tongue in cheek.

'Would you want him to tell you to take it easy?' Matt Turner said.

'My moneys on Matt to make the best improvement,' Gary Slater predicted.

'That's what I'm here for,' Matt replied.

'What about you, Andy?' Stuart asked.

'I'm so nervous – where's the bog? Andy Swearman said.

'Why's that – you can beat us all,' Jim said.

'Listen up lads: you're here for a breakthrough, and a fistful of personal bests. In thirty years you can tell your grandchildren what you did on a cold December day in Leeds. Hey up lads it's Bud on the PA,' I uttered.

'What a great day, my club Tipton Harriers are here, and one of the favourites for the team medals. But so are Liverpool, Salford, Derby, Morpeth, and not forgetting Leeds the host club…' Bud said.

'You've forgotten Kingston upon Hull, Bud,' I said in dismay.

'Who are they?' Bud chided.

'Have your little chuckle, old friend – it might crack your face later,' I said through gritted teeth.

'Pete Flatman thinks Kingston upon Hull have a chance this afternoon. But the only big fish to come out of Hull were landed off trawlers,' Bud said.

'OK, nice joke, Bud. You'll see my boys will pull the rest in on a rope,' I said.

'I think Pete will have Bud's job one day,' Stuart said.

I go with my team to the start near Leeds Town Hall, and give them some last instructions to help them on their way,

'Remember you must be on the start line – or you'll get slowed up by fun runners. Expect the first mile to be your fastest then you will have a clear run. If you're not hurting, you should be running faster. If you are hurting, and tempted to slow down, remember the pain you'll have later for giving in. Good luck and make yourselves proud.' I said. *Hoping we could get team medals*, I thought, with my fingers crossed.

'The leaders are in the last mile, and the team race is Leeds to lose – their flying vests are everywhere,' Bud announced.

'Sorry, Bud my spotters reckon Kingston have won by a few points,' I reckoned.

'The leaders are in sight and it's a home win for Leeds,' Bud said.

'Kingston upon Hull have won – mark my words,' I was sure.

An hour later we gather in a council office in Leeds Town Hall for the prize-giving, and Bud Badaro takes the microphone,

'Now we come to the men's team prize, but first I owe Pete Flatman – Kingston's coach an apology, who twice told me his team had won the team prize. It's a remarkable achievement for a club only formed last year. Well done, Hull,' Bud said.

'What a day, Pete. I ran 31:16 and Gary 31:27,' Stuart said.

'That's great Stuart -probably puts you in the top 100 in the UK,' I said.

'I came 13th in 30:41 – I think it is my best time at 10k, and Andy Swearman came 7th in 30:27,' Darren Bilton said.

'Hi Matt, how did you fare?'

'I'm really chuffed, I've knocked off nearly four minutes, with 33:17. It's made all the hard-work worthwhile,' Matt said with a beaming smile.

Results: 1. Martin Yelling (Bedford) 29:58 2. Mark Hudspith (Morpeth) 30:03 3. Neil Wilkinson (Salford) 30:04 4. Simon Deakin (Leeds) 30:05 5. Stephen Heppies (Loftus) 30:23 6. Mathew Piano (Trafford) 30:23 7. Andy Swearman (Kingston) 30:27 8. Tom Hearle (Kilbarchan) 30:30 9. Ray Ward (Sheff) 30:37 10. Lee Hurst (Belgrave) 30:38 11. Steve Platts (Morpeth) 30:40 12. Dave Norman (Altrincham) 30:40 13. Darren Bilton (Kingston) 30:41 14. Kevin Sheppard (Tipton) 30:43 15. Craig Wheeler (Trafford) 31:13 16. Stuart Carmichael (Kingston) 31:16 17. Philip Leybourne (Salford) 31:16 18. Laurence Hellawell (Keighley) V40 31:16 19. Martin Hilton (Leeds) 31:17 20. Greg Hull (Leeds) 31:17 21. Mike Burrett (Leeds) 31:18 22. Paul Dobson (Leeds) 31:19 23. Willy Smith (Keighley) 31:20 24. Andrew Jones (E Ches) 31:25 25. Gary Slater (Kingston) 31:28 51, Matt Turner (Kingston) 33:17. **M40:** 1. L Hellawell (K&C) 31:15 2. M Hawkins (Bing) 31:33 3. J Convery (Bing) 31:48 **M45:** 1. P Kelly (Hart) 32:44 2. S Richardson (Pock) 34:15 3. R Griffiths (Bing) 31:33 **M50:** 1. B Hilton (Leeds) 34:33 2. P Probin (Bing) 34:51 3. N Robson (Bing) 35:33 **M55:** 1. K O'Hara (N Vets) 36:27 2.

B Wells (RRC) 36:40 3. J Robinson (R&Z) 36:41 **M60:** 1. F Gibbs (Bing) 35:55 2. D Barber (Bing) 40:22 3. M Mahoney (St Bedes) 42:21 **M70:** M Jones (Bir) 47:50 **Team:** 1 Kingston upon Hull 36pts 2 Leeds City 43pts 3 Morpeth Harriers 72pts. **Women:** 1. P Thackery (Wakefield) 33:50 2. D Robinson (Unatt) 34:08 3. J Heath (Sale) 35:26 4. G Keddie (Bingley) 35:59 5. D Elmore (Wold Vets-50) 36:19 6. C Humphrey (Harrogate) 37:02 6. L Whitaker (Unatt) 37:09 7. E Nutter (Ripon) 37:55 8. A Butler (Wakefield) 37:57. **W35:** 2. Sutton (Vall) 38:50 3. C Cramer (Perth) 39:05 4. J Atkinson ((Quak) 39:31 **W40:** 1. T Carney (Dews) 38:20 2. S Milburn (New A) 39:43 3. G Roby (Hali) 38:59 **W45:** 1. B Hodgson (Knaves) 41:56 2. S Ratcliff (Sadd) 42:56 3. S Haslam (Scar) 43:34 **W50:** 2. S Caariss (Bing) 38:23 3. F Garland) (Red) 41:46 **W55:** 1. I Bass (Harr) 47:12 2. G Wolff (PFR) 48:51 3. G Buck (R&Z) 51:57

On 13th January 2002, I took seven runners to run the Morpeth to Newcastle Half Marathon race that had formerly been a road race of 14-miles was first run in 1904. I believed that we had a chance to beat Morpeth Harriers in their own back yard and I hoped four of my Scorpions squad Andy Swearman, Stuart Carmichael, Gary Slater and Jim Crisp could make it happen along with in-form Darran Bilton, Andy Hughes and Jim Abel. The weather was cold with some bright spells. I drove up and down the course to give encouragement. Dominic Bannister was soon in charge of the race with Morpeth's Craig McBurney holding off Darran and Andy. Kingston's third runner was Gary running well in the first ten with his pal and training partner Stuart Carmichael not far behind. Stuart and Gary had set personal bests in the Leeds Abbey Dash, but a half marathon was new territory for them. Therefore, I was alarmed when I saw Gary at nine miles, alone and looking tired as though he might drop out, I knew I had to do something. Yet how could I help Gary wearing an Adidas sports coat with runner's tops tied around my waste and car keys jangling in my pockets? In an instant, I knew what to do, when he approached me I ran alongside for a few hundred metres. Gary did not look up and I started a one-sided chat with him, *'Hi Gary are you OK?'* while he stared ahead, *'We're doing well, but the lads need you to keep going,'* I said, then noticed he'd picked up his pace, *'Hold that pace, and I'll see you at the finish,'* Now, I had to run back to my car and park near the finish line and a large sign that read, *400 metres to the finish.* Gary needed inspiration, because he was being pressed by Morpeth's wily Les Atkinson and as they approached, I looked at Gary's fatigued eyes and bellowed,

'Go Gary go!' He took off as though it was an 800m track race. Les was dumbfounded.

'There's nae way am going with that!' He lamented in his Geordie twang.

Gary took nine-seconds out of Les on the run-in, and Stuart also passed Les and was just three-seconds behind his Kingston team-mate at the tape. We all gathered in a local sports hall for the results – hoping our club had scored an away win against one of the North's great club teams. Because the showers were near to the prize-giving all the windows had misted against a brooding sky. Finally, a Morpeth official stood up to announce the results, and there was deafening hush when it came to the team prizes,

'The first team prize … goes to Kingston upon Hull AC. Darran Bilton, Andy Swearman and Gary Slater.' Against a back drop of mutterings from Morpeth supporters was quiet applause for the winners.

'The second prize … goes to Morpeth Harriers. Craig McBurney, Terry Wall and Les Atkinson.' Greeted with ironic applause, and genuine incredulity that such an unknown team had beaten their Morpeth boys.

'The third prize … goes to Kingston upon Hull. Stuart Carmichael, Andy Hughes and Jim Abel.' How much more humiliation could our hosts take…

Men 1. D Bannister (SB) 67:24 2. C McBurney (Morp) 68 3. D Bilton (KuH) 68:46 4. A Swearman 69:34 5. R Hand (Dur) 69:49 6.T Wall (Morp) 70:38 7. D Cavers(Bord) 70:59 8. S Murdoch (Bord M40) 72:10 9. G Slater (KuH) 72:25 10. S Carmichael (KuH) 72:28 11. L Atkinson (Morp M45) 72:37 12. D Robertson (Sun M40) 72:51 13. I Tweddle (NSP) 73:20 14. I Handyside (Dur) 74:28 15. A Hughes (KuH) 75:21 16. A Tatham (Quak) 75:36 17. M McDonald (Low F) 75:40 18. D Kirkland 75:49 19. G Dixon (Morp M40) 75:54 20. T Cummings (Thurr M40) 75:58.

TEAM: 1. Kingston upon Hull 16 2. Morpeth 19 3. Kingston upon Hull B 65 4. Elswick 77.

Women 1. J Roxburgh (Irvine) 81:16 2. S Allen (H&P W40) 32:33 3. D Richardson (Quak) 88:52 4. F Shenton (Elv W40) 89:25 5. E Nutter (Ripon) 89:40 6. A Banner (Els) 90:52.